Racism, Dissent,
and Asian Americans
from 1850 to the Present

Recent Titles in
Contributions in American History

Campaigning in America: A History of Election Practices
Robert J. Dinkin

Looking South: Chapters in the Story of an American Region
Winfred B. Moore, Jr., and Joseph F. Tripp, editors

News in the Mail: The Press, Post Office, and Public Information, 1700-1860s
Richard B. Kielbowicz

North from Mexico: The Spanish-Speaking People of the United States.
New Edition, Updated by Matt S. Meier
Carey McWilliams

Reagan and the World
David E. Kyvig, editor

The American Consul: A History of the United States Consular Service, 1776-1914
Charles Stuart Kennedy

Reform and Reaction in Twentieth Century American Politics
John J. Broesamle

A Quest for Security: The Life of Samuel Parris, 1653-1720
Larry Gragg

Anti-Racism in U.S. History: The First Two Hundred Years
Herbert Aptheker

James Kirke Paulding: The Last Republican
Lorman Ratner

New York at Mid-Century: The Impellitteri Years
Salvatore J. LaGumina

Alternative Constitutions for the United States: A Documentary History
Steven R. Boyd

Racism, Dissent, and Asian Americans from 1850 to the Present

A Documentary History

Edited by
Philip S. Foner
and **Daniel Rosenberg**

973.0495
R121

Contributions in American History, Number 148

Greenwood Press
Westport, Connecticut • London

Library of Congress Cataloging-in-Publication Data

Racism, dissent, and Asian Americans from 1850 to the present : a documentary
  history / edited by Philip S. Foner and Daniel Rosenberg.
     p.   cm.—(Contributions in American history, ISSN 0084-9219
; no. 148)
   Includes bibliographical references and index.
   ISBN 0-313-27913-6 (alk. paper)
   1. Asian Americans—History—Sources. 2. Chinese Americans—
History—Sources. 3. Japanese Americans—History—Sources.
4. United States—Race relations—Sources.   I. Foner, Philip
Sheldon, 1910- . II. Rosenberg, Daniel, 1953- . III. Series.
E184.O6R33 1993
973′.0495—dc20   92-38451

British Library Cataloguing in Publication Data is available.

Library of Congress Catalog Card Number: 92-38451
ISBN: 0-313-27913-6
ISSN: 0084-9219

First published in 1993

Greenwood Press, 88 Post Road West, Westport, CT 06881
An imprint of Greenwood Publishing Group, Inc.

Printed in the United States of America

The paper used in this book complies with the
Permanent Paper Standard issued by the National
Information Standards Organization (Z39.48-1984).

10 9 8 7 6 5 4 3 2 1

Contents

Acknowledgments

A host of libraries, historical societies, and researchers assisted the editors in the completion of this work. Tillie Pevzner was especially helpful in obtaining materials from the Bancroft Library of the University of California at Berkeley. Saw Wei Chi Poon, of the Asian Studies Library at Berkeley, also gave freely of her advice. Gracious assistance in forwarding materials was rendered by the staffs of the libraries of the University of Washington, Lincoln University, Adelphi University, Hofstra University, the State University of New York at Stony Brook, the State University of New York at Albany, the University Research Center at UCLA, the Immigration History Research Center at the University of Minnesota, the Tamiment Institute of New York, San Francisco State University, and the Catholic University of America.

In addition, Richard Oestreicher, Gerald Horne, H. Mark Lai, Rockwell J. Chin, Nina Greenpan, Yuri Kochiyama, and Karl Yoneda were generous in suggesting leads and sources. Nora Bonosky played a crucial role in the completion of the book, and Gabriel Rosenberg provided essential professional guidance. Peter Katopes contributed useful insights and steady encouragement as the collection took shape. The editors express special appreciation to John Donohue, for his technical and intellectual support throughout.

Introduction

The dominance of racism in American society - resting upon centuries of federal and state sanction, legal segregation, biological "proof" of ethnic rank, divisive hiring and discriminatory housing, the phobias and fulminations of presidents, the expeditions of the Klan, bias in school curricula, the propaganda in the press, and the officially administered doses of hysteria which accompanied the birth of imperialism and the growth of U.S. foreign involvement - is beyond doubt. But a substantial body of evidence shows that race relations in American history have been more complex than previously supposed. Native Americans, African-Americans, Mexican-Americans, Asian Americans and other direct victims of racism have resisted the stamp of inferiority. In addition, people who have been expected to sustain the prevalent prejudices have also challenged racism. Deviations from prevailing winds have ranged from humanitarian sympathy, to episodes of labor solidarity, to simple protest against one or another incidence of racist violence, to acceptance of intermarriage, to outright anti-racism.

The following documents are intended to indicate the existence of more than one view among whites, Blacks, and others not of Asian descent, on the position of Asians in the United States. It is simplistic to impute racist views to all who belong to that group whose other members expound them. That an ethnic group may regard itself as special does not necessarily connote hostility to other groups. That the sense of ethnic, even racial, difference may turn antagonistic generally involves the development of forces in society with a stake in and a rationale for the long-term perpetuation of their hegemony. The assumed naturalness of the perception of racial differences and the fears these may insinuate cannot explain the strength and application of racism - politically-economically-ideologically-socially-culturally-educationally systematized oppression - in the United States. Historian Sucheng Chan makes this apt distinction: "Because ethnocentrism is a worldwide phenomenon, Asian immigrants, as foreigners and newcomers, were looked upon with disdain and curiosity by earlier arrivals. Like most European immigrants, they started at the bottom of the economic ladder. Unlike their European counterparts, however, their upward climb was impeded not only by a poor knowledge of the English language, a lack of familiarity with the American way of doing things, limited education, and the absence of relevant job skills, but also by laws that severely limited - on racial grounds - the opportunities, they could pursue. Like other people of color, they were victims of legally sanctioned color prejudice."[1] John Higham's contrast between overt "race-thinking" and what he somewhat rigidly terms the "habitual suspicion" characterizing race relations in American history can be useful in understanding that racism was more than a natural force. Indeed, "the evolution of white supremacy into a comprehensive philosophy of life, grounding human values in the innate constitution of nature, required a major theoretical effort. It was the task of the race-thinkers to organize specific antipathies toward dark-hued peoples into a generalized, ideological structure."[2]

Racism may be built upon primary human concerns. But it assumes organized historical form and application, in actual contexts, which invite scholarly analysis linking psychology, economics, sociology, anthropology, and history, following human behavior over time and identifying variations in perceptions according to class, group, gender, ancestry, period, region, religion, occupation, and so forth. Though circumstances may contribute to the formation of attitudes and moods held in common, other factors may induce challenge to widely-shared assumptions. Many instances of multiethnic and multiracial cooperation dot the American past. In the case of attitudes by non-Asians, the breaches in prejudice were not necessarily deep, nor of long duration. But they did exist, and still do. Past and present differences raise important questions about how people think and how future concepts of American community might evolve.

This volume essentially spans the one-hundred years between the mid-nineteenth and mid-twentieth centuries. During that period, Chinese and Japanese people came to play an important part in the growth of American industry and agriculture. The immigrants and their children became key components of the labor force. Many lived in cities, experiencing and helping to shape the contours of American urbanization. The history of Asian Americans in general, the Chinese and Japanese in particular, is inseparable from the mining, railroad, fruit, vegetable, canning, garment, culinary, and longshore trades. Their presence decisively influenced immigration law, becoming an axis around which many battles revolved. Many statutes governing race relations were shaped in the context of Asian immigration. Important policies of major churches, significant international decisions, and a host of other critical questions in American society were built upon the notion of subordinating, if not excluding, Asians.

The support, sympathy, and solidarity registered in the following documents clearly appeared in a most inhospitable climate. In many cases, their expression required great effort and determination. The material suggests the scope and type of American dissent from anti-Asian thought and practice. As the latter concentrated in great part on the exclusion of Chinese and Japanese people from these shores, sympathetic commentary on their right to settle here naturally constitutes a theme running through the following chapters. While support for the immigration rights of Asians never pre-supposed an all-encompassing anti-racist stance by the non-Asians who so advocated, it nevertheless clashed with the chauvinistic charges of Asian barbarism, clannishness, and depravity, which saturated the ideology of exclusion.[3] Linked with practice and policy, these assumptions held great influence and distinction: "No variety of anti-European sentiment has ever approached the violent extremes to which anti-Chinese agitation went in the 1870's and 1880's."[4]

Historically, it was impossible to espouse the justice of Asian settlement and opportunities without doing battle with racist policies and conceptions. Certainly, a number of supporters exaggerated or distorted other qualities, even employed stereotypes, to show the desirability of non-exclusion; several of the sympathizers attest to meekness as a Chinese trait, one preferable to the unruliness apparently characteristic of, for example, the Irish. And, as Ronald Takaki has noted, American capitalists often opposed Chinese exclusion out of their desire to drive down the costs of labor, use Chinese workers as a "wedge" against unions, and promote the idea among white workers that the entry of the Chinese as society's mudsills would elevate their own status.[5] But the great body of anti-Asian racism denied that the Chinese and Japanese possessed any of the physical and spiritual features recognizable as human and admissible as "American": the argument was considered proven. To show otherwise, sometimes amidst vigilante attacks (as in the 1870's), or in the aftermath of the Pearl Harbor bombing which precipitated the evacuation of Japanese Americans from the West Coast, often required acceptance of Asians as members of the human family. While some advocates condescended to a degree, the material which follows includes statements of a more egalitarian character, manifesting unyielding support for Chinese and Japanese rights and absolute condemnation of their violation.

The documents include criticism of anti-Asian discrimination by protagonists of the abolitionist movement and the Radical Reconstruction policies favoring significant advances for African-American former slaves. The heaviest concentration of material concerns the rights of the Chinese and Japanese during America's late nineteenth and early twentieth century industrial explosion. That moment and phenomenon are considered crucial in the evolution of the American population and labor force, basic to the political and economic intertwining of government and capital, central to the birth of imperialism, and significant in the history of race relations, highlighted by enforced segregation and disfranchisement of African-Americans in the South. It was likewise the era in which anti-Asian sentiment reaped a bumper crop of exclusion laws and violence. The dominant view and treatment were best exemplified in the volatile San Francisco-based exclusion campaigns of the 1870's and 1880's, involving many laborers, which spread throughout the Western states and territories; the story is superbly told in Alexander Saxton's *The Indispensable Enemy*. Not coincidentally, the peak of the anti-Chinese surge coincided with the depths of the depression of the 1870's.

Articulate dissenters emerged as supporters of the rights of Asians in that period: Frederick Douglass (no stranger to dissent), Radical Republicans Charles Sumner and George Hoar, leading women reformers and radicals like Victoria Woodhull, such outstanding clergymen as Otis Gibson and George Washington Woodbey, well-known writers like Mark Twain, important figures in the Gilded Age labor movement, including J.P. McDonnell of the Workingmen's Party and the *Labor Standard*. The roster of those from the public, religious, labor, business, academic and African-American communities of the non-Asian majority who sympathized with Chinese and Japanese rights includes little-known figures, trends, and organizations, represented in many of the following documents. Significant for this period are the remarks by those African-Americans who opposed Asian exclusion. These statements suggested a vision of cooperation among racially oppressed groups, a theme important enough to highlight in Part V, but which finds reiteration by African-Americans in other sections of this volume.

While the late nineteenth and early twentieth centuries marked a particularly concentrated moment of resistance to anti-Asian racism, later periods witnessed a recurrence of the theme. The history of the Industrial Workers of the World shows dogged adherence to principles of multi-racial solidarity, opposing the disparagement of Chinese and Japanese laborers.

Efforts to limit the property-holding rights of Japanese Americans bore legal fruit in the Far Western states during the 1920's but also produced expressions of outrage both within and outside the Japanese American community. The exigencies of the Great Depression often engendered endeavors for reform that crossed racial lines, linking whites, Blacks, Mexican Americans and Asian Americans.

The Pearl Harbor attack produced the most difficult circumstances for resistance to anti-Asian, specifically anti-Japanese chauvinism. It unleashed repression of a group unmatched since the end of slavery, charged by the tensions of genuine war. Amidst all-out defamation of Japanese Americans, many non-Asian voices previously critical of racism became still, or merged with the national mood. But there were others - Norman Thomas, Carey McWilliams, and W.E.B. DuBois, to name a few - who joined the protests of Japanese Americans and spoke out against the internment.

The historical literature discussing both the racism against Asians and Asian Americans and their movements for equal treatment has grown impressively. Notable in a by-no-means exhaustive survey are the works by such scholars as Ronald Takaki, Roger Daniels, Gary Okihiro, Sucheng Chan, Shih-Shan Henry Tsai, Alexander Saxton, Lawrence H. Fuchs, Yuji Ichioka, Peter Kwong, Robert Parmet, Lucie Cheng and Edna Bodnacich.[6] In illuminating the exploitation of and resistance by Asian Americans, some have also alluded - without amplification - to the operation of sympathetic trends among non-Asians, while necessarily emphasizing the prevalence of racism. Hence, Daniels makes clear that the proposal to exclude the Japanese in the early twentieth century was endorsed "well nigh unanimously" in California and other Western states.[7] Both Daniels and Saxton demonstrate the abusive treatment, policy, and atmosphere in which Asian Americans worked and built communities, yet both refer to the humane stance of former abolitionists toward the Chinese.[8] Chan mentions the Reverend William Speer, who labored on behalf of both the souls and the rights of the Chinese in California in the 1850's.[9] Recalling an important and controversial figure who defended the Chinese, Takaki links the Reverend Otis Gibson - burned in effigy during the height of the San Francisco anti-Chinese campaign in the 1870's - with the cheap labor arguments used against Chinese exclusion.[10] Saxton favorably assesses the anti-exclusion position of Henry Ward Beecher and other clerics - he is among the few to deal with the contrasting views of the clergy - while noting that they often made a case for the degradation of labor.[11] In general, those scholars who have mentioned dissent from anti-Asian racism have done so in passing.

A number of works dealing with labor provide a sampling of the scholarly treatment of the relationships between Asians and non-Asians, and of variations in attitudes. Indeed, white workers engaged in particularly violent attacks on Asian Americans in the periods covered by the present volume; unions often became an important buttress of exclusion and discrimination. Nevertheless, the literature gives pause before the conclusion that labor - white, Black, Mexican-American - was an undifferentiated mass when it came to the Chinese and Japanese, or was itself the generator of racism. For in discussing the sphere of the greatest contact between national and racial groups (Yuji Ichioka notes that "Japanese immigrant history is also labor history"[12]), scholars have not always found labor's position clear-cut. Alexander Saxton's devastating review of labor's late nineteenth-century anti-Chinese activities establishes its irony and ambivalence: white workers "have been both exploited and exploiters....Ideologically they were drawn in opposite directions. Racial identification cut at right angles to class consciousness."[13] Inferring that racism was often consciously evoked or concretely provoked, others make the related point that employers used anti-Asian antagonism to obstruct unified labor organizations. They developed, writes Takaki, a "dual wage system to pay Asian laborers less than white workers and pitted the groups against each other in order to depress wages for both." Demonstrating that the initial impetus against the Chinese in California came from self-employed white miners and a relatively better off "petite bourgeoisie," June Mei avers that "it was basically the capitalistic system that pitted Chinese capital against white capital and Chinese workers against white workers, in the incessant competition for profit and jobs." On a similar note, Sucheng Chan points out, "economic dislocations" inspired much of the anti-Chinese racism of the 1870's.[14] Though Saxton could find few viable exceptions in the labor movement,[15] the present volume includes many, within both the most intense anti-Asian periods and at later points.

In this light, Richard E. Lingenfelter's discussion of the demand in 1876 by gold miners along California's Inter-Yuba Ridge for equal pay for Chinese workers is worthy of note, as is his perception of resistance to anti-Chinese violence by several unions elsewhere in the hardrock mining districts.[16] Takaki empathetically addresses the "possibility of class unity in a multiethnic working class," describing the cooperation practiced by Filipino,

Chinese, Japanese, Portuguese, and Spanish workers in a Hawaii sugar strike in 1920.[17] Yuji Ichioka devotes great attention to joint action occurring across national and racial lines earlier in the century, from the joint Japanese-Mexican farmworkers strike at Oxnard, California in 1903 to the building of a United Mine Workers local at Rock Springs, Wyoming (site of an outright pogrom twenty years before) comprising workers of 32 nationalities, including over 300 Japanese by 1908. Japanese American officers and interpreters served the UMW.[18] A number of writers have remarked upon the participation of Asian American workers in the strikes and labor organizations which arose during and after the Great Depression. They give numerous examples of solidarity between Asian and non-Asian workers in the labor movement: the "racially mixed coalition" formed by gardeners in Hollywood,[19] the "interethnic cooperation" strategy of the International Longshoremen's and Warehousemen's Union in Hawaii and on the U.S. mainland,[20] the multiracial principles of the National Maritime Union, which welcomed Chinese and other Asian members, leading one historian to conclude: "Such active participation in the NMU was a step forward not only for the seamen but for all Chinese workers in the United States, laying the foundation for their integration in other areas of the U.S. labor movement."[21]

In spite of the foregoing, neither the sympathetic relationships that occasionally evolved between Asian and non-Asian working people, nor the broader currents of support for the liberties of Asian Americans have been well-chronicled. In light of the overall neglect of the subject, African-American views of the rights of Chinese and Japanese Americans have all but escaped scholarly attention. Insofar as African-American observers offered comment on the conditions and struggles of Asians in America, and to the extent that both industrialists and planters contemplated and briefly attempted the employment of Asian workers in trades occupied by Blacks, several historians have studied the relationship between Asian Americans and African-Americans. Ronald Takaki, who has subjected the variant strains of racism to particularly sharp and revealing scrutiny, remarks that anti-Chinese attitudes were rooted in anti-Black racism: "The language used to describe the Chinese had been employed before: Racial qualities that had been assigned to blacks became Chinese characteristics."[22] The hiring of Chinese immigrants in the South was designed, writes Takaki, to speed up the pace of work: "Louisiana and Mississippi planters imported Chinese laborers and pitted them against black workers during the 1870's. They praised the workers from

Asia for outproducing blacks in per-worker competition, and used the Chinese to 'regulate' the 'detestable system of black labor.'"[23]

Others have recorded similar findings.[24] Among those who have addressed the attitudes of African-Americans, the most suggestive indicate the complexity of relationships between these oppressed groups, locating many instances of competition and resentment. In several cases, the point is made that African-Americans opposed anti-Asian exclusion and discrimination laws for their white supremacist thrust, while endorsing widely-believed prejudices against Asians. Essentially, writes Leigh Dana Johnsen of anti-Chinese sentiments in the 1870's, "these antagonisms...occupied a significant place in the activism of San Francisco's blacks."[25] Arnold Shankman, who has done substantial work in this area, explains that, though many Blacks accepted derogatory stereotypes, they were offended by racist treatment: "Even if the Chinese were of dubious value as settlers, it was unjust and un-American to treat them as sub-humans."[26] Acknowledging Frederick Douglass' strong views on the subject (an issue well-developed by Douglass scholar Waldo E. Martin, Jr.[27]), David J. Hellwig puts a more emphatic spin on African-American sympathies, stressing, "The significance of the black reaction to the Chinese and their opponents, however, is not that Afro-Americans shared the prejudices of other Americans or that they did not find the foreigners exemplary....As citizens they shared the larger society's revulsion at the newcomers; but as victims of oppression, they rejected special treatment for people, who, like themselves, were physically distinct from the white majority. Racism as well as ethnocentrism and rivalry for jobs and housing was involved in the anti-Chinese movement and in future years in the attacks on the Japanese. The enemies of the Asian were those of the black American."[28] Consideration of the diverse dimensions of this relationship, along the lines indicated by Hellwig, would be an important contribution to the understanding of racism and race relations.

Protest against the internment of Japanese Americans during the Second World War constitutes another divergence from the policies and demands of prejudice, in unprecedented circumstances. Dissent by non-Japanese in this case defied the racist and undemocratic measures adopted in the name of national security, the apparent requirements of which were acceptable to most, though resistance by Japanese Americans themselves was common. Despite the important and necessary publication of crucial studies, fine biographies, revealing reminiscences, and pertinent documents, describing concentration camp experiences and struggles, policy deliberations, and legal questions,[29] one is left with the impression that this legal, racist, assault and battery was universally accepted, if not welcomed, outside the Japanese community. One of the few to recognize the actuality of dissent, Roger Daniels notes that it flew in the face of a national consensus that even embraced forces otherwise thought to favor equality and civil rights. At the government level, "there was some, but not much dissent"; more challenge came from the California state CIO (Congress of Industrial Organizations), the Southern California American Civil Liberties Union, and a "group of religious leaders and educators called the Committee on National Security and Fair Play."[30] Perceiving that the indispensability of Japanese workers in Hawaii made their internment problematical, and recognizing the operation there of a somewhat different set of race relations (against glorification of which Gary Y. Okihiro cautions[31]), Ronald Takaki presents the rejection of internment in Hawaii as "counterpoint to the reality of racial hierarchy in the islands," and, by implication, to the atmosphere on the mainland.[32] Though historians like Daniels and Takaki are a minority in mentioning dissident approaches, materials in the present volume demonstrate the need to probe this area more deeply.

Six themes comprise the collection which follows. Though a number of documents point out the struggle against bigotry conducted by Chinese and Japanese Americans, the focus is dissent from anti-Asian policies and conceptions by Americans who were not of Asian descent. The editors have left the spelling of Chinese names and places in the original Wade Gillis transcription in which they first appeared.

The federal and state sanction given to anti-Chinese and anti-Japanese racism and direct resistance to that official course form the body of Part I.

Part II presents the sympathetic sentiments of public figures and organizations opposed to exclusion; as in Part I, a picture is given of the debate on the issues. Editorials supporting free immigration and pamphlets expressing like sentiments also appear here.

Part III embraces the demands of members of the clergy, dating back to the 1850's, for humane treatment of Asian immigrants.

Part IV demonstrates that while hostility to Chinese and Japanese workers generally characterized the position of organized labor, another view surfaced as well. Supportive statements, resolutions, speeches, articles, and pamphlets drawn from a seventy-year period are contrasted with discriminatory union policies and practices, which descended to violence during the late nineteenth century. Included among the arguments favoring multiracial cooperation are materials from the socialist and communist movements, the Industrial Workers of the World, and the United Mine Workers.

Part V documents the debate between the 1850's and 1870's among African-Americans. Though materials illustrating the views and sympathies of Blacks appear throughout the volume, the materials here concentrate the distinctive concerns of that community most experienced with racial oppression.

Indicating both the legal undercurrents and the response of the Japanese community, Part VI focuses on the wartime appeals in behalf of the evacuated and interned Japanese Americans. In the face of genuine hysteria, during which many previous supporters of fair treatment fell silent, voices of protest were raised nonetheless. The documents also trace the course of the movement for redress for the survivors of the USA's concentration camps. Reference notes are provided for background at various points and to indicate seminal and supplemental literature.

While the parts group thematically related material, there is both interconnection and overlap between the different sections and their contents. It may be seen, for example, that while there is a large segment devoted to labor, documents reflecting sympathetic views within the labor movement may also be found in Part I's Congressional hearings, in Part V's focus upon statements by African-Americans, and in the protests against the Japanese American evacuation in Part VI. Part V highlights statements by African-Americans, but Part VI includes W.E.B. DuBois' castigation of the Japanese American internment and Part IV presents the anti-exclusion position of the African-American socialist, the Reverend George Washington Woodbey. While Part III assembles particularly significant ministerial appeals, the clergy - including the African-American clergy - are also represented in other sections of the volume.

The documents are of more than historical interest. Contemporary trends - "Japan-bashing," physical assaults on Asian Americans, exploitation of Asian American workers, biased portrayals in American culture, new forms of pigeonholing and stereotyping - indicate that discriminatory treatment and views are alive and well in American life. Despite the increasing contribution of Asian Americans to all aspects of society, white actors continue to play

Asian characters, universities have employed quotas to limit Asian American enrollment, unskilled Asian workers, including children, have yet to achieve a liveable wage, and commercials by major automobile corporations persist in lampooning everything Asian.[33] All manner of media have catered to, if not promoted, the types of anti-Asian mythology and fears that commonly erupt as physical assault, as in the past. Bigoted slanders of Asians pass from the lips of officials at the highest levels of government.[34] Measures calculated to discourage multilingual usage and education, in favor of "English-only," reflect forms of discrimination which came into vogue during the 1980's.[35] Japanese Americans have attested that the policy of Federal reparations to the survivors of the evacuation - a potential national coming to terms with racism at its worst, with unprecedented opportunity to confront and "redress" profound societal ills - has not facilitated equal treatment or freedom from discrimination. On the contrary, the end of the twentieth century has witnessed a "growing bias," the increasingly sharp "sting of prejudice."[36] As with racism historically, new twists in discrimination against Asian Americans are both distinctive and suggestive of racial inequality overall, particularly as it affects African-Americans. In that regard, the discrepancies between white and Black have grown and racist attitudes have persisted, even as the living standards of all have declined.[37] W.E.B. DuBois' observation in 1903 that "the problem of the Twentieth Century is the problem of the color-line" appears equally appropriate at the dawn of the twenty-first century.[38]

Notes

1. Sucheng Chan, *Asian Americans: An Interpretive History*, Boston, 1991, p. 61.

2. John Higham, *Strangers in the Land: Patterns of American Nativism, 1860-1925*, New York, 1978, pp. 132-133.

3. A superb collection assessing exclusion is Sucheng Chan, ed., *Entry Denied: Exclusion and the Chinese Community in America, 1882-1943*, Philadelphia, 1991.

4. Higham, p. 25.

5. Ronald T. Takaki, *Iron Cages: Race and Culture in Nineteenth Century America*, New York, 1979, pp. 232-240.

6. Takaki, *Iron Cages*; Takaki, *Strangers from a Different Shore: A History of Asian Americans*, Boston, 1989; Roger Daniels, *Coming to America: A History of Immigration and Ethnicity in American Life*, New York, 1990; Gary Okihiro, *Cane Fires: The Anti-Japanese Movement in Hawaii, 1865-1945*, Philadelphia, 1991; Sucheng Chan, *This Bittersweet Soil: The Chinese in California Agriculture, 1860-1910*, Berkeley, 1986; Chan, *Asian Americans*; Shih-Shan Henry Tsai, *The Chinese Experience in America*, Bloomington, 1986; Alexander Saxton, *The Indispensable Enemy: Labor and the Anti-Chinese Movement in California*, Berkeley, 1971; Lawrence H. Fuchs, *The American Kaleidoscope: Race, Ethnicity, and The Civic Culture*, Hanover, 1990; Yuji Ichioka, *The Issei: The World of the First Generation Japanese Immigrants, 1885-1924*, New York, 1988; Peter Kwong, *Chinatown, New York: Labor and Politics, 1930-1950*, New York, 1979; Robert D. Parmet, *Labor and Immigration in Industrial America*, Boston, 1981; Lucie Cheng and Edna Bodnacich, ed., *Labor Immigration Under Capitalism: Asian Workers in the United States Before World War II*, Berkeley, 1984.

7. Daniels, p. 254.

8. Daniels, p. 271; Saxton, pp. 132-134.

9. Chan, *Asian Americans*, p. 73.

10. Takaki, *Strangers from a Different Shore*, p. 88.

11. Saxton, p. 134-137.

12. Ichioka, p. 2.

13. Saxton, p. 1.

14. Takaki, *Strangers from a Different Shore*, p. 13; June Mei, "Socio-economic Developments among the Chinese in San Francisco, 1848-1906," in Cheng and Bodnacich, p. 391, 395; Chan, *This Bittersweet Soil*, p. 370.

15. Saxton, p. 221-223.

16. Richard E. Lingenfelter, *The Hardrock Miners: A History of the Mining Labor Movement in the American West, 1863-1893*, Berkeley, 1981, p. 119-124.

17. Takaki, *Strangers from a Different Shore*, p. 152-155.

18. Ichioka, pp. 77, 96-99, 116-123.

19. Nobuya Tsuchida, "Japanese Gardeners in Southern California, 1900-1941," in Cheng and Bodnacich, p. 450.

20. Takaki, *Strangers from a Different Shore*, p. 407-411.

21. Kwong, p. 130, chapter 5 passim. See also Chan, *Asian Americans*, pp. 89-90.

22. Takaki, *Iron Cages*, p. 217. See the excellent article by Luther W. Spoehr, "Sambo and the Heathen Chinee: Californians' Racist Stereotypes in the Late 1870's," *Pacific Historical Review*, Vol. XLII, No. 2 (May 1973).

23. Takaki, *Strangers from a Different Shore*, p. 94.

24. See for example Parmet, p. 29; William Ivy Hair, p. 24. *Bourbonism and Agrarian Protest: Louisiana Politics, 1877-1900*, Baton Rouge, 1969, pp. 94-95; Philip S. Foner and Ronald L. Lewis, eds., *The Black Worker, Volume II: The Black Worker During the Era of the National Labor Union*, Philadelphia, 1978, p. 167.

25. Leigh Dana Johnsen, "Equal Rights and the 'Heathen Chinee': Black Activism in San Francisco, 1865-1875," *Western Historical Quarterly*, January 1980, p. 68.

26. Arnold Shankman, "Black on Yellow: Afro-Americans View Chinese-Americans, 1850-1935," *Phylon*, Vol. XXXIX, No. 1 (Spring 1978), p.9. See also Shankman's fascinating *Ambivalent Friends: Afro-Americans View the Immigrant*, Westport, CT., 1982.

27. Waldo E. Martin, Jr., *The Mind of Frederick Douglass*, Chapel Hill, 1984, pp. 213, 217-219.

28. David J. Hellwig, "Black Reactions to Chinese Immigration and the Anti-Chinese Movement: 1850-1910," *Amerasia*, Vol. 6, No. 2 (Fall 1979), pp. 27-29, 38-39.

29. Roger Daniels, *Concentration Camps USA: Japanese Americans and World War II*, New York, 1971; Peter Irons, ed., *Justice Delayed: The Record of the Japanese American Internment Cases*, Middletown, CT., 1989; Roger Daniels, Sandra C. Taylor, and Harry H.L. Kitano, eds., *Japanese Americans: From Relocation to Redress*, Salt Lake City, 1986; Edward H. Spicer, Asael T. Hansen, Katherine Luomala, and Marvin K. Opler, *Impounded People: Japanese-Americans in the Relocation Centers*, Tucson, 1969; John Christgau, *"Enemies": World War II Alien Internment*, Ames, IA., 1985; Audrie Girdner and Anne Loftis, *The Great Betrayal: The Evacuation of the Japanese-Americans During World War II*, New York, 1969; Daisuke Kitigawa, *Issei and Nisei: The Internment Years*, New York, 1967; Dillon Myer, *Uprooted Americans: The Japanese Americans and the War Relocation Authority during World War II*, Tucson, 1971; John Tateishi, *And Justice For All: An Oral History of the Japanese American Detention Camps*, New York, 1984; Donald E. Collins, *Native American Aliens: Disloyalty and the Renunciation of Citizenship by Japanese Americans During World War II*, Westport, CT., 1985.

30. Daniels, *Concentration Camps USA*, pp. 78-79.

31. Okihiro, pp. ix-xv, 195-276.

32. Takaki, *Strangers from a Different Shore*, p. 384.

33. "Asian-Americans protest 'Yellowface,': Issues in the Arts - Behind the 'Miss Saigon' controversy," *Peoples Daily World*, August 25, 1990; "Fighting Asian Stereotypes in 'Yellow Punk Dolls,'" *New York Times*, January 17, 1991; "Harvard and U.C.L.A. Face Inquires on Quotas," *New York Times*, November 20, 1988; "Chosun Daily News on Strike," *Justice*, November 1990; "Slaving Away: Chinese Illegals Oppressed at Home, Exploited Here," *Village Voice*, February 5, 1991.

34. "Treasury Secretary Criticized for Using Term 'Japs,'" *New York Times*, August 2, 1992.

35. Edward Chan and Wayne Henderson, "'The English-Only Movement,'" *East Wind*, Vol. VI, No. 1 (Spring/Summer 1987), pp. 2-5.

36. "Orientals in The U.S.: Hostility is Not New," *New York Times*, May 5, 1975; "Anti-Japanese Bias Spreading Again," *San Francisco Chronicle*, May 17, 1982; "Asian-Americans See Growing Bias," *New York Times*, September 10, 1983; "Japanese in the New York Region Begin to Feel the Sting of Prejudice," *New York Times*, July 22, 1990; "50 Years After Pearl Harbor, Reconciliation Is Still Elusive," *New York Times*, September 1, 1991.

37. Thomas Byrne Edsall, with Mary D. Edsall, "Race," *The Atlantic Monthly*, May 1991, pp. 53-86.

38. W.E.B. DuBois, *The Souls of Black Folk*, in Nathan Huggins, ed., *W.E.B. DuBois: Writings*, New York, 1986, p. 359.

Part I: Law and Dissent

Racism became institutionalized at an early point in American history. As a rationale for the removal of and genocide against Native Americans and the enslavement of Africans and African-Americans, it also served as an instrument of ruling elites to dilute lower-class opposition. During the mid-19th century, it became legal and codified with respect to Asians in the United States, as an expression of a required and enforced inferior status. [Documents 1 and 2]

The Burlingame Treaty (1868) permitted free immigration of Chinese people to the United States, and generally reflected a tolerant view. It did, however, deny the right of naturalization to Chinese immigrants. Increasingly exclusive laws, highlighted by the Chinese Exclusion Act of 1882 and the notorious Geary Bill of 1892, followed.[1] [Documents 3a-c]. Later restrictions drew heavily on such assumptions as those presented at the Joint Congressional Investigation of 1876 [Documents 4a-h, particularly a-d]. The statements of Senator Charles Sumner [Document 5], and of Frederick Bee and Benjamin Brooks [Documents 6 and 7] demonstrate that the prevailing racism of the period did not go unchallenged in the governmental arena. Senator George Hoar [Documents 8a and b] was particularly outspoken in his opposition to discrimination against the Chinese. Pressure on Congress to lift Chinese exclusion was always the activity of a minority of the nation's non-Asian population, but the humanity of that effort may be gleaned from the 1892 petition [Document 9] and the pamphlet sent to Congress in 1902 [Document 10].

Exclusion and bigotry were policy at both the state and national levels well into the 20th century. The Washington and California Alien Land Acts affecting Japanese-American property ownership in the 1920's [Documents 11a and b] attest to official discrimination on the West Coast, in the wake of the Gentlemen's Agreement (1907) between the U.S. and Japan, which reduced Japanese emigration to this country. Opponents of discrimination undertook to challenge much of the reasoning behind those Acts in testimony and statements of protest [Documents 12a-d].

1

In People v. Hall *(1854), the California Supreme Court ruled 2 to 1 that a white man charged with murder had been wrongly convicted because Chinese witnesses had testified against him: inadmissibility of their evidence, according to the decision, was covered by the proscription on testimony by Blacks and Indians in the California state constitution. Ironically, the concurring justice, Solomon Heydenfeldt, later appeared before Congress in defense of the rights of the Chinese: see Document 4f below.*

....We are of the opinion that the words "White," "Negro," "Mulatto," "Indian," and "Black person," wherever they occur in our Constitution and laws, must be taken in their generic sense, and that, even admitting the Indian of this Continent is not of the Mongolian type, that the words "Black person," in the 14th section must be taken as contradistinguished from White, and necessarily excludes all races other than the Caucasian.

We have carefully considered all the consequences resulting from a different rule of construction, and are satisfied that even in a doubtful case would be impelled to this decision on grounds of public policy.

The same rule which would admit them to testify, would admit them to all the equal rights of citizenship, and we might soon see them at the polls, in the jury box, upon the bench, and in our legislative halls.

This is not a speculation which exists in the excited and over-heated imagination of the patriot and statesman, but it is an actual and present danger.

The anomalous spectacle of a distinct people, living in our community, recognizing no laws of this State, except through necessity, bringing with them their prejudices and national feuds in which they indulge in open violation of law; whose mendacity is proverbial; a race of people whom nature has marked as inferior, and who are incapable of progress or intellectual development beyond a certain point, as their history has shown; differing in language, opinions, color, and physical conformation; between whom and ourselves nature has placed an impassable difference, is now presented, and for them is claimed, not only the right to swear away the life of a citizen, but the further privilege of participating with us in administering the affairs of our Government.

These facts were before the Legislature that framed this Act, and have been known as matters of public history to every subsequent Legislature.

There can be no doubt as to the intention of the Legislature, and that if it had ever been anticipated that this class of people were not embraced in the prohibition, then such specific words would have been employed as would have put the matter beyond any possible controversy.

For these reasons, we are of the opinion that the testimony was inadmissible.

The judgment is reversed and the cause remanded.

4 Cal 399

2

The House Commerce Committee's Report on the "Coolie Trade" (1860) was one of the earliest calls at the government level for Chinese exclusion.

This trade is of recent origin. It seems to have commenced about the time when the laws against the prosecution of the African slave trade were enforce with the greatest stringency, and resting in theory upon the voluntary action of the emigrants themselves, it seemed at first an innocent and worthy source of mercantile profit. Several merchants of unquestioned honor and of high integrity of character in the commercial cities on our Atlantic seaboard engaged without hesitation and without suspicion of wrong in the shipment of Asiatic coolies from Chinese ports to Cuba and to the Brazils, and to other places upon the South American coast....But before the public attention had been drawn to this subject in this country they had ascertained so much of the true character of this trade as to induce their immediate abandonment of it at large personal loss.

....It is a mortifying fact that up to the present time American shipmasters and northern owners are found willing to connect themselves with a trade in many of its features as barbarous as the African slave trade. In one respect it is more abhorrent to an honorable mind than that trade which the civilized world condemns as piracy. The captured African is not made to believe that he is changing his condition for the better; but the Asiatic coolie is entrapped and deceived by false pretences of promised gain into the power of men who, having cheated him of freedom, enslave him for gain.

....Your committee proceed now to state the manner in which this involuntary coolie emigration is conducted. Until the recent treaties with England, Canton was the only Chinese port free to foreign vessels. But within a few years four other ports have been opened, to wit: Amoy, Foo Chow, Ningpo and Shanghai....On the 31st of December 1845, a treaty was ratified between China and the United States, which contained the essential provisions of the treaties with England, and provided for the erection at the five ports of chapels, cemeteries, and hospitals. Permission was given to ships-of-war to visit Chinese ports. Similar treaties have been made between France and the Emperor of China.

From these ports, but chiefly from Amoy, the shipments of coolies were made during the earlier emigration. But as the traffic enlarged itself, and its great profits enticed lawless men to engage in it, the coolie traders have found it more easy to evade the few provisions of law which could be enforced at the legal ports where consuls resided by carrying their vessels to illegal ports and loading them there.

....The coolies are procured by purchase, and are, in fact, as truly the subject of barter and sale as the negroes upon the coast of Africa. Native Chinese are employed to entice from their homes such as may be persuaded by hope of profit to themselves to leave their friends. These men are employed by "brokers," who themselves deal with the shipmasters or agents. The brokers send their emissaries into all parts of the country in search of men and boys, who are deceived by false pretences to place themselves in the power of men who are remorseless as death. They are sometimes beguiled and sometimes kidnapped. But whether they are obtained by fraud or force, when once they are in the custody of the broker they are his merchandise. The pretence of contract is sometimes continued, but the disguise imperfectly conceals the fact of slavery. "The men being inveigled to barbarian houses and ships, are publicly sold. When once amongst them, they cannot understand their gibberish, and they are kept in close confinement. They may implore Heaven, and their tears may wet the earth, but their complaints are uttered in vain."

....The following, which is the latest account of a coolie tragedy, is extracted from newspapers of March 24, 1860. The voyage now so fearfully interrupted is not probably the first voyage of the kind in which the *Norway* has been engaged. Mr. Reed [William B. Reed, U.S. minister to China], in his communication to the Department of State, dated April 10, 1858, says: "A large ship of two thousand tons, called the *Norway*, fitted out expressly for this trade at New York, arrived at Hong Kong soon after my circular of the 18th February." Mr. Reed expresses the belief that the threatened penalties and some pecuniary embarrassments in which the parties were interested were involved, prevented at that time the intended prosecution of the voyage.

"Terrible Mutiny of Coolies at sea. - Thirty shot and over ninety wounded. - We are indebted to the Merchant's News Room for the following: A very serious case of mutiny occurred on board the ship *Norway*, (of New York), Capt. Major, on her recent passage from Macao to Havan, which came very near proving disastrously to the officers, passengers, and crew. The *Norway* sailed from Macao, November 26, with about one thousand coolies aboard, and when five days out, at about six o'clock in the evening, the captain being below at the time, a mutiny broke out among the coolies, who set fire to the ship in two places and endeavored to force the hatches. Mr. Stimpson, of Boston, one of the mates, had charge of the deck, and the watch, with the exception of the man at the wheel, was aloft taking in sail, Mr. Stimpson rushed to the hatch and commenced the struggle. The crew from aloft and those below, tried to seize the boats and leave the ship, when the surgeon, and English gentleman, drew his pistol and threatened to shoot the first man who dared to make that attempt.

"The crew then rallied and went to the assistance of the officers, and a fight ensued, which continued from six in the evening until after daylight the next morning. Thirty of the coolies were killed and more than ninety wounded before the mutiny was quelled. The captain then gave the coolies one hour to deliver up the arms in their possession; if they did not, he threatened to cut away the masts, set fire to the ship, take the boats and provisions and leave them to their fate. The mutineers soon came to terms.

"Capt. Major had his wife and two daughters with him, and also a lady passenger and child, but during the night the lady died of fright, and in the morning the child also died."

It is difficult to obtain satisfactory information as to the extent to which this trade has been carried on from the different ports in China, during the last ten years. At the illegal ports, where the largest shipments are made, no official returns are kept. Nor is it probable that parties engaged in such business, would be careful to disclose the extent of their iniquitous commerce.

....Your committee are instructed to inquire into the expediency of prohibiting by law all American vessels from engaging in the coolie trade, or from transporting apprentices, so called, to the West Indies or other parts of the world.

They believe it to be within the power of Congress so to legislate, and that the time has fully arrived when such legislation is clearly demanded. Your committee therefore report the accompanying bill.

U.S. Congress. House Committee on Commerce. *Coolie Trade.* [Report of Mr. Eliot, April 16, 1860]. 30th Congress, 1st Session. H.R. Report No. 443, pp. 4, 5, 9-10, 27-28, 30

3

The Burlingame Treaty (a) denied the rights of naturalization to Chinese immigrants, but permitted free "voluntary emigration" (as contrasted with the "coolie trade"). Democratically-minded Americans, including Mark Twain (see Part II), generally welcomed the Treaty. The Chinese Exclusion Act of 1882 (b) became the law upon which all future exclusion measures were based. The Geary Bill of 1892 (c), though subsequently modified, represented the extent to which racism against the Chinese had become public policy.

(a)

Article V

The United States of America and the Emperor of China cordially recognize the inherent and inalienable right of man to change his home and allegiance, and also the mutual advantage of the free migration and emigration of their citizens and subjects, respectively, from the one country to the other, for purposes of curiosity, of trade, or as permanent residents. The high contracting parties, therefore, join in reprobating any other than an entirely voluntary emigration for these purposes. They consequently agree to pass laws making it a penal offense for a citizen of the United States or Chinese subjects to take Chinese subjects either to the United States or to any other foreign country, or for a Chinese subject or citizen of the United States to take citizens of the United States to China or to any other foreign country, without their free and voluntary consent respectively.

Article VI

Citizens of the United States visiting or residing in China shall enjoy the same privileges, immunities, or exemptions in respect to travel or residence as may there be enjoyed by the citizens or subjects of the most favored nation. And, reciprocally, Chinese subjects visiting or residing in the United States, shall enjoy the same privileges, immunities, and exemptions in respect to travel or residence as may there be enjoyed by the citizens or subjects of the most favored nation. But nothing herein contained shall be held to confer naturalization upon citizens of the United States in China, nor upon the subjects of China in the United States.

Burlingame Treaty, July 28, 1868, in *Report of the Joint Special Committee to Investigate Chinese Immigration*, 44th Congress, 2nd Session, Washington, 1877, pp. 1182-1183

(b)

Be it enacted. &c., That from and after the expiration of ninety days next after passage of this act, and until the expiration of ten years next after the passage of this act, the coming of Chinese laborers to the United States be, and the same is hereby, suspended; and during such suspension it shall not be lawful for any Chinese laborer to come, or having so come after the expiration of said ninety days, to remain within the United States.

Sec. 2. That any master of any vessel, of whatever nationality, who shall knowingly on such vessel bring within the jurisdiction of the United States, and permit to be landed, any Chinese laborer from any foreign port or place shall be deemed guilty of a misdemeanor, and on conviction thereof shall be punished by a fine of not more than $500 for each and every such Chinese laborer so brought, and may be also imprisoned for a term not exceeding one year.

Sec. 4 That in order to the faithful execution articles 1 and 2 of the treaty of the United States and the Empire of China ratified July 19, 1881, in case any Chinese residing in the United States on the 17th day of November 1880, or shall have come into the same before the expiration of ninety days next after the passage of this act, shall depart therefrom, they shall, before such departure, cause themselves to be duly registered at a custom-house in the United States, and produce to the collector of the district at which they shall seek to re-enter the United States the certificate of such registration properly vised by the indorsement of the proper diplomatic representatives or consul of the United States as required in cases of passports by the fifth section of this act.

Sec. 16 That hereafter no State court or court of the United States shall admit Chinese to citizenship; and all laws in conflict with this act are hearby repealed.

Sec. 17 That the words "Chinese laborers," wherever used in this act, shall be construed to mean both skilled and unskilled laborers and Chinese employed in mining.

H.R. 3540, *Congressional Record*, March 14, 1882, vol. 13, 47th Congress, 1st Session, pp. 1899-1900 [passed May 6, 1882, as 22 Stat. 58]

(c)

Mr. GEARY. Mr. Speaker, I move to suspend the rules and pass the bill (H.R. 6185) to absolutely prohibit the coming of Chinese persons into the United States.

The SPEAKER. The bill will be read.

Be it enacted, etc. That from and after the passage of this act it shall be unlawful for any Chinese person or persons, whether subjects of the Chinese Empire or otherwise, as well those who are now within the limits of the United States, and those who may hereafter leave the United States and attempt to return as those who have never been here, or having been here, have departed from the United States (save and excepting only the following classes, that is to say: Such Chinese person or persons as may be duly accredited to the Government of the United States as minister plenipotentiary or other diplomatic representatives, consuls-general, consular and commercial agents, including other officer of the Chinese or other governments traveling upon the business of that Government, with their body and household servants), to come to or within, or to land at any port or place within the United States; and the coming of Chinese persons of the United States, whether for the purpose of transit only or otherwise, excepting the classes hereinbefore specifically described and excepted from and after the passage of this act, be, and the same is hereby, prohibited....

Sec. 7 That any Chinese person, or persons of Chinese descent, entering the United States or any of its Territories by crossing its boundary lines, or entering therein in any other manner whatever contrary to the provisions of this act, or found unlawfully in the United States or its Territories, may be arrested..., and when convicted upon a hearing, and found and adjudged to be one not lawfully entitled to be or remain in the United States, such person shall be imprisoned in a penitentiary for a term of not exceeding five years, and at the expiration of such term of imprisonment be removed from the United States to the country from whence he came: Provided, That when Chinese persons found unlawfully in the United States shall have come into the United States from China by way of contiguous foreign territory they shall be returned to China....

Sec. 12 That it shall be the duty of all Chinese persons within the limits of the United States, at the time of the passage of this act, to apply to the commissioner of internal revenue of their respective districts within one year after the passage of this act for a certificate of residence, and any Chinese person...who shall fail or refuse to comply with the provisions of this act, or who, within one year after the passage hereof, shall be found without such certificate of residence, shall be adjudged by the court before whom he may be brought as being unlawfully within the limits of the United States and subject to the same fines and penalties as though he had unlawfully come into the United States in the first instance.

H.R. 6185, *Congressional Record*, February 18, 1892, vol. 23, 52nd Congress, 1st Session, p. 2911 [passed May 5, 1892, as 27 Stat. 25]

4

Testimony before the Congressional Joint Special Committee's investigation of Chinese immigration, held on the West Coast in 1876 (a-d), lent substantial impetus to the ensuing exclusion laws. A number of witnesses attested to the very real exigencies of life during the nation's first industrial depression, a major factor in the scapegoating of the Chinese. Included below are statements by single-taxer (and, at the time, California State Inspector of Gas Meters) Henry George[2] and prominent Bay Area trade union leader Albert Winn.[3] There were, however, witnesses - workers among them - who supported the right of the Chinese to settle and work in the U.S. and to enjoy basic liberties (e-h).

(a)

Henry George sworn and examined....

Question. I understand that the theory is advanced by those who are in favor of Chinese immigration that they are a great benefit to the State, and that our industries are carried on by them? - Answer. That theory will not hold water a minute, and I do not think it is entertained by anybody who ever thought upon the subject.

Q. Explain that theory? - A. I understand that theory is that if you get type set so much less a thousand, you produce a cheaper newspaper; if you get boots made at so much less, you produce cheaper boots; and if you raise and harvest wheat so much cheaper, you produce cheaper flour; so that Chinese labor is really a benefit to all classes in giving cheaper commodities.

Q. That is the argument? - A. That is the theory.

Q. What is your response to that argument? - A. I do not think that will hold water a minute. It seems to me, in the first place, that when we speak of the wages of labor, we generally mean the wages of manual labor. There are other things that enter into the cost of production. There is the wages of the superintendent, and rent, which is a most important element.

By the Chairman:

Q. Do you think that the theory of protection....is an exploded theory? - A. Yes, sir.

Q. You think that there ought to be free trade? - A. Undoubtedly.

Q. That people should be allowed to buy where they can the cheapest? - A. Yes, sir.

Q. And employ where they can the cheapest? - A. No, sir; I did not say that.

Q. You do not carry your free-trade doctrine so far? - A. No, sir; unless you give men and women what I call absolute free trade, and then I will....Between a Chinaman working here cheaply and a Chinaman working cheaply in China, there is a very great difference. He can work as cheaply as he pleases in China, and, in my opinion, only benefit us if we exchange freely with him. Here he only injures us. If their race there works cheaply and exchanges with us, it really adds to our production. Here he affects the distribution of the product between the various classes by reducing the share which the laborer gets, and increasing the share of the capitalist.

Q. As this is a sort of political discussion, allow me to ask you if you get your theory mixed? Are you now proposing to protect American y excluding Chinese cheap labor? - A. That certainly would be my tion.

Q. If you propose to protect American labor by excluding cheap Chinese labor, what is the difference in theory between excluding a cheap product in China that comes in contact with our own products? - A. I was trying to explain that very point.

Q. That is the point I should like you to explain, because if you can do that you can answer a great problem which we have been discussing in this country for a great many years. - A. The Chinaman by laboring in China cheaply does not affect the rate of wages here, that is, he does not affect the distribution of our production. If we ship a cargo of flour to China and get back a cargo of tea, the more tea we can get for our flour the better we are off - the greater is the aggregate sum that we have to divide among all classes; but when the Chinaman comes here and works for low wages the effect is to make a great many other men also work for low wages and to lessen the rate of wages that is given to the working classes.

Q. I should like to understand if I can, (perhaps it is my difficulty of understanding,) the difference in principle between excluding cheap labor from China, keeping it out of this country, and excluding an article from our market manufactured more cheaply in China than we can make it here? - A. The difference is this: Excluding the cheap labor would prevent the reduction of wages; excluding the cheap product has no effect on wages except to decrease them....

By Mr. Piper:

Q. You are acquainted with the working and mechanical population of San Francisco? - A. Yes, sir.

Q. Are you well acquainted with it? - A. Yes, sir; pretty well.

Q. Is the working and mechanical portion of this community a respectable portion of it? - A. Yes, sir.

Q. It is the large portion of the white population? - A. Yes, sir. As to the character of those who are opposed to Chinese immigration, instead of being confined to the idle and dissolute as stated here, I do not know any man who really thinks for himself who does not take that view. I think it is the thinking portion of the community who are opposed to Chinese immigration.

Q. How do the mechanical and laboring portion of our community live? Have they, generally, families? - A To a very great extent.

Q. Have they not families to a greater extent than any other classes of our community? Is there not a greater percentage of the laboring and mechanical citizens of San Francisco, who have families, than the so-called upper class? - A I am not competent to answer the question. I think the proportion is as great as among the laboring classes.

Q. How do our mechanics and laboring men, our operatives, live generally? - A They do not live as well as they ought to live.

Q. Do not a great many of them live in their own houses? - A A good many of them do. The number who do of course in proportion is gradually becoming less and less.

Q. They send their children to school, I presume? - A O, yes; they all send their children to school.

Q. Has this influx of Chinese tended to degrade the dignity of labor? - A Undoubtedly.

Q. Has it had a tendency to bring white labor into the same repute that slavery did in the Southern States? - A I think its ultimate effects are precisely the same upon the white race as slavery.

Q. You think there is no doubt of that? - A None whatsoever.

Q. Is there not a general distrust and perturbation among the mechanical portion of this community in relation to Chinese labor? Is it not held in terrorem over them by their employers that if they do not submit to their exactions as to price of labor, they will employ Chinese? - A Yes, sir.

Q. That is a fact? - A Yes, sir; I think that is one reason why some of the employers really favor Chinese immigration; it gives them a rod.

Q. So that they may subjugate the American or white laborers to their prices and demands? - A Yes, sir; the effect is to break the power of trades unions and workingmen's combinations....

By Mr. King:

Q. You say that in your opinion the Chinese government would not object to the abrogation of that clause of the treaty which allows immigration here? - A That is my opinion.

Q. If that clause should be abrogated, do you think they would insist on the abrogation of the entire treaty? - A Not at all.

Q. Do you not think that if they found this a profitable market for their products they would wish to continue the treaty so far as it related to commerce? - A I do not think the Chinese government has any relations with the outside world of its own wish. We forced the opening of the ports, and we forced the extension of the treaty upon them.

By Mr. Piper:

Q. You think that was a mistaken policy on our part? - A. Not at all. The more trade we have with China the better for us. I think the only mistake is in opening the doors to the Chinese population.

Testimony of Henry George, *Report of the Joint Special Committee to Investigate Chinese Immigration*, 44th Congress, 2nd Session, Washington, 1877, pp. 280-282, 285

(b)

Edward L. Cortage sworn and examined.

By Mr. King:

Question. What is your occupation? - Answer. My occupation is a workingman in a broom factory.

Q. For whom do you work? - A. For Gillespie, Zan & Co., 114 Sacramento street.

Q. How many Chinese do you think there are employed on the coast in broom-making? - A. Somewhere between ninety and one hundred. I cannot exactly tell to a t, but there is pretty nearly that amount, exclusively of Oregon. There are a few small factories. I do not know that they have one, two, or three, but they all have some Chinese.

Q. What is your opinion as to whether that industry can be carried on without the use of Chinese labor on this coast? - A. It can be carried on just as well without Chinese, because it has been carried on without to the same full extent to what it is carried on now.

Q. Can we compete with the eastern manufacturers by white labor? - A. We have driven them out of this market by white labor.

Q. State anything else in connection with broom-manufacturing, so far as it is affected by Chinese labor, that occurs to you. - A. Gentlemen, I had no notion to come up here until yesterday at dinner-time I was invited to come. My object is not to run against the Chinamen. I am in favor of anybody making a living that possibly can, but I am a married man and have a family of four little children suffering here, and I would like to see them do something in the world. Years ago I could average $20 and $21 a week. By being a married man I have been expressly favored by my employer. I must say he is a gentleman in every respect. I know he would not discharge me if he could help it; but it is said what you call the power behind the throne will compel us to take Chinamen. We have carried it so far that it is almost impossible to employ a man without the Chinamen going beyond him. My average wages for the last week is $14.89. I put in about fourteen hours a day, including traveling backward an forward from Oakland. If the Chinaman has a mind to work for my firm he gets employment and I have to compete with him. He offers to work for about one-third less the price I am working for now. That would reduce my wages to a little above $9, not quite $10, and I think it is impossible to live on $10 a week in this country....

By Senator Cooper:

Q. You say that the lower wages of the Chinese operate to reduce your wages? - A. Yes, sir.

Q. And you cannot live upon the wages which they receive? - A. Not very well. $10 a week for a family, a wife and four children, is hardly sufficient to live on. Rents in our days for white men are seldom less than $15 a month. If a man wants to live anywhere decently with three little rooms he has to pay that, and if he has a trifle of elbow-room to give his children he cannot live for less, unless he moves in the fourth story of a tenement, and then it will cost him $12 a month, where they all live together.

Q. So the competition is in living? You could not afford to live like a Chinaman? - A. No, we could not, because a Chinaman is single and can live on 19 cents a day, at the same rate as our prisoners live in jail.

Q. He could live better in his mode of living than you can upon your wages? - A. So could I if I was single. If I was single I could live on $4 or $5 a week, by putting it down to the lowest possible figure.

By Senator Sargent:

Q. You do not like a bare struggle for existence? You want some comforts for your family? - A. I do not talk particularly for comforts. I like to clothe them decently and give them an education. I have a tolerably good schooling, because I was instructed in the German language; but I want to learn my children something a little better than merely to be in competition with Chinamen, if they are capable.

Testimony of Edward L. Cortage, pp. 359-360, 361

(c)

Chinese immigration and cheap labor presents to our consideration a complicated question of political economy. It has two sides, each possessing the elements of discussion for every class of people. Most of the rich want cheap labor to carry on their shops and farms to the best advantage for an increase of profits; the poor cannot afford to compete with labor so far below the American standard of industry. This creates a conflict of opinion between the rich and the poor.

The question is no longer treated from an individual standpoint; it is national in its character; the nation's Representatives have treated it in that way; and I have seen the necessity of furnishing the committee with all the information we can obtain. The question has been in a state of agitation for twenty-five years. Those who then discussed its merits are getting old, while a new generation has been born and grown to manhood....

Comparisons are often made as between the Chinese and other foreigners without taking into consideration that Chinese can never assimilate with our people, and will always be Chinamen; while from every other country the people delight in becoming American citizens, and their children are native Americans as much as those who descend from the revolutionary fathers. The free schools form their mind, while our contact with them in everyday life establishes their republican principles.

China can send her millions of men to this country who may become a Trojan horse in time of war with any power opposed to a republican form of government. I do not believe in underrating the skill and power of an enemy. With a few brave, energetic white men they would be a formidable army, when their prejudices are ripened into revenge. The cornered coward often exhibits astonishing courage; and it might be so with them.

A government formed by and for the people is a failure unless it can arrange commerce so as to benefit its citizens and keep them employed. We are told that a high tariff is as much for the protection of the mechanic and the farmer as for revenue; yet we bring the same labor here to compete with those we claim to protect. Such inconsistency is too plain to argue.

Statement of Albert M. Winn, pp. 321-322

(d)

Dennis L. McCarty sworn and examined.

By Mr. King:

Question. What is your occupation? - Answer. I am a boot-maker.

Q. How long have you been in that business on this coast? - A. Nearly eleven years, between ten and eleven years.

Q. What is your opinion as to whether or not that trade can be carried on profitably by the use of white labor? - A. I think it can.

Q. How many Chinese are there in that business? - A. I think at the present time there are between two thousand and three thousand in the city.

Q. State anything else that you wish to mention in connection with that trade. - A. I am connected with the United Workingmen's Co-operative Association, and we are employing altogether white labor. We are confined almost entirely to the manufacturing of men's boots. That is the line of goods the Chinamen have not got into as yet, but in ladies' work and misses' work and children's work they have, I may say, almost the entire control. The slipper business they have altogether, and in this other line of work, ladies' shoes, misses' shoes, &c., they have got the entire control. We make only a small portion in our business of that line of work, only that which it is really necessary for us to make. One year we employed a few Chinamen to make that line of work. At the prices that we have paid white labor for that line of work we could not sell them, so that we put on a few Chinamen just to make up that class of work, cheap shoes, and we employed them for one year. After that year we had some white men apply to us for that line of work, and they said they would make them as cheap as the Chinamen so as to get employment. So we discharged the few Chinamen we had, and we have employed the white men ever since. We employed only some fifteen Chinamen for one year. Now we have altogether between sixty and seventy white people on the class of work that we have worked on, as I have said, men's boots, which the Chinamen have not got into as yet, but I suppose it is only a question of time when they will.

Q. What is the comparative rapidity with which whites and Chinese labor, and what is the result of their labor as compared? - A. From the experience we had with them I think a white man will do about one-fourth more work than a Chinaman will. They work in teams of four men. The Chinaman would make about thirty pairs and the white men by working very hard would make fourty pairs of these misses' and children's shoes, which I would consider about a fair average. The same number of Chinamen would do about three-fourths the amount of work that white men would. Some five or six years ago there were no Chinamen employed at all in this business. We had then in the neighborhood of eight hundred white men but the manufacturers considered that there was more money by employing Chinamen, so that they gradually introduced them and I think to-day only about four hundred to five hundred white men are employed; whereas, if the Chinese were not in that business, we would have, I think, about two thousand white men in that line of business right now.

Testimony of Dennis L. McCarty, pp. 363-364

(e)

Rev. John Francis sworn and examined.

By Mr. Bee:

Question. You have been in charge of the mission-schools here? - Answer. Yes, sir.

Q. State to the commission your experience while you have been in charge in educating the Chinese, how long you have been, and what sect you represent. - A. The Baptist. I received an appointment as Chinese missionary by the American Baptist Home Missionary Society about five years since, and have continued, excepting a short interval of a few months, up to the present time, and am still engaged as a missionary in this city....

By Mr. Brooks:

Q. Will you state, from your intercourse with the Chinese, what is their general character? - A. I find the Chinese to be just like other people. I cannot perceive any difference at all. When we bring religious truths to bear upon them they appreciate and exemplify religious principles just like other people. I have been to some extent connected with almost all nationalities in both hemispheres; I hold the office of a minister, and I am not able to point out any differences between a Chinese and other nationalities, Welsh, Irish, Scotch, &c. When I bring the truth to bear upon their intellects and hearts, the effect is alike.

Q. What is their general character as members of society? - A. All our young men with whom we have been connected have proved themselves, with very few exceptions, to be honorable, just, reasonable, and honest in their character and in their dealings with us. A number of them are in different occupations in the city, photograph galleries, and other occupations. I find there is a demand for our young men, and we are not able to supply that demand. I think the same is felt by other missions. Our Christian community, our converts, are in demand. The people want them in their service and in their employ....

By Mr. Bee:

Q. Would not your work be facilitated to a great extent if the Chinese were permitted to attend our schools and get an English education? - A. Certainly; it would take away a great deal of labor that we are now obliged to perform. We could instruct them in the Christian religion at once, if they were to come prepared to read the scriptures, and it would save a great deal of time. I must say that it is amazing to me that in this Christian America (I am a British subject) the privileges of education are not secured to all alike.

Testimony of the Reverend John Francis, pp. 484-485, 486, 487-488

(f)

Solomon Heydenfeldt sworn and examined.

By Mr. Bee:

Question. How long have you resided in California? - Answer. Nearly twenty-seven years.

Q. Were you at one time associate justice of the supreme court of this State? - A. Yes, sir.

Q. How many years did you keep that position? - A. Five years.

Q. You are conversant with the various institutions of California, mining, manufacturing, and farming? - A. Tolerably, sir; practically from observation, &c.

Q. And with the Chinese question and legislation in reference to it? - A. I have been an observer of what has been going on for the last twenty-seven years.

Q. The committee are here to get information. I should like to have you detail your information as to the facts, if any, since the Chinese advent to California. - A. I think California owes its prosperity to the industry of the Chinese who have come to this country. I think without them we would not have had our harbor filled with ships; we would not have had railroads crossing our mountains, and we would have been behind, probably, a great number of years. I think we would not have had as many white people here if the Chinese had not come.

Q. You think, then, that the Chinese who are among us have

duced to bring white people here and give white people homes and employment? - A. I do.

Q. As to the construction of this new railroad, the Southern Pacific, which is some 400 hundred miles in length, would that have been built but for the Chinese, in your opinion? - A. I think not; and I have been assured so by those who are interested in completing it.

Q. It has opened a vast new territory of farming land to the immigration of this State? - A. It has.

Q. Do you think that the benefits of the Chinese among us have been wide-spread? - A. I do.

Q. How do you look upon the Chinese, as a class, for honesty, integrity, &c.? - A. I think they are the best laboring class we have among us.

Q. Do you think they compare favorably with other laboring classes? - A. I think they are the best we have....

Q. Do you think we have a surplus of labor in this State, either white or yellow? - A. No, sir; I think there is employment enough for everybody.

Q. To what class of labor do we owe our present success in manufacturing? - A. I think to the Chinese, except foundaries and such things as that....

By the Chairman:

Q. How long have you lived on this coast? - A. Nearly twenty-seven years.

Q. Have you, by your profession, been brought in contact with the Chinese? - A. Sometimes.

Q. You have a general knowledge of their condition and habits? - A. I have observed a great deal of them since I have been in the State.

Q. What is your opinion of the unrestricted immigration of the Chinese? - A. I will answer the question by stating in the first place that I am not in favor of the immigration of anybody to the United States. I think we have people enough for production and for progress. I am very much in favor of leaving some room for the descendants of the people we have; but if people will come we cannot help it; and if people will come I think it is as much to our advantage to have Chinese as any other people.

Q. Do you think it desirable that a limit should be fixed upon this immigration? - A. I do not; and I do not see how it can be done. If a mere matter of opinion is asked I do not see that it is possible for it to be done. I think that any attempt to make a proposal of that kind to the Chinese government would be an insult to that government in the eyes of all the world, if it would not be a disgrace to ourselves.

By Mr. Brooks:

Q. Suppose we attempt to limit the emigration from China, without the consent of the Chinese government, by simple legislation, how would that be regarded by the Chinese government? - A. I should say that it would be an infraction of the treaty. They would regard it, as a matter of course, as a breach of good faith.

Q. Would that be more or less an insult than asking them to abrogate the treaty on the subject? - A. I do not think that there is much difference. That is getting rather too far below a good system of ethics for comparison....

By Mr. Pixley:

Q. If immigration is to come, do you think there is no choice in the character of the immigration; in other words, are European families not better than the people who come from China? - A. Not a particle better.

Q. Do they assimilate with us soon? - A. Hardly. Give the Chinese a chance and I think they will assimilate with us.

Q. That chance would embrace the elective franchise. - A. Certainly.

Q. Would you be in favor of giving the franchise to the Chinese the same as to European immigrants? - A. Unquestionably. If the one is entitled to it I would give it to the other; and if the negro is entitled to it, I do not see why it should not be given to the Chinese.

Q. Then you regard the Chinaman as equal in all respects to the European immigrants? - A. I see no reason why he is not equal.

Q. Is the Chinaman equal in his civilization and morals? - A. In every respect....

By Senator Sargent:

Q. The cry used to be "Would you have your daughter marry a negro?" I was going to ask you, in the same sense, would you have your daughter marry a Chinaman? - A. I do not see why the Chinese should not intermarry. I think if you will look at the question practically, as a question of providing for family by industry and frugality, and in regard to that kindness and consideration which is due a woman, that the Chinamen would make better husbands than usually fall to the lot of our poor girls.

Testimony of Solomon Heydenfeldt, pp. 504, 505-506, 508

(g)

Charles S. Peck sworn and examined.

By Mr. Bee:

Question. How long have you been in this country? - Answer. A little over 18 years.

Q. What is your occupation? - A. Drayman or teamster, whichever you please to call it; drayman, I suppose.

Q. What class of people do you do business for principally? - A. With the Chinese almost exclusively. We, however, do other work if we are called upon....

Q. How have you found them as to their honesty and integrity in dealing with them? - A. We have found them very honest; indeed I may say strictly honest. I do not know that we ever lost anything by them....

Q. Have you an extensive acquaintance among the draymen and laboring classes, the white people you are brought in contact with? - A. I have.

Q. What is their opinion in reference to Chinese immigration? - A. The general opinion seems to be that the Chinese have been beneficial to the State, and that what is here is well enough; but they think there should be some measures taken perhaps to limit the immigration in the future; some think so and some do not. Some think that the immigration will be according to supply and demand.

Q. How many draymen are there in the city engaged in the business of driving drays? - A. Perhaps 3,000.

Q. Do you speak on this question in reference to their opinion as covering this 3,000, or a portion of them? - A. A portion of them, of course. I do not come in contact with all of them.

Q. About what proportion of that 3,000 would that portion be that you have conversed with and with whose ideas you are familiar? - A. Probably two-thirds of them.

Q. You say that some of them are favorable to restricting and others are not. What do you mean by restricting? Say that 500 went back, would you bring 500 here? Would that be satisfactory to that class? - A. If more came, that is if the Chinese population should increase in a certain ratio with the white population, it would be beneficial to the State and country.

Q. Suppose they did not increase with the ratio of white people, then how would it be? - A. I do not know that I am capable of judging.

Q. From your experience of what we have had here, with a population of seven hundred or eight hundred thousand white people at the present time, which is about the population of the State, suppose that we had a population of 1,200,000 people, could we endure another 50,000 Chinese? - A. I think we could....

Q. Do you think there is a very large element here opposed to Chinese immigration? - A. There is a certain class; I do not think it is a very large element.

Q. From your observation, who are that class; what are they composed of? - A. The laboring classes....

By Senator Sargent:

Q. Speaking of the opinion of different classes, do I understand you to say that a majority of those engaged in doing the draying business in this town think that we can stand an increase in the number of Chinese here? - A. I think so.

Q. You think that is a prevailing opinion among them? - A. I do.

Q. You have not hesitation in expressing that opinion? - A. No, sir.

Q. Do they ever attend anti-Chinese meetings and sign anti-Chinese petitions? - A. I do not know that they do. I never saw one of those petitions.

Q. On what do you base your statement that is their opinion, if you never saw the petitions nor attended those meetings. - A. I never attended those meetings. The draymen have a union here, and I have heard them express their sentiments there.

Q. At the Draymen's Union do they express sentiments in favor of the Chinese? - A. I do not know that they do at the meeting; but I have heard individual members express themselves. The question never has been brought up.

Q. Was it in general discussion you heard this? - A. No, sir; not in general discussion of that question. That question has never been agitated in the meeting.

Q. You have heard individuals express their opinion that way? - A. Yes, sir.

Q. Have you ever heard any individuals express the opposite opinion? - A. Yes, sir.

Q. Then you simply say there is a division of opinion among them? - A. O, yes; of course. Some would say they ought all to be driven out of the country.

Q. I think that is an extreme view? - A. I think so, too.

Q. I do not think that is shared by many? - A. No, sir; by very few.

Testimony of Charles S. Peck, pp. 728, 729, 730, 731

(h)

The frenzied appeals of a blatant daily press have fired the hoodlum heart against the Chinese to a pitch of enthusiastic venom which has on several occasions narrowly escaped manifesting itself by a resort to violence. That we have been spared scenes of the most revolting nature has been mainly attributable to the treaty relations of the Federal Government with China, and the quiet but ominous disapproval of our best and most influential citizens. We are emphatically not admirers of the Chinese; we see nothing loving or lovable about them. They possess no single trait in common with our people, and their presence among us in large numbers is not desirable. Nevertheless, there are certain features of the question which do not seem to have sufficiently impressed themselves upon the popular mind. It is certain that but for their cheap labor this State and this city would not occupy to-day the commercial and agricultural rank they now boast, and it is no less positive that our maritime relations with China have been materially furthered by the Burlingame treaty. The trade of the Orient, in which China occupies the most prominent position, has always been the subject of a covetous struggle between the maritime nations of the Old World. It was a source of wealth and commercial prosperity worth having. It not only fostered ship-building and every interest connected with it, but has been a wonderful incentive to manufactures, furnishing employment to thousands upon thousands, and finding a profitable outlet for domestic products in large variety. It is true that the remoteness of China from European nations and from the Atlantic States was a bar to Chinese immigration, and before our transcontinental railways were laid down it was rare to see one of that race in Europe or America. All over the christianized world a determination was manifested to break down the "Chinese wall of exclusion," and force them to open the doors of their valuable commerce to the enterprise of "outside barbarians." This desideratum was only partially secured by England and France at a great sacrifice of blood and treasure. The United States Government adopted a totally different role. All its efforts were those of peace, argument, and reason, and they proved more effective than cannons and bayonets. Recognizing the wide difference between the approaches of America and those of her European competitors, the Chinese government readily accorded us greater privileges than she had yielded to them, a circumstance of which European governments were not slow to take advantage under the treaty stipulations which placed them on a footing "with the most favored nations." It was made manifest, however, that Americans were held in greater esteem as a rule, and that a disposition was shown to give them the preference whenever it could be done without exciting suspicion, and our commerce with China soon began to unfold itself into ever-enlarging circles of mutual profit. After California became a part of the American Union, with San Francisco confronting the Orient as its great commercial metropolis, it became apparent that the United States would eventually become the central figure of intercourse between Christendom and the Orient. Our geographical position, and the unlimited abundance of natural resources possessed by the Pacific slope, clearly indicated by its ultimate success in grasping for a trade that had been for ages so eagerly sought by Europe. Chinese confidence in our frequent protestations of amity induced them to abandon the determination and usages of centuries, and come among us without fear of molestation. It is this confidence which the Federal government has relied upon as the lever with which to open the treasure-vaults of Oriental trade and commerce. It is this confidence which has been the *sesame* that flung wide the doors of Japanese preference and intercourse. It is this confidence which was impressing itself upon other Oriental people, and inducing them to extend special favors upon our country. The main question for our present consideration is, whether it is better to renounce at once and forever all the golden opportunities within our reach, or by the exercise of cool judgment, clear and unimpassioned reflection, and the adoption of some acceptable, just policy, maintain possession of our advantages and reap the ripening harvest? Shall we, by a coarse, violent, and repulsive policy against the Chinese, disgust the people of Japan, India, and the Pacific isles, by disgusting and ostracizing the Chinese? Is it wise to permit far-distant Europe to monopolize so vast a trade, and make this country tributary to its broader humanity, more admirable forbearance, and greater scope of enterprise? These are the salient points which will suggest themselves to our Representatives in Congress, to the men whose business is to legislate for the whole nation, to those who are intrusted with the very solution of international problems, and on whose action must depend the future to a very large extent. Local maladies will be consigned to local treatment for mitigation or cure, within the scope of national supervision and under the regimen of international obligations. If California be permitted to exclude the Chinese, China will exclude our people. We are, probably, no less repulsive to them than they to us, but we are less so now than the people of other countries, and it is well worth our while to hold fast to so valuable a possession.

Appendix O, Article submitted by Henry C. Beals (*San Francisco Commercial Herald and Market Review*, May 11, 1876), pp. 1184-1185

5

> *Famed Radical Republican Senator Charles Sumner of Massachusetts came forward fairly early as a supporter of naturalization rights for all peoples, regardless of race, nationality, or color.*

Mr. SUMNER. I offer a new section, which has already been reported upon favorably by the Judiciary Committee:

And be it further enacted, That all acts of Congress relating to naturalization be, and the same are hereby, amended by striking out the word "white" wherever it occurs, so that in naturalization there shall be no distinction of race or color....

Mr. SUMNER. The remark of the Senator from Vermont makes it necessary for me to make a brief statement. Some time during the last Congress I had the honor of introducing a bill to strike out the word "white" from our naturalization laws. I tried to have it put on its passage. I was resisted then by the Senator from Vermont, who moved its reference to the Committee on the Judiciary. There it remained without any report until that Congress expired. During the first week of the present Congress, now more than a year ago, I introduced the same bill. It remained in the room of the Judiciary Committee from March, 1869, until very recently, when it was reported favorably.

Such, sir, have been my efforts to bring the Senate to a vote on this question. Never till this moment has it been in my power to have a vote on a question which I deem of vital importance. I have here on my table at this moment letters from different States - from California, from Florida, from Virginia - all showing a considerable number of colored persons - shall I say of African blood? - aliens under our laws, who cannot be naturalized on account of that word "white."

Now, sir, there is a practical grievance which needs a remedy. This is the first time that I have been able to vote upon it, and I should be unworthy of my seat here if, because Senators rise and say they will vote it down on the ground that it is out place, I should hesitate to persevere. Senators will vote as they please; I shall vote for it....You are now revising the naturalization system, and I propose to strike out from that system a requirement disgraceful to this country and to this age. I propose to bring our system in harmony with the Declaration of Independence and the Constitution of the United States. The word "white" cannot be found in either of these two great title-deeds of this Republic. How can you place it in your statutes?

Congressional Globe, 41st Congress, 2nd Session, Part 6, July 2, 1870, pp. 5121, 5123

6

Frederick Bee was among the more forceful speakers in defense of the Chinese before the 1876 Congressional Investigation. A prominent San Francisco lawyer, he acted as a defense attorney during the hearings. He had the support of the important local Chinese merchants who constituted the so-called "Six Companies."[4]

The creation of this Commission by the Congress of the United States, is received by the Chinese residents of California with pleasure as a good omen, and in their behalf I am requested to return to you their heartfelt thanks and appreciation of your consideration in permitting them to be represented before your honorable committee. They ask to be heard before you as the representatives of a great nation, which, for a century, has been the asylum and refuge of the poor, oppressed and down-trodden of every nation on the globe, regardless or race or color.

The giant strides of this young empire opened up fresh fields for enterprise on the Pacific coast. Thousands of miles, across the trackless deserts, came thousands of hardy pioneers, under whose hands millions upon millions was added to the nation's wealth of gold. Closely following in their tracks came the farmer with his household goods and implements of toil, and like magic, the golden grain covered the great valleys of California. The fame and wonders of this new el dorado reached the remotest confines of civilized and semi-civilized countries. Hordes of emigrants poured in upon us from every clime. Australia landed its hundreds of convicts upon our shores, freely and without protest. Our mines and rich soil was free to all. China, in due course of time, learned of this wonderful eastern country, and soon the Mongolian, or "moon-eyed celestial," as we are wont to call them, ceased to be a curiosity in our midst; but, to the contrary, was pronounced a blessing. He filled a vacuum. He came to labor and found ready employment. The cute Yankee was quick to discover that John Chinaman was a mere labor machine, and utilized him accordingly.

Well do I remember when the question of a free or slave constitution was agitated in this State. The men from New England and the men south of Mason and Dixon's line stood shoulder to shoulder for a free constitution, and the only real fact that controlled and carried the election was that China would furnish us cheap labor, and the supply only limited by demand.

Legislation and Congressional action was sought as time rolled on, to frame nearer reciprocal and commercial relations between China and the United States, which culminated in the Burlingame treaty. I wish to say, by way of parenthesis, that I regret exceedingly that San Francisco should have so soon forgotten the magnificent reception given Mr. Burlingame on his return from negotiating this treaty. It was sought in negotiating this treaty, and used as an argument, that a portion of the vast foreign commerce of the Orient was controlled by a few favored nations, while our more favorable geographical location entitle us to a larger share of this trade. England early established a line of subsidized steamships, and at the time this treaty was negotiated, controlled 90 per cent of the whole commerce of the Orient. The number of our ships engaged in the tea trade could be counted on your fingers. The American merchant bought the bulk of his teas in the English market. But what a change is going on? Our merchant marine is making sad inroads on England's former supremacy in that quarter. Our magnificent steamships, thanks to a liberal government, have aided wonderfully in building up a large commerce with China and Japan. True to our go-ahead-ativeness, the people and the government demanded the construction of the great national highway, the Pacific railroad, not only to bind together our own territory, but to bring the Occident and Orient nearer together, and over this great highway transport the silks and teas of Asia to our own doors, inside of thirty days - an established fact today. England and France, alarmed at the advances made by the United States, constructed the Suez Canal to checkmate, in a measure, American enterprise in those seas.

Well do I remember our present Senator, (Mr. Sargent) a member of this committee, when he was in the National House of Representatives. I listened to his eloquence as he portrayed to members of Congress the immense advantages of opening up and constructing this trans-continental railway. He pictured in his eloquent way the immense advantage it would be to us, the great traffic which we would open. He showed by statistical information that of the whole commerce of the Orient, amounting from $350,000,000 to $400,000,000, we had not 3 per cent.

He claimed, and justly too, that it was an enterprise national in its character, and its benefits wide spread. The north, south, east, and west would all alike reap its benefits. He pictured in glowing words the future of the empire of the west, the valley of the Mississippi as the central mart of commerce of the world.

How prophetic his words! look around you to-day and witness the great strides made in fulfillment of his predictions.

Those arguments were used not only by the Senator but by all the distinguished statesmen of the day. Go still further. Go back to the time of Tom Benton, and examine the congressional records, and you will see all those statesmen of his time advocating in strong terms a mode by which the United States would secure a portion of the trade of China. There was no one in Congress, or out of Congress - Whig, Democrat, pro-slavery, barn-burner or Tammany Hall politician, who at that time opposed any of these measures. A Democratic Congress subsidized the Pacific Mail to the amount of $5,000,000. Now, after consuming these great achievements and becoming living witnesses to a growing trade and commerce, with a glorious future unfolding for the coming generation, will we, who are so directly interested, will the great empire of the States lying east of the Rocky Mountains, submit to the demands of a few demagogues, the forced mouth-pieces of anti-coolie leagues, and abrogate these treaty relations, close our ports to trade and commerce with the Orient? I answer, no!

The facts in reference to the export and import trade will be brought to your attention in a manner that you may judge of its advantages not only to California, but to the whole country.

And now, Mr. Chairman and gentlemen of the committee, in these few words I have sketched to the committee the outlines or the pedigree of this so-called Chinese question. You are here as a court of inquiry. A demand has been made for the modification or the complete abrogation of our treaty relations with China. It is charged that the Chinese residents among us are like a cancer eating into our vitals, breeding disease, corrupting the morals of our youth, monopolizing the labor of the country and bringing desolation throughout our fair land. It is openly advocated that it is far better to close the doors of trade and commerce, abrogate all treaty relations between the two countries, rather than endure or foster this so called evil. If those charges are proved true to your satisfaction, it would be well to inquire who sought this alliance? Was it the Chinese Empire? By no means. The Government of the United States fairly forced the present relations upon the Government of China. First, to break down the exclusiveness of that government we send a fleet of war ships, and obtain a few concessions. Later, we negotiate a treaty which opens up the whole country to the trade and commerce of our people.

It is under these solemn treaty obligations that the Chinese immigrant has been brought to our shores, opened up the riches of China to our merchant marine, dotted the ocean with our merchant ships, and maintained a line of steamships which is a pride to every American citizen. All these advantages we are willing to forego, and why? Because this great empire of boundless extent, whose shores are washed by two oceans, three thousand miles apart is invaded by 150,000 honest toilers. The great State of California, sufficient to support 10,000,000 people, is threatened with destruction because during a period of 24 years, 150,000 Chinese have come here and by willing industry have contributed largely to her present standing and wealth.

Let us see under what circumstances he comes and how he is received in this free and enlightened republic - the land of the free and oppressed. I regret exceedingly, Mr. Chairman and gentlemen, to bring to your attention scenes and acts which have transpired upon the streets of this city [San Francisco], which are a disgrace to any and all civilization. No country, no government, I undertake to say, on the face of God's footstool, has ever permitted indignities to be cast upon any race of people that the government and municipality of San Francisco and the State of California have permitted upon this class of people. I have seen, myself, one of the Pacific Mail steamships hauled into the docks here in this city, loaded, probably, with a thousand or fifteen hundred of these people. I have seen them loaded into express wagons to be taken to the Chinese quarter. What I say has been seen by thousands of our citizens. I have seen them stoned from the time they passed out of the ship, rocks thrown at them, until they reached Kearny street.

I have seen them leaning over the sides of the wagons with their scalps cut open. I have seen them stoned when going afoot from the steamships. No arrests were made, no police interfered. I do not recollect, within my knowledge, (I may be wrong in an instance or two), of ever an arrest being made when these street hoodlums and Arabs attacked these people on their landing here. It does not stop there. There are portions of this city, and I say it with shame, where none of these people dare frequent. There are portions of the city of San Francisco where these Chinamen dare not visit. If they do so, they go in large numbers, and they must have large numbers; because one of these hoodlums will drive fifty of them. That is not an exaggeration. I am speaking of those who first land here.

I say, and I say it with shame, that these people have no privileges. They do not seem to have extended to them the protection of the law in any particular. When a Chinaman lands upon this coasts he seeks for work. He comes here as a laborer. He comes here for the purpose of bettering his condition. He comes here a law-abiding citizen. We shall show upon investigation that the Chinese residents of this city and of the State of California compare favorably, and I think are the peer of any foreign population which comes here, in their appreciation of the laws and usage of the country.

Opening Argument of F.A. Bee before the Joint Committee of the Two Houses of Congress on Chinese Immigration (pamphlet), San Francisco, 1876, pp.3-9

7

> *Lawyer Benjamin Brooks' contribution to the same forum*
> *included a veiled attack on Irish Americans and a paternalistic appeal*
> *to the benefits of Chinese cheap labor, but contained as well a number*
> *of humanistic propositions.*

I do not sympathize at all with the view of the subject which has been presented on the other side. The very people who raise all this clamor, who fill the halls, pass resolutions and elect delegates, would never have been in this country, if their views had prevailed. It seems strange to me that one class of emigrants should be permitted to rise against another class of emigrants, because they come in competition with them. I deny the right of any foreigner, who comes to this country to do that. We permit them to come here. They come here by virtue of our laws. No foreigner has a right as a *foreigner*, simply to come into this country, and to establish himself and become an owner of the soil. It is *our law* which gives him that right. I have no sympathy for the argument made by an Irishman, a German, or a foreigner of any nation, who has come here and been naturalized, and been made a citizen, and allowed to hold land, when he talks about *our* land being land for the *white* man, and says that this yellow colored man comes in competition with the white man. It is nothing to me if he does. I do not think it concerns the nation or humanity, or the world at large, that the yellow man's labor comes in competition with the black man's, the red man's, or the labor of any other man. I do not subscribe to the creed of my friend on the other side. I believe these men *have* souls. I believe in the common humanity and brotherhood of all men. I do not claim any rights whatever as against a red man, or a black man, or a yellow man. If he can compete with me on a fair footing, let him compete. If he diminishes my earnings, I have no right to complain. He has a good a right to earn a living on God's footstool as I.

....I have lived here from the beginning of the American occupation. I came here in 1849 with my family, and with my family I have resided here ever since. I have seen San Francisco grow from a few tents and adobe houses to a great commercial city, I have seen this State grow up. I love it as any man loves his native land. I love her prosperity. Everything that touches it interests me. It is for that reason that when I was at the East and read the memorial which was presented to the Congress of the United States by the representative of these emigrants, demanding legislation for them, my indignation was excited, and I wrote a reply to it which I sent to the Committee on Foreign Relations of the United States Senate. In that paper I answered each of the charges which was made against these people. I did that at no man's solicitation. I did it simply as a Californian and as a man.

The Almighty has blessed us beyond all other people. He has placed in our hands the means of prosperity and happiness greater than any other people had. I feel as if we were throwing away this great prosperity, as if we were casting back in the face of the Almighty the gifts which he presented to us; that we are throwing back upon him his bounty with scorn and seeking to destroy the foundations of the prosperity of our State and its great and glorious future.

It is therefore that I take my stand here, not for the Chinaman but for the State of California and her people, and ask that they may be heard.

They do not go to these torchlight processions; they never go to these mass meetings. During the day they are at their counters and about their business, following their trades, working upon their farms. At night they are at home with their families. But if you pass through these streets day or night you will see thousands of idle people - people who, if you offer them work, will ask you all sorts of conditions, "Where is it, how is it, what is it, when is it, shall I have this, shall I have that, shall I have the other thing." They dictate terms to you, and these must be just so and so; otherwise they will stay as they are....That is the class of men who throng your mass-meetings, and pass resolutions, and dictate the future of this State.

I hope the committee will look into the bottom of this question and see what is to be the effect of the measures proposed. I hope they will direct their own eyes in the matter and not allow anybody to say to them, "look at this, and see that. This is so and so, and that is so and so."

I would remark that all that is bad, all that is noxious, about this thing, is the creature of our own legislation, our own neglect, and our own mismanagement.

When a stream of water overflows its banks and becomes a flood, it is a terrible engine of destruction, but when it runs its natural course and is used and utilized, what can be more beneficent? The Chinese element is an element of prosperity, of future greatness, of wealth, but you can make an evil of it, as you can of anything. When you look at this matter, I think you will see that all that is noxious about it comes from ourselves, and not from the Chinese.

Opening Statement of B.S. Brooks before the Joint Committee of the Two Houses of Congress on Chinese Immigration (pamphlet), San Francisco, October 21, 1876, pp. 2-6

8

Senator George Hoar, Republican of Massachusetts, consistently supported the rights of the Chinese, opposed exclusion, and strove to defeat or revise the various hostile bills. The speeches below are excerpted from proceedings in the Senate; the second was delivered during the debate on the most important law to bar the Chinese.[5]

(a)

Mr. HOAR. Mr. President, I had not proposed to take any part in this debate, and I do not propose to enter into any extended discussion of this amendment or bill; but I wish to call the attention of the Senate briefly to one or two very important practical considerations, as I conceive them.

I do not doubt that there may be cases where an imperative danger of national destruction may warrant or excuse a people in breaking its faith; but such a case is not the case of a breach of national faith; it is the case of an impossibility to keep the promise. If a nation cannot keep a treaty without destruction, then of course it becomes impossible that the treaty shall be kept, because the destruction of a nation is of itself a destruction of the power to observe the obligation that is in question. But does anybody pretend that there exists to-day in California, or in Nevada, or in Oregon, or anywhere on the Pacific coast, a state of things which threatens such imminent and present peril and destruction to our civilization, to our national life, to our national interests, as warrants this nation in resorting to the extreme and harsh measure of abrogating at once a treaty without even a notice or a request to the power with whom the treaty has been made?

We have a thick volume on which the international rights, the international obligations, large commercial interests, and large personal interests of the citizens of the United States depend. It has been a triumph of our recent diplomacy, a triumph due not to the skill of our Secretaries of State or our foreign ministers, but to the recognition of the growing power of this country and increased respect abroad for our flag, that we have within the last ten or twelve years made treaties with the principal powers of the earth in regard to the right of expatriation and the right of their citizens to take up their abode in this country and to form new ties here. On the validity of those treaties depend some of the most valuable rights of large numbers of our adopted fellow-citizens, Germans, Irish, English, Swedes, and men of other nationalities. Yet the Senator from Ohio and the Senator from Delaware declare that those treaties are but rags, whenever Germany or England or any of the powers from whom they were extorted by respect for the growing of this nation chooses to determine that it is for its interest to abrogate them. There is not a page of this volume which contains the record of any right which the United States has a right to enforce against any foreign country, if the large doctrine which is avowed here be true.

Mr. President, this treaty with China is one upon which very large commercial and business interests depend. The men of New York, the men of Boston, the men of Philadelphia, the men of Baltimore, and of our other commercial cities, have large interests in the trade with China. Our citizens are domiciled there; our large commercial houses, who have obtained large wealth and have large relations throughout the civilized world, are established in China to-day on the faith of this treaty. Yet it is proposed by the Senator from California at one blow, without any necessity for adopting this course, to cut up by the roots every right which an American citizen has, depending upon this treaty, to his property, to his established business, his right to prosecute his commercial relations with that people. Suppose the rights exists, it seems to me that there never was a more crude, a more unjustifiable, and more indefensible measure of statesmanship proposed in the American Congress than the method which the Senators propose to adopt to terminate the treaty.

Will any Senator get up here and claim that if this bill passes to-night and is signed by the President to-morrow there is a single treaty right which this country can enforce in favor of any of its citizens against the Empire of China? Yet this is to be given up rather than give six months' notice to our own citizens who are concerned; rather than make an attempt by diplomatic methods to induce the Emperor of China to abandon a right for his subjects which these very gentlemen who argue for this bill say he is indifferent to. Both the Senators from California and the Senator from Nevada have told us that the Emperor of China is opposed, or, at least, is indifferent to the emigration of his subjects; and yet rather than ask him to abandon voluntarily a right which he does not desire to have exercised on behalf of his subjects, if the full and careful studies of the Senator from Nevada can be depended upon as authority, it is proposed to overthrow by a single blow every right to the commerce which the merchants of the United States have depending upon treaty stipulations with China.

But, as I said, Mr. President, I do not wish to detain the Senate at this late hour; I wish simply to put on record my own individual opposition to this measure. I am opposed to it, first, because it violates without necessity and in the absence of danger the public faith. I am opposed to it because, if we had the right to accomplish the result by this method, it overthrows the guaranteed rights of so large a portion of our fellow-citizens, on which so much of their wealth and their commerce depends. I am opposed to it for another reason. I am opposed to it because it violates the fundamental principle announced in the Declaration of Independence upon which the whole institutions of this country are founded, and to which by our whole history the American people are pledged.

Mr. President, the function of this people, the duty which God has committed to this people, is in my opinion to work out in practical history the truth, that wherever God has placed in a human frame a human soul, that which he so created is the equal of every other like creature on the face of the earth - equal, among other things, in the right to go everywhere on this globe that he shall see fit to go, and to seek and enjoy the blessings of life, liberty, and the pursuit of happiness at his own will. That truth, declared in the Declaration of Independence, declared in more august words and by higher authority in the Gospel of Christ, is the truth which lies at the foundation of the institutions of the American people.

I do not mean to give any vote based on the theory that obedience to that divine law of justice and of liberty is to work destruction to any people who undertake to obey it. The argument of the Senators from California, and of the junior Senator from Maine, and the Senator from Nevada, is the old argument of the slaveholder and the tyrant over and over again with which the ears of the American people have been deafened and which they have overthrown....

The Senator from California charges me with having uttered what he calls sentimentalities, and with seeking to make sentimentality the guide of our legislative action. Mr. President, I do not understand that those simple rules of conduct which are laid down by the founder of our religion, by the founders of our Republic, by the sense of honor and the sense of honesty of mankind, are properly described by the scornful term which the Senator from California applies to them. The rule which requires nations to keep their faith, which demands that governments shall have regard to the laws of justice, which declares the equality of every human soul with every other human soul in the right to use the gifts which God has created for His children in this world - these are the eternal and practical verities which, through all time and everywhere acted upon, lead to prosperity, to wealth, to greatness, and which departed from lead the government or individual who departs from them to disaster, to poverty, to destruction. You might as well say that the mariner who trusts that the compass points to the north is relying upon a sentimentality, as to say that the nation which governs itself by these rules of conduct in its legislation is resting upon sentimentality.

Mr. President, I agree with the Senator from California in the desire to accomplish all that he says he desires to accomplish by this legislation. I agree that the cooly trade should be broken up. I agree that laborers imported, not coming in as immigrants but imported by their employers, may properly be excluded from our ports. I agree that contracts for terms of time by capital for the employment of human beings, contracts in which the laborer has no volition, are illegal and immoral, and should be broken up. But this legislation does not undertake alone or simply to do that. It starts by a denial of the obligation of national faith. It starts by the abrogation at the mere will of one party of a solemn treaty. It starts by relieving the Emperor of China of obligations upon which depend the rights and the property and the business of large number of our own fellow-citizens, who are as much entitled to the protection of the Government in their business as any other class of our fellow-citizens; and it does all these things without the slightest necessity. It does all these things because the people of California tell us that in some remote future a population which in thirty years has left with its immigration, according to their own account, but a hundred thousand excess of the immigrants who have stayed above those of the emigrants who have returned, will some time in distant ages swamp their civilization.

Mr. President, the argument which I addressed to the Senate was not that the cooly trade ought not be broken up; not that labor contracts were not immoral; but that this bill was in violation of the true principles of government. I said that the Senator from California in his argument struck hands with the Senator from Alabama and but repeated the old taunts and the old arguments which had been ringing in our ears for two generations. I do not believe that it is necessary for the future of this Republic to prohibit to any man who seeks its shores of his own volition the right to enter in the mode and at the time he choose, and to remain as a citizen or as a laborer or as a resident as long as he may choose. I believe that right is the right to the pursuit of happiness with which the Creator has clothed every human being, and I am willing to trust the power which creates a planet, which sets it in motion in its course, and which brings it back at the end of a thousand years true to its hour, to the due execution of His own laws.

Congressional Record, 45th Congress, 3rd Session, February 14, 1879, pp. 1311-1312, 1314

(b)

Nothing is more in conflict with the genius of American institutions than legal distinctions between individuals based upon race or upon occupation. The framers of our Constitution believed in the safety and wisdom of abstract principles. They meant that their laws should make no distinction between men except such as were required by personal conduct and character. The prejudices of race, the last of human delusions to be overcome, has been found until lately in our constitutions and statutes, and has left its hideous and ineradicable stains on our history in crimes committed by every generation. The negro, the Irishman, and the Indian have in turn been its victims here, as the Jew and the Greek and the Hindoo in Europe and Asia. But it is reserved for us at the present day, for the first time, to put into public law of the world and into the national legislation of the foremost of republican nations a distinction inflicting upon a large class of men a degradation by reason of their race and by reason of their occupation.

The bill which passed Congress two years ago and was vetoed by President Hayes,[6] the treaty of 1881, and the bill now before the Senate, have the same origin and are parts of the same measure. Two years ago it was proposed to exclude Chinese laborers from our borders, in express disregard of our solemn treaty obligations. This measure was arrested by President Hayes. The treaty of 1881 extorted from unwilling China her consent that we might regulate, limit, or suspend the coming of Chinese laborers into this country - a consent of which it is proposed by this bill to take advantage. This is entitled "A bill to enforce treaty stipulations with China."

It seems necessary in discussing the statute briefly to review the history of the treaty. First let me say that the title of this bill is deceptive. There is no stipulation of the treaty which the bill enforces. The bill where it is not inconsistent with the compact only avails itself of a privilege which that concedes. China only relaxed the Burlingame treaty so far as to permit us to "regulate, limit, or suspend the coming or residence" of Chinese laborers, "but not absolutely to prohibit it." The treaty expressly declares "such limitation or suspension shall be reasonable." But here is proposed a statute which for twenty years, under the severest penalties, absolutely inhibits the coming of Chinese laborers to this country. The bill is intended absolutely to prohibit it.

....Here is a declaration made by a compact between the two greatest nations of the Pacific, and now to be re-enforced by a solemn act of legislation, which places in the public law of the world and in the jurisprudence of America the principle that it is fit that there should hereafter be a distinction in the treatment of men by governments and in the recognition of their rights to the pursuit of happiness by a peaceful change of their homes, based not on conduct, not on character, but upon race and upon occupation. You may justly deny to the Chinese what you may not justly deny to the Irishman. You may deny to the laborer what you may not justly deny to the scholar or to the idler. And this declaration is extorted from unwilling China by the demand of America. With paupers, lazzaroni, harlots, persons afflicted with pestilential diseases, laborers are henceforth to be classed in the enumerations of American public law.

Certainly, Mr. President, this is an interesting and important transaction. It is impossible to overstate or calculate the consequences which are likely to spring from a declaration made by the United States limiting human rights, especially a declaration in a treaty which is to become international law governing these two great nations. As my friend from California [Mr. Miller] well said, it is of the earth, earthy. The United States within twenty years has taken its place as the chief power on the Pacific. Whatever rivalry or whatever superiority we may be compelled to submit to elsewhere, our advantage of position, unless the inferiority be in ourselves, must give us superiority there. Are we to hold out two faces to the world, one to Europe and another to Asia? Or are we to admit that the doctrine we have proclaimed so constantly for the first century of our history is a mere empty phrase or a lie?

For myself and for the State of Massachusetts, so far as it is my privilege to represent her, I refuse consent to this legislation. I will not consent to a denial by the United States of the right of every man who desires to improve his condition by honest labor - his labor being no man's property but his own - to go anywhere on the face of the earth that he pleases....

The number of immigrants of all nations was 720,045 in 1881. Of these 20,711 were Chinese. There is no record in the Bureau of Statistics of the number who departed within the year. But a very high anti-Chinese authority places it above 10,000. Perhaps the expectation that the hostile legislation under the treaty would not affect persons who entered before it took effect stimulated somewhat their coming. But the addition to the Chinese population was less than one seventy-second of the whole immigration. All the Chinese in California hardly surpass the number which is easily governed in Shanghai by a police of one hundred men. There are as many pure blooded

Gypsies wandering about the country as there are Chinese in California. What an insult to American intelligence to ask leave of China to keep out her people, because this little handful of almond-eyed Asians threaten to destroy our boasted civilization. We go boasting of our democracy and our superiority, and our strength. The flag bears the stars of hope to all nations. A hundred thousand Chinese land in California and every thing has changed. God has not made of one blood all the nations any longer. The self-evident truth becomes a self-evident lie. The golden rule does not apply to the natives of the continent where it was first uttered.

Speech of the Hon. George F. Hoar of Massachusetts delivered in the Senate of the United States, March 1, 1882, (pamphlet), Washington, 1882, pp. 6-7, 9, 13-14

9

> *The petition below was one of hundreds protesting anti-Asian legislation during the late nineteenth century. Its target was the Geary Bill, to which it gave basic, if conditional, disapproval. Those of its 2500 signers named in the* Congressional Record *include leading reformers (the Garrisons, Stone, Livermore, Hallowell), clergymen (who clearly predominated), educators (Goodwin, Thayer, and others), and businessmen (Baldwin, Capen, and the former Republican congressman Rice). The* New York Times *of December 10, 1892 noted that the House of Representatives' decision to have the entire appeal printed - not simply mentioned - in the* Congressional Record *was unusual.*

Mr. ANDREW. [John Andrew, R - Massachusetts] Mr. Speaker, I ask unanimous consent to offer at this time a petition of citizens of Massachusetts, and have it referred to the Committee on Foreign Affairs; and also request that the body of the petition may be printed in the RECORD, as it will only occupy a very small space.

There being no objection, the body of the petition was ordered to be printed in the RECORD, and referred as requested.

It is as follows:

Petition of Bishop Phillips Brooks, Charles W. Eliot, William Endicott, jr., William Lloyd Garrison [II], Samuel Johnson, Robert Treat Paine, Rufus S. Frost, Archibald M. Howe, Norwood P. Hallowell, Richard P. Hallowell, Alexander H. Rice, A.E. Pillsbury, John E. Sanford, William M. Olin, Jabez Fox, Rev. Solon W. Bush, Rev. Minot J. Savage, Rev. A.H. Plumb, Rev. George C. Lorimer, Rev. A.P. Peabody, Rev. John Cuckson, Rev. William E. Griffiths, Rev. Robert Macdonald, Rev. Samuel May, Rev. Frederick B. Allen, Rev. Reuben Kidner, Rev. C.A. Bartol, Rev. S.H. Hayes, Rev. A.J. Gordon, Rev. Charles Follen Lee, Prof. F.J. Childs, Prof. W.W. Goodwin, Prof. J.B. Thayer, Prof. Charles E. Fay, Darwin E. Ware, William H. Baldwin, Samuel B. Capen, George S. Hale, Mary A. Livermore, Rev. Percy Browne, Francis J. Garrison, Edna Dean Proctor, Rev. O.B. Frothingham, Rev. Louis Albert Banks, Rev. Samuel E. Herrick, Lucy Stone, Rev. Charles G. Ames, Charles R. Codman, Osborne Howes, jr., and twenty-five hundred other citizens of Massachusetts asking for the repeal of an act to prohibit the coming of Chinese persons into the United States, approved May 5, 1892, and known as the "Geary bill," excepting, however, the first section thereof, whereby all laws now in force prohibiting and regulating the coming of Chinese persons into the United States are hereby continued in force for a period of ten years from May 5, 1892.

Congressional Record, 52nd Congress, 2nd Session, December 9, 1892, p. 72

10

Excerpts follow from a statement against exclusion legislation debated in Congress in 1902, replying point-by-point to a labor pamphlet endorsing that legislation. [The Act of April 29, 1902 extended all contemporary exclusion laws and obligated the Chinese laborer in the continental U.S. "to obtain within one year after the passage of this act a certificate of residence," warning that "he shall be deported upon failure to obtain the same." - Section 4]. The authors, identifying themselves in the introduction as "thinking men and patriotic Americans," set forth as their objective "to bring home to the American people the facts that surround this Chinese exclusion legislation..." Anti-labor union argument and tone colored part of the statement's content; but important data was presented which challenged the assumption that the Chinese lowered the standard of living. The document was referred to the Senate Committee on Immigration.

The pamphlet of the labor union, among other things, says:

....That there had arrived in California in 1868 about 80,000 Chinese.

This is wrong. According to the United States Census there were in the whole United States, in 1860, 34,933 Chinese, and, in 1870, 63,249 Chinese.

The statement that the Chinese who came to California were slaves of the Six Companies, and practically chattels, is absolutely false.

The so-called Six Companies are really benevolent associations. They give relief to the needy and take care of them in trouble. They do not control the persons or movements of the Chinese in this country in any way. It is true that there are some Chinese secret societies in San Francisco called "Tongs." The "Tongs" have aims something like those of the labor unions, and have just as much control over their members as the labor unions have over their members.

As to the Chinese in other parts of the country than the State of California, they have nothing to do with the Six Companies or Tongs....

In regard to Chinese competition, it may be said that Chinese do not work for less wages than other people. According to the information furnished by an employment bureau, a Chinese cook cannot be had for less than $40 or $50 a month. This does not look like cheap labor....

The table purporting to give the class of labor, average wages, etc., of Chinese in California, compiled by John S. Enos, Commissioner of the Bureau of Labor Statistics of the State of California from 1883 to 1886, is not particularly reliable. In any case he describes the condition of things nearly twenty years ago. The times have changed since then. It is a fact that the Chinese appreciate the value of their labor now, and they will not work for less than white laborers.

It is absurd to say that the Chinese in the United States obtain 75 per cent. of their food from China and send 75 per cent. of their earnings to China. Chinese have acquired extravagant habits from their contact with the American people. It is a well-known fact that thousands of Chinese in California, who have been in this country many years, have spent all that they have made, and saved nothing....

It is stated that Chinese labor degrades labor as slave labor did. This is not so. It is a well-known fact that there is a scarcity of labor in the agricultural districts. Owing to the exclusion law, fields lie uncultivated for lack of labor. It is to the interest of farmers to be able to obtain any other kind of labor when white labor cannot be had....

The old story about the Chinese, in their habits and customs, violating every principle and rule of hygiene is here repeated, but the Chinese in this regard, are no worse than the Italians or the Hungarians, in cities or places where there are no Chinese. Sanitary laws have to be enacted and enforced to meet such a situation. In every country there are some people who are filthy in their habits....

It is not necessary to say much in reply to what is said there in regard to the moral standard of the Chinese. Suffice it to say that any one who takes up a copy of the *New York Journal* can find a state of things equally bad among the people of other nationalities....

Opium is imported into this country by Americans. Chinese are prohibited from bringing opium into this country, by treaty between China and the United States. If there are opium dens in San Francisco and other American cities, the Americans have only themselves to blame, for China has done her utmost to put a stop to that traffic....

Page 33 [of the labor pamphlet]. Reply to Memorial to Congress.

"When Chinese flocked in." The Chinese have contributed largely to the opening up and development of California and the Western States. They worked mines, they reclaimed waste lands, they constructed the transcontinental railroads connecting the Pacific coast with the Atlantic seaboard.

"Effects of the Geary Act." Its effects are disastrous to California. According to the fifteenth report of the Commissioner of Labor, the average rate of wages in California fell to $1.73 per day in 1893, the year when the Geary Act went into effect, while the average rate of wages was $2.00 per day before the exclusion of the Chinese.

"Chinese are not assimilative." Americans do not give them a chance. They are not allowed by law to become citizens; it is hardly fair to deny them the right to become naturalized and, in the same breath, find fault with them for not being assimilative....

"Exclusion an aid to industrial peace." From what has been said, it is not the real laborers who do not want the Chinese, but the walking delegates, and others of that class. They are the real disturbers of the peace, not the Chinese....

"Experience with slave labor." Chinese labor is voluntary, and not slave labor.

"Our civilization is involved." The historical allusions are rather far-fetched. They have no bearing whatever on the question at hand.

The Americans have often boasted of their fair dealing and consideration for the oppressed of mankind. The exclusion laws against the Chinese give a lie to their professions. They do not dare to do the same thing to a stronger power. They simply take advantage of the weakness of China and do as they please about this matter. This is like kicking a man when he is down. Nothing is more cowardly than this.

The Chinese do not come here to commit any criminal offence. They come to trade and to work. But it is the practice for custom officials to look upon their attempt to enter the country as criminal offences, and treat them worse than thieves or robbers. Is this fair? Should it be done by a civilized people?

Truth versus Fiction: Justice versus Prejudice - Meat for All, Not for a Few. A Plain and Unvarnished Statement: Why Exclusion Laws Against the Chinese Should Not be Re-enacted - Respect Treaties and Make General, Not Special Laws, 1902, pp. 3-4, 6-7, 8, 10, 11, 12

11

Laws limiting the right of Japanese immigrants in the United States to own land were passed in several Far Western states during the early twentieth century. The laws compounded the pressures upon people who already had been denied citizenship.[7]

(a)

Section 1. All aliens eligible to citizenship under the laws of the United States may acquire, possess, enjoy, transmit and inherit real property, or any interest therein, in this state, in the same manner and to the same extent as citizens of the United States, except as otherwise provided by the laws of this state. Section 2. All aliens other than those mentioned in section one of this act may acquire, possess, enjoy and transfer real property, or any interest therein, in this state, in the manner and to the extent and for the purpose prescribed by any treaty now existing between the government of the United States and the nation or country of which such alien is a citizen or subject, and not otherwise.

Section 4. Hereafter no alien mentioned in section two hereof and no company, association or corporation...may be appointed guardian of that portion of the estate of a minor which consists of property which such alien or such company, association or corporation is inhibited from acquiring, possessing, enjoying or transferring by reason of the provisions of this act. The public administration of the proper county, or any other competent person or corporation, may be appointed guardian by the estate of a minor citizen whose parents are ineligible to appointment under the provisions of this section.

On such notice to the guardian as the court may require, the superior court may remove the guardian of such as estate whenever it appears to the satisfaction of the court:

(a) That the guardian has failed to file the report required by the provisions of section five hereof; or

(b) That the property of the ward has not been or is not being administered with due regard to the primary interest of the ward; or

(c) That facts exist which would make the guardian ineligible to appointment in the first instance; or

(d) That facts establishing any other legal ground for removal exist.

Section 6. Whenever it appears to the court in any probate proceeding that by reason of the provisions of this act any heir or devisee cannot take real property of in this state or membership or shares of stock in a company, association or corporation which, but for said provisions, said heir or devisee would take as such, the court, instead of ordering a distribution of such property to such heir or devisee, shall order sale of said property to be made in the manner provided by law for probate sales of property and the proceeds of such sale shall be distributed to such heir or devisee in lieu of such property.

Section 7. Any real property hereafter acquired in fee in violation of the provisions of this act by any alien mentioned in section two of this act, or by any company, association or corporation mentioned in section three of this act, shall escheat to, and become and remain the property of the State of California. The attorney general or district attorney of the proper county shall institute proceedings to have the escheat of such real property adjudged and enforced in the manner provided by section four hundred seventy-four of the Political Code and title eight, part three of the Code of Civil Procedure. Upon the entry of final judgment in such proceedings, the title to such real property shall pass to the State of California. The provisions of this section and of sections two and three of this act shall not apply to any real property hereafter acquired in the enforcement or in satisfaction of any lien now existing upon, or interest in such property, so long as such real property so acquired shall remain the property of the alien, company, association or corporation acquiring the same in such manner. No alien, company, association or corporation mentioned in section two or section three hereof shall hold for a longer period than two years the possession of any agricultural land acquired in the enforcement or in satisfaction of a mortgage or other lien hereafter made or acquired in good faith to secure a debt.

California Anti-Alien Land Law, 1920

(b)

Section 2. An alien shall not own land or take or hold title thereto. No person shall take or hold land or title to land for an alien. Land now held by or for aliens in violation of the constitution of the state is forfeited to and declared to be the property of the state. Land hereafter conveyed to or for the use of aliens in violation of the constitution or of this act shall thereby be forfeited and become the property of the state.

Section 3. An alien is not qualified to be trustee under a will, executor, administrator or guardian, if any part of the estate is land; Provided, An alien now lawfully acting in any such capacity may continue for not more than two years.

Section 4. If hereafter an alien acquire land by inheritance or in good faith either under mortgage or in the ordinary course of justice in the collection of debts, and remaining an alien, hold the same for more than twelve years from the date title was so acquired or control or possession taken, the land shall be forfeited to the state.

Section 5. If an alien claiming or holding under a mortgage has control, possession, use or enjoyment of the mortgaged land, the obligation secured by the mortgage shall be deemed matured and the mortgage shall be foreclosed; and if the land not be sold under foreclosure within three years after the alien has obtained control, possession, use or enjoyment, the mortgage and the obligation thereby secured shall be forfeited to the state and shall be foreclosed for the use of the state.

Section 6. Unless an alien who has declared his intention to become a citizen of the United States be admitted to citizenship within seven years after his declaration was made, it shall be presumed that he declared his intention in bad faith.

Washington Anti-Alien Land Law, 1921

12

While the Alien Land Acts represented a wave of discriminatory legislation against Japanese immigrants (Issei), they also generated opposition. Through diverse channels and activities, Japanese on the West Coast launched a series of appeals,[8] while supporters demanded that the Japanese be accorded equal rights. Although the hearings on Japanese immigration, held by the House Committee on Immigration and Naturalization on the West Coast in 1920, served essentially as a forum for anti-immigrant diatribes, there were a number of witnesses who testified in favor of the Japanese and who made a number of clearly anti-racist arguments. Among them were the Los Angeles Baptist minister C.C. Pierce (a), whose statement below was incorporated with his answers to questions; John P. Irish (b), a wealthy farmer and member of the Oakland Chamber of Commerce whose pamphlet on the "anti-Japanese pogrom" was incorporated into the published proceedings as Exhibit B, and who refused to denounce interracial marriage and relationships despite the prodding of his questioners[9]; and Erwin B. Ault (c), editor of the Seattle Union Record, *voice of the Seattle Central Labor Council; Ault had been a major player in the Seattle General Strike in 1919.[10] The Oakland-based American Committee of Justice, which included political figures, landowners, merchants, clergymen, academicians, and John Irish, among others, produced a pamphlet (d), from which a passage against the Alien Land Act is excerpted.[11] The Committee's efforts were not all in vain: over a third of the voters in California opposed the Act in the November 1920 election.*

(a)

There is no real Japanese problem in California. The so-called Japanese problem is based upon a number of facts and considerations, some of which are real, but some are imaginary and the outgrowth of prejudice, ignorance, and selfishness. That the Japanese people are here in considerable numbers, that they carry on their activities upon some of the best land in California, that they are fairly prolific as a race, that they live in rather simple conditions in many cases, that they are diligent workers, that they are increasing in numbers, and doubtless some other things which might be mentioned, either for or against them, present various phases of the truth. But most of the things which are urged against the Japanese and which are true or contain an element of the truth present a very different aspect when viewed from the standpoint of international comity, friendship, and true Americanism than when presented in an unqualified manner and in the spirit of misunderstanding.

Many things urged against the Japanese are wholly untrue or are so nearly wholly untrue that to state them is to deceive and mislead. It is not true at all that they have "crowded the young white men off the farm and the ranch," that they are a people coming to possess this country who hold "a divided allegiance," that they "do not understand or appreciate our institutions," that the Americans are beholding their "possessions wiped out," that they are "an unassimilable race," that "they send the most of their money earned here back to Japan," and maintain an unswerving loyalty to their native country any more than do those of other nations.

Unfortunately, there exists a rather positive element of race prejudice in the minds of many people, and in the case of the Japanese and our relations to them and our estimation of the various elements introduced by their presence it is quite evident that this prejudice is rather widely and generally manifested in the State of California. Most of the facts which exist in connection with the presence of the Japanese people in this State, however, exist wherever people of one nationality come in considerable numbers to take up their residence among those of another race.

Practically all of the things, or at least many of them, which I hear constantly urged against the Japanese I heard as a boy urged against the Scotch and the Irish in rural New York, and later in the city of New York and Boston against practically all of the people of southern Europe who came there in throngs to live....

If we have a real Japanese problem, there is one and only one just and wide solution of it. Admit the Japanese to this country on precisely the same basis that we admit other foreigner. When here, treat them precisely as we treat the others. Naturalize those who desire to be naturalized, give them the same advantages as we do others, continue to extend to them the same hand of friendship which we have heretofore in the main extended to them, test out by actual experiment their ability to assimilate and measure their deserts, not by unreasoning race prejudice, but by an honest recognition of the actual facts.

Statement of C.C. Pierce, House of Representatives, Committee on Immigration and Naturalization, *Hearings on Japanese Immigration*, 66th Congress, 2nd Session, Part I, July 12, 13, and 14, 1920, Washington, 1921, pp. 938-939

(b)

Let it be repeated that the present anti-Japanese agitation, like the anti-Chinese movement of years ago, has the same psychology as the Russian anti-Jewish pogrom, which always starts with the lie that Jews have murdered Christian children to use their blood in the rites of the synagogue. The leader of the anti-Japanese pogrom is Senator Phelan [of California]. An election is approaching. He has made no record of any benefit to the State in the Senate, so he must divert attention from his uselessness as a Senator by attacking the Japanese and trying to stampede the State by lying about them.

It is my purpose to take up his public statements and those of his helpers in this ignoble work and prove them false, not by my word but by official and other indisputable authority.

Senator Phelan began his pogrom by publishing that an American company has sold to Japanese 800,000 acres of land on the Mexican side of the Imperial Valley.

The American company at once proved this to be a lie. It had not sold land anywhere to Japanese.

Mr. Phelan then changed his statement and charged that the Mexican Government had sold 800,000 acres of land adjoining our boundary to Japanese, and that this was a violation of the Monroe Doctrine.

The Mexican Government immediately replied with proof that it had not sold land anywhere to Japanese, and, as Senator Phelan had claimed that under the Monroe Doctrine the United States can dictate to the States of Central and South America what private parties may own land in their jurisdiction, President Carranza very promptly and properly repudiated the Monroe Doctrine.

In November Mr. Phelan published in the *Chico Enterprise* that he had been approached by a Japanese, who presented a letter from our ambassador to Tokyo, and who proposed that we should surrender the whole Imperial Valley to the Japanese.

But the Senator had furnished a clue to test the truth of the story by naming a letter from our ambassador, and soon changed the story; and in its new form, it was published in the *California Cultivator* of January 31, 1920, as follows:

"When I left Washington an American representing powerful Japanese organizations said to be backed by the Japanese Government proposed that Americans be ousted from the Imperial Valley and it be turned over to the Japanese."

Notice that in this last version no names are mentioned and no clue given, not even finger marks. As no Japanese and no American can be thought of to be fool enough to go to Mr. Phelan with such an idiotic proposition, the statement has the face of a lie in both versions.

In November he made a speech to the Chamber of Commerce of Oakland. After some vagrant vituperation of the Japanese, he ventured upon a specific statement to call attention to the "horrible condition of Merced County, overrun by Japanese, who own there 5,000 acres of the best farm land in the county."

I immediately wrote to the recorder of Merced County to let me know the acreage owned by Japanese. In reply he sent me the 1919 report of the county assessor, just made to the State controller. The assessor says there are 185 Japanese in Merced County. They own 395 acres of farm land and 36 town lots. There are 27 Japanese children in the primary schools and 2 in the high school. The white neighbors of the Japanese all say they are good people to do business with, unobjectionable.

On the 18th of last December Mr. Phelan made an anti-Japanese speech to the Commonwealth Club in San Francisco, in which he said that Japanese births in California were three to one white birth.

The official report of the State board of health, sent to me by Mr. Ross, registrar of vital statistics, show for 1919:

White births.. 50,898

Japanese births.................................... 4,378

The records of the board of health show more white births in the single year 1919 than Japanese births in the ten years preceding. His speech on that occasion strung together other lies on this birth rate lie, like beads on a string.

In their statements made to the Committee on Immigration of the United States Senate, both Senator Phelan and Mr. McClatchy said that there were in California 20,000 picture brides and that "usually each give birth to a child once a year." The official report of the California Board of Health for 1919 records 4,378 Japanese births in the State for that year. So that of the imaginary picture brides, 20,000 in number, reported by Phelan and McClatchy, more than 16,000 must have been asleep at the switch.

After Gov. Stephens refused to call an extra session of legislature to pass anti-Japanese laws, Phelan said in Washington that the governor had received a letter from the Japanese Association warmly thanking him for his refusal, and Phelan published the letter.

I wrote the governor's office asking if he had received such a letter. The answer was: "Phelan's statement is an absolute lie."

There are men in San Francisco who know the inside facts about this little comedy. When those facts are made public, as they undoubtedly will be, the Senator will have to face an embarrassing situation. In the meantime, it is sufficient to say that the governor never received the letter.

Recently a questionable item in a naval appropriation bill was before the Senate. Mr. Phelan demanded its passage as necessary to the defense of this coast, for as he said, "the largest Japanese warship lies in the harbor of Honolulu."

A few days later the Associated Press published from its agent in Honolulu that no Japanese warship was in Hawaiian waters, nor had been for a long time. Commenting on this, the *New York Sun* said maybe Senator Phelan does not know where Hawaii is.

The Senator has uttered other defamatory statements, and every one is a lie. They are as thick in his record as cooties in a battle trench. I leave him now to attend to the cases of his companions in falsehood and exaggeration.

I dislike to say that Mr. McClatchy, of the *Sacramento Bee*, intentionally lies, but his bitter prejudice and hatred had fed his credulity until he has become a "carrier" of falsehoods, as some people are "carriers" of typhoid. Mr. McClatchy has published that during the 12 months ending June 30, 1919, 9,678 Japanese were found to be illegally in this country and were arrested and deported.

Now, the official report of the Commissioner of Immigration shows 9 Japanese deported for being illegally in the country in the year ending June 30, 1918.

The commissioner's report for the next year, ending June 30, 1919, shows 117 contraband Japanese were apprehended and deported. So, for the full year covered by Mr. McClatchy's statement, the official report shows only 126 Japanese illegally in the country and deported.

I wrote the Commissioner General of Immigration asking the foundation for Mr. McClatchy's statement, and that official seems to think that his official report, above quoted, is sufficient answer. The circumstantial evidence is against the truth of Mr. McClatchy's figures, since the arrest of so large a number could not have escaped the notice of the newspapers and of the Japanese consul. Mr. McClatchy follows his apocryphal figures with the statement that "No account is taken of the picture brides who arrived." This is not true. They all had to land at the immigration station and be registered, undergo a physical examination, and their names and those of their husbands recorded.

In Mr. McClatchy's statement to the immigration section of the Commonwealth Club he said the Japanese on landing at first drive white labor out by working for low wages and then proceed to conquer everything. This statement is not true. I am a farmer, and know, as do all farmers, there was no white labor to drive out. Instead of working for low wages, the Japanese in California are paid the highest farm wages in the world, and they are the most industrious and skillful land people in the State.

The glaring falsehoods of Hon. John S. Chambers I have already answered. The lies in the newspapers are too numerous to mention. One in the *Call* may suffice. That paper, under infuriating headlines, published that Japanese stevedores in loading an American cargo of vegetable oils had maliciously punched holes in the tin containers with loading hooks, and the oil leaked out, and this was done to damage American commerce. The owner of the oil in San Francisco and the officers of the ship at once exposed the story as a malicious lie, as did Lloyd's, whose surveyor in Kobe watched the loading and certified to the proper condition of the cargo. Then it was shown by the same parties that Japanese stevedores use no loading hooks. But did the *Call* correct the lie? Not up to date.

Another member of Phelan's pogrom gang publishes that Japanese have leased 10,000,000 acres of land in the Sutter Basin. Go to the maps in the office of the State reclamation board and you find that in the whole Sutter Basin, from the mouth of Butte Slough to the confluence of the Sacramento and Feather Rivers, there are only 60,000 acres. But people who don't know what or where Sutter Basin is, read that 10,000,000 lie and rush to join the anti-Japanese pogrom.

Senator Phelan has published a study of the "hybrids," as he calls them, half Japanese and half white children. I refuse to accept his expert opinion.

During the anti-Chinese pogrom there were long and hot discussions over Chinese and white hybrids, impossibility of assimilation, etc. But the multimillionaire Chinese Ah Fong, of Honolulu, had a bevy of charming daughters by his wife, who was half Portuguese and Hawaiian. The Ah Fong girls were the toast of the Pacific, beautiful and accomplished, and they all married well, to white gentlemen, several of the husbands being officers in the American Army and Navy.

It is demonstrated by the foregoing that politicians are trying to stampede the people of California to do an act of dishonor against an industrious, cleanly, and law-abiding people. The proposed initiative measure has to go back to the cruelties attending the expulsion of the Jews from Spain to find an equal in cruelty, inhumanity, and dishonor. It violates our treaty with Japan and the fourteenth amendment of our own Constitution, and is a proper offspring of the disgraceful lies from which it comes. I stand for American honor, decency, and fair play; I stand for what is called our Christian civilization and wonder if there is enough of its spirit in California to save the honor of the State.

Exhibit B, "The Anti-Japanese Pogrom - Facts Versus the Falsehoods of Senator Phelan and Others" (1920), by Col. John P. Irish, in *Hearings on Japanese Immigration and Naturalization*, pp. 5-7

(c)

The Chairman. Now, speaking of the central labor council, have you a membership in that order?

Mr. Ault. Yes; I am a delegate to the central labor council from the typographical union. I am also elected manager or editor of the *Union Record* by the central labor council.

The Chairman. So that the views expressed in your paper might be considered the views of organized labor?

Mr. Ault. Yes; with certain limitations. There is a certain amount of personal expression.

The Chairman. We all have that.

Mr. Ault. I have not yet been successfully opposed as editor of the *Union Record.*

The Chairman. The faction that elects you is a majority in the Central Labor Council of Seattle?

Mr. Ault. Yes.

The Chairman. Now, we have been confronted with statements in this record to the effect that labor in Seattle had ceased to object to the admission of the Japanese on the ground that he had ceased to become a competitor of labor itself and was a competitor of the small business man.

Mr. Ault. I started to explain that.

The Chairman. If you will.

Mr. Ault (continuing). That tendency has arisen - the workers made a losing fight without receiving any assistance from the business element. The Japanese were admitted as a convenience to both the big and small businesses. There would never any of them have found any lodgment here if a business man did not give them employment. When they originally came here they could not provide employment for themselves. I believe that the Great Northern Railway was the chief offender in that respect. It employed more of them than any other single employer. The lumber interests in the sawmills have employed more Hindus that any other single employer - Hindus and orientals - I distinguish between the Hindus and the Japanese and the Chinese - they are different racial stock. And labor has, I believe, become rather luke warm on the subject of immigration; that is, of oriental immigration, as distinguished from all immigration. Having admitted them, having brought them here to serve the interests of the employing class - we certainly did not bring them here - we feel that it is - I say "we" - that again is a point of issue - it is a debatable point - a certain proportion of the labor movement believes in organizing the Japanese, believes in raising the standard of living of the Japanese to that of the white man, believes in making him economically equal, and I believe that a very considerable portion of the labor movement in the Northwest has come to that conclusion. It would not be hard, however, for you to find many witnesses in the ranks of labor and prominent in the ranks of labor who will take a contrary attitude. That would be particularly true amongst the culinary crafts, in which the Japanese are the principal competitors of white workingmen.

The Chairman. And the barbers?

Mr. Ault. The barbers are less affected. The Japanese have a large number of barber shops, but the number of white barbers is constantly increasing, and I doubt if the Japanese have made any great inroad on them.

The Chairman. Have any of the unions taken in Japanese members?

Mr. Ault. The machinists take in Japanese members, and I believe the timber workers, though I am not so sure of that.

The Chairman. Will you endeavor to ascertain, and when you receive this record put in a statement as to whether the timber workers do take in the Japanese? When you say "Japanese" do you mean all orientals, or just the Japanese?

Mr. Ault. I believe that the machinists have specifically admitted Japanese. I do not know that they have admitted any other orientals.

The Chairman. The machinists have delegates in your -

Mr. Ault (interposing). In the central labor council.

The Chairman. A large number of delegates?

Mr. Ault. Well, quite a considerable number. Five or six; I don't know exactly how many.

The Chairman. So, then, they propose to unionize all ranks of Japanese?

Mr. Ault. Those who are here. I think that the machinists, as well as other organizations, will stand with any program that will not cause international complication; that will tend to limit the further introduction of Japanese, or any other oriental labor. What we are trying to do generally is to wipe out, to avoid, all considerations of race prejudice in the discussion of this question; we consider it almost purely an economic question....

Mr. Raker. Now, in regard to wiping out the race question, you made a statement a while ago that we ought to wipe out the racial question. What do you mean by that?

Mr. Ault. I say any prejudice, simply because a man's skin is dark or fair - I don't think it is a fair estimate of a man's ability or capacity or usefulness to society or of his right to life, liberty, and the pursuit of happiness. I believe that the color of the man's skin has not anything to do with it.

Statement of Erwin B. Ault, *Hearings on Japanese Immigration and Naturalization*, pp. 1417-1418, 1421

(d)

Defeat It

....Initiative No. 1 aims to dispossess a helpless minority of aliens who have come here at our invitation and who are tilling California's soil in compliance with our laws. This Initiative, totally ineffective in restricting future Oriental immigration, merely persecutes the aliens against who it is directed, and sows the seeds of distrust in their minds. No fair-minded, far-seeing Californian could endorse such a proposition.

Only 2 per cent of California's total population is Japanese....We should not be placed in the ridiculous position of 98 per cent of our population being in fear of 2 per cent. We would be confessing ourselves weaklings and fools if we were to think that our institutions and civilization are being endangered by the presence of such a small number of Japanese, unobtrusive, law-abiding, minding their own business, and bothering nobody.

The area of land cultivated by Japanese in California amounts to only 1.6 per cent of our farm land. Even of this 1.6 per cent only a very small portion is actually owned or controlled by them. No man with a healthy mind can believe that this is a grave menace to the State.

Neither organized commerce nor organized labor is in sympathy with this Initiative. The San Francisco Chamber of Commerce has taken a definite stand against it. The labor councils of Sacramento and Stockton oppose it. Why? Because they know that this Initiative is not based upon the real need of the State, but upon the unreal fear conjured up by designing persons.

Japan permits a corporation, though composed entirely of non-Japanese, to own land. It allows alien individuals to lease land for fifty years, and to acquire superficies for unlimited period. Yet this Initiative denies this reciprocal privilege to a handful of Japanese in California.

This Initiative is an affront to the American tradition of honor and fair play. Our innate sense of justice revolts against it. It should be defeated because it insults the American people, rather than because it works hardship for the Japanese.

Defeat this Initiative, and we shall be in a stronger position in urging the Federal Government to protect California against further influx of Oriental immigration. Adopt it, and we shall merely embarrass our Government and make the solution of the real trouble all the more difficult.

Vote NO on Initiative No. 1 on November 2.

The American Committee of Justice, *California and the Japanese: A Compilation of Arguments Advertised in Newspapers by the American Committee of Justice, Together With the Memorial Addressed to Congress by the Said Committee*, Oakland, 1920, pp. 6-7

Notes

1. A comprehensive analysis of the fate of exclusion laws in the courts is provided by Lucy Salyer, "Captives of the Law: Judicial Enforcement of the Chinese Exclusion Laws, 1891-1905," *Journal of American History*, Vol. 76, No. 1 (June 1989), pp. 91-117. Connie Young Yu surveys the broader legal history in "The Chinese in American Courts," *Bulletin of Concerned Asian Scholars*, Vol. 4, No. 3 (Fall 1972), pp. 22-30.

2. There is much on George and the Chinese in Alexander Saxton, *The Indispensable Enemy: Labor and the Anti-Chinese Movement in California*, Berkeley, 1971, chapters 5 and 6. See also Edward J. Rose, *Henry George*, New York, 1968, pp. 40-43; Anna George de Mille, *Henry George: Citizen of the World*, Chapel Hill, 1950, pp. 57-59.

3. Winn's background and activities are detailed in Saxton, pp. 79-108.

4. Good surveys of the make-up and social function of the Six Companies can be found in Shih-Shan Henry Tsai, *The Chinese Experience in America*, Bloomington, 1986, pp. 45-50; Sucheng Chan, *Asian Americans: An Interpretative History*, Boston, 1991, pp. 63-67.

5. Hoar's career is described in Richard E. Welch, *George Frisbie Hoar and the Half-breed Republicans*, Cambridge, 1971. Hoar became active in the Anti-Imperialist League in the late nineteenth century: see Philip S. Foner, *The Spanish-Cuban-American War and the Birth of American Imperialism*, New York, 1972, pp. 186, 416, 580, 582.

6. The Chinese Exclusion Act of 1882; see document 3b.

7. Ronald Takaki supplies a clear analysis of the alien land laws in *Strangers from a different Shore: A History of Asian Americans*, Boston, 1989, pp. 203-208. See also the pioneering study by K.K. Kawakami, *The Real Japanese Question*, New York, 1921. A detailed account is Teruka Okada Kachi's dissertation, *The Treaty of 1911 and the Immigration and Alien Land Law Issue Between the United States and Japan, 1911-1913*, published by Arno Press (New York) in 1978.

8. See for example, Toyoji Chiba, *Truth of the Japanese Farming in California*, in U.S. House of Representatives, Committee on Immigration and Naturalization, *Hearings on Japanese Immigration*, 66th Congress, 2nd Session, Part I, July 12, 13, and 14, 1920, Washington, 1921, pp. 182-191; *Text of Resolution Adopted by the Japanese Agricultural Association at its Convention at the State Fair at Sacramento, September 4, 1918*, in *Hearings*, p. 768; *Memorial Presented to the President while at San Francisco on September 18, 1919*, in *Hearings*, pp. 174-182; *Summary Statement Presented by United North American Japanese Associations, July 29, 1920, Seattle, Wash.*, in *Hearings*, pp. 1202-1209.

9. Member of the House Committee asked many witnesses about their views on intermarriage during the hearings. Dissent from the racial superiority explicit in that line of questioning can also be found in the testimony of Ms. L.S. Woodruff, a Stockton, California public school teacher, in *Hearings*, pp. 496-497.

10. Harvey O'Connor's *Revolution in Seattle: A Memoir*, New York, 1964, remains a leading account of the general strike and includes material on Ault. Substantial material on Ault and Seattle labor is in Carlos A. Schwantes, *Radical Heritage: Labor, Socialism, and Reform in Washington and British Columbia, 1885-1917*, Seattle, 1979.

11. Other appeals by both non-Japanese and Japanese groups were included in Appendices I through IV. The second edition of the pamphlet was published, with permission of the Committee, by the Japanese Association of America.

Part II: Statements by Public Figures and Organizations

Rooted in antebellum times, discrimination against Asian immigrants intensified dramatically during the last quarter of the nineteenth century. At the same time, resistance to racism and exclusion persisted and grew. Through organizations, petitions, pamphlets, speeches, and articles, public figures - both Asian and non-Asian - spoke against racist restrictions, treaties, and pogroms. Chinese organizations challenged discrimination from the very beginning [Document 1]. Few Americans were as adamant in support of Chinese rights as Mark Twain, whose major essays on the subject cover the period of its greatest controversy [Documents 2 and 3a and b]. The exchange between Henry George and John Stuart Mill in 1869 offers a comparison between the anti-immigrant views of the former and the more tolerant approach of the latter [Documents 4a and b]. Well-known abolitionist and reformer Wendell Phillips supported the right of free, voluntary Chinese immigration to the United States [Document 5], as did his longtime friend and colleague William Lloyd Garrison [Document 10].

In response to the crystallization of anti-Chinese sentiment in legal form, significant voices were raised in opposition. No sooner had the 1876 Congressional hearings concluded than there appeared Augustus Layres' strong denunciation of exclusion and its chief Senatorial protagonist, Aaron Sargent of California [Document 6]; Joseph C.G. Kennedy's critique of Sargent's report was in the same vein [Document 7]. Chung Wai Hsin Pao's pamphlet [Document 8] and the satiric *Uncle Sam-ee and his Little Chin-ee* [Document 9] came out in 1879. Violence and threats against the Chinese in San Francisco provoked the articles comprising Documents 11, 12a and b.

Anti-Chinese attacks were by no means confined to California: the 1880's witnessed a wave of assaults in the Pacific Northwest, in Seattle, Portland, and Tacoma, and in the Territories of Montana and Wyoming. Judge Roger S. Greene's speech and the reaction in the press [Document 13] indicate the bitterness of the debate. As exclusion became more entrenched in policy, the Chinese community again spoke in resistance [Documents 14, 15, and 19];an

Irish-American co-authored one of the statements herein. An article from 1893 illustrates that on the East Coast too, burdens on the Chinese could take a tragic course [Document 16]. Another piece demonstrates that at least one West Coast daily deviated from he prevailing attitude toward the Chinese [Document 17]. In a statement made at the dawn of the twentieth century, the writer Joaquin Miller denounces those who would bar or "bully" the Chinese [Document 18].

1

Responding to an anti-Chinese speech by Governor Bigler of California in 1855, a committee of Chinese merchants in San Francisco submitted the following message, penned by businessman Lai Chun-chung of the Chai Lung firm. The remarks defend the integrity of Chinese in America, their thriftiness, honesty and fidelity to law; the pamphlet exhibits a certain anti-working class tone.

We have read the message of the Governor.

Firstly - it is stated that "too large a number of the men of the Flowery Kingdom have emigrated to this country, and that they have come here alone, without their families." We may state among the reasons for this that the wives and families of the better families of China have generally compressed feet; they live in the utmost privacy; they are unused to winds and waves; and it is exceedingly difficult to bring families upon distant journies over great oceans. Yet a few have come; nor are they all. And further, there have been several injunctions warning the people of the Flowery land not to come here, which have fostered doubts; nor have our hearts found peace in regard to bringing families. Suppose you say, "we will restrain only those who work in the mines; we would not forbid merchants," it is replied, that the merchandize imported by Chinese merchants chiefly depends upon Chinese consumption. If there be no Chinese miners allowed, what business can we have to do? The occupations are mutually dependent, like tooth and lip; neither can spare the other.

It is, we are assured, the principle of your honorable country to protect the people; and it has benevolence to mankind at heart. Now, the natives of China, or of any strange country, have one nature. All consider that good and evil cannot be in unison. All nations are really the same. Confucius says: "Though a city had but ten houses, there must be some in it honest and true." Suppose then we see it declared that "the people of the Flowery land are altogether without good," we can not but fear that the rulers do not exercise a liberal public spirit, and that they defer their own knowledge of right to an undue desire to please men....

If it be observed that the "number of our merchants in your honorable State is not great," we reply, that nevertheless the amount of merchandize arriving here is not small, embracing imports by men of all other nations, as well as the business of our own traders. And this mutual general traffic fills the coffers of thousands, and involves the interests of myriads of people. But the miner in the mountain, and the workman in the shop, do no less than the merchant, pay respect to your customs....

Some have remarked that "emigrants from other countries bring their families; that their homes are distributed over the State; that some engage in manual employments, and amass wealth; that thus mutual interests are created, mutual civilities extended, and common sympathies excited; that while in every respect they adopt your customs, on the contrary the Chinese do not." To this we rejoin, that the manners and customs of China and of foreign countries are not alike. This is an ancient principle, and is prevalent now. What if other countries do differ somewhat from your honorable nation in hats, and clothes, and letters, and other things, while there is much that is common? In China itself, the people differ. In China, there are some distinctions in the inhabitants of various provinces, or departments, or counties, or townships, or even villages. Their dialects, their manners, their sentiments, do not wholly accord. Their articles of use are not all made by one rule. Their common customs all differ. One line cannot be drawn for all. And just so it must be in all parts of the world. It would certainly appear unreasonable, when the officers and the merchants of your honorable country come to our Middle Kingdom, were they rebuked for not knowing our language, or for not being acquainted with our affairs....

Finally. It is said that "henceforth you would prevent the emigration of people of the Flowery land." Hitherto our people have been imbued with your sacred doctrines; we have tried to exercise modesty and reason. If we can henceforth be treated with mutual courtesy, then we shall be glad to dwell within your honorable boundaries. But if the rabble are to harass us, we wish to return to our former homes. We will speedily send and arrest the embarkation of any that have not yet come. And now we, who are here, do earnestly request that a definite time be fixed, by which we may be governed, within which we can return our merchandize, and make any necessary arrangements. We trust that in that case the friendly intercourse of previous days will not be interrupted; and that your honorable nation may maintain its principles in tenderly cherishing the strangers from afar. If there be no definite regulation upon this subject, but only these incessant rumors about forbidding the Chinese emigration, we fear the result will be that the class who know nothing, of every nation, will be seeking occasions to make trouble; that our Chinese people in the mines will be subjected to much concealed violence, to robbery of their property, and quarrels about their claims. Thus there will be unlimited trouble; and where will be the end of it?

Remarks of the Chinese Merchants of San Francisco Upon Governor Bigler's Message, And Some Common Questions; With Some Explanations of the Character of the Chinese Companies, and the Laboring Class in California, pamphlet, San Francisco, Whitton, Towne, & Co., 1855, pp. 3, 4, 5-6

2

Mark Twain was a leading supporter of the rights of Asian immigrants in the United States. Not coincidentally, he became a sharp critic of American imperialism, and not least of all, U.S. intervention in Asian nations during the late nineteenth and early twentieth century. Though the Burlingame Treaty [see Part I] barred the Chinese from naturalization, it promised to protect the rights of the Chinese in the United States, which greatly encouraged Twain and prompted him to write the article excerpted below.

They can never beat and bang and set the dogs on the Chinamen any more. These pastimes are lost to them forever. In San Francisco, a large part of the most interesting local news in the daily papers consists of gorgeous compliments to the 'able and efficient' Officer This and That for arresting Ah Foo, or Ching Wang, or Song Hi for stealing a chicken; but when some white brute breaks an unoffending Chinaman's head with a brick, the paper does not compliment any officer for arresting the assaulter, for the simple reason that the officer does not make the arrest; the shedding of Chinese blood only makes him laugh; he considers it fun of the most entertaining description. I have seen dogs almost tear helpless Chinamen to pieces in broad daylight in San Francisco, and I have seen hod-carriers who help to make Presidents stand around and enjoy the sport. I have seen troops of boys assault a Chinaman with stones when he was walking quietly along about his business, and send him bruised and bleeding home. I have seen Chinamen abused and maltreated in all the mean, cowardly ways possible to the invention of a degraded nature, but I never saw a Chinaman righted in a court of justice for wrongs thus done him. The California laws do not allow Chinamen to testify against white men. California is one of the most liberal and progressive States in the Union, and the best and worthiest of her citizens will be glad to know that the days of persecuting Chinamen are over, in California.

"The Treaty with China," *New York Tribune,* August 9, 1868

3

In a series of satirical pieces in The Galaxy *in 1870-1871, Mark Twain assailed the hypocrisy of American democracy in its treatment of Chinese immigrants.*

(a)

In San Francisco, the other day, "A well-dressed boy, on his way to Sunday school, was arrested and thrown into the city prison for stoning Chinamen." What a commentary is this upon human justice! What sad prominence it gives to our human disposition to tyrannize over the weak! San Francisco has little right to take credit to herself for her treatment of this poor boy. What had the child's education been? How should he suppose it was wrong to stone a Chinaman? Before we side against him, along with outraged San Francisco, let us give him a chance - let us hear the testimony for the defence.

He was a "well-dressed" boy, and a Sunday-school scholar, and therefore, the chances are that his parents were intelligent, well-to-do people, with just enough natural villainy in their composition to make them yearn after the daily papers, and enjoy them; and so this boy had opportunities to learn all through the week how to do right, as well as on Sunday.

It was in this way that he found out that the great common-wealth of

California imposes an unlawful mining-tax upon John the foreigner, and allows Patrick the foreigner to dig gold for nothing - probably because the degraded Mongol is at no expense for whisky, and the refined Celt cannot exist without it.

It was in this way that he found out that a respectable number of the tax-gatherers - it would be unkind to say all of them - collect the taxes twice, instead of once; and that, inasmuch as they do it solely to discourage Chinese immigration into the mines, it is a thing that is much applauded, and likewise regarded as singularly facetious.

It was in this way that he found out that when a white man robs a sluice box (by the term white man is meant Spaniards, Mexicans, Portuguese, Irish, Hondurans, Peruvians, Chileans, etc., etc.), they make him leave the camp; and when a Chinaman does that thing, they hang him.

It was in this way that he found out that in many districts of the vast Pacific coast, so strong is the wild free love of justice in the hearts of the people, that whenever any secret and mysterious crime is committed, they say, "Let justice be done, though the heavens fall," and go straightway and swing a Chinaman.

It was in this way that he found out that by studying one half of each day's "local items," it would appear that the police of San Francisco were either asleep or dead, and by studying the other half it would seem that the reporters were gone mad with admiration of the energy, the virtue, the high effectiveness, and the daredevil intrepidity of that very police-making exultant mention of how "the Argus-eyed officer So-an-so," captured a wretched knave of a Chinaman who was stealing chickens, and brought him gloriously to the city prison; and how "the gallant officer Such-and-such-a-one," quietly kept an eye on the movements of an "un-suspecting, almond-eyed son of Confucius" (your reporter is nothing if not facetious), following him around with that far-off look of vacancy and unconsciousness always so finely affected by that inscrutable being, the forty-dollar policeman, during a walking interval, and captured him at last in the very act of placing his hands in a suspicious manner upon a paper of tacks, left by the owner in an exposed situation; and how one officer performed this prodigious thing, and another officer that, and another the other - and pretty much every one of these performances having for a dazzling central incident a Chinaman guilty of a shilling's worth of crime, an unfortunate, whose misdemeanor must be hurrahed into something enormous in order to keep the public from noticing how many really important rascals went uncaptured in the meantime, and how overrated those glorified policemen actually are.

It was in this way that the boy found out that the legislature, being aware that the Constitution has made America an asylum for the poor and the oppressed of all nations, and that therefore the poor and oppressed who fly to our shelter must not be charged a disabling admission fee, made a law that every Chinaman, upon landing, must be *vaccinated* upon the wharf and pay to the State's appointed officer *ten dollars* for the service, when there are plenty of doctors in San Francisco who would be glad enough to do it for him for fifty cents.

It was in this way that the boy found out that a Chinaman had no rights that any man was bound to respect; that he had no sorrows that any man was bound to pity, that neither his life nor his liberty was worth the purchase of a penny when a white man needed a scapegoat; that nobody loved Chinamen, that nobody befriended them, nobody spared them suffering when it was convenient to inflict it; everybody, individuals, communities, the majesty of the State itself, joined in hating, abusing, and persecuting these humble strangers.

And, therefore, what could have been more natural than for this sunny-hearted boy, tripping along to Sunday school, with his mind teeming with freshly-learned incentives to high and virtuous action, to say to himself-

"Ah, there goes a Chinaman! God will not love me if I do not stone him."

And for this he was arrested and put in the city jail.

Everything conspired to teach him that it was a high and holy thing to stone a Chinamen, and yet he no sooner attempts to do his duty than he is punished for it - he, poor chap, who has been aware all his life that one of the principal recreations of the police, out toward the Gold Refinery, is to look on with tranquil enjoyment while the butchers of Brennan Street set their dogs on unoffending Chinamen, and make them flee for their lives.*

Keeping in mind the tuition in the humanities which the entire "Pacific coast" gives its youth, there is a very sublimity of incongruity in the virtuous flourish with which the good city fathers of San Francisco proclaim (as they have lately done) that "The police are positively ordered to arrest all boys of every description and wherever found, who engage in assaulting Chinamen."

Still, let us be truly glad they have made the order, notwithstanding its inconsistency; and let us rest perfectly confident that the police are glad, too. Because there is no personal peril in arresting boys, provided they be of the small kind, and the reporters will have to laud their performances just as loyally as ever, or go without items.

The new form for local items in San Francisco will now be: "The ever vigilant and efficient officer So-and-so succeeded, yesterday afternoon, in arresting Master Tommy Jones, after a determined resistance," etc., etc., followed by the customary statistics and final hurrah, with its unconscious sarcasm: "We are happy in being able to state that this is the forty-seventh boy arrested by this gallant officer since the new ordinance went into effect. The most extraordinary activity prevails in the police department. Nothing like it has been seen since we can remember."

* I have many such memories in my mind, but am thinking just at present of one particular one, where the Brennan Street butchers set their dogs on a Chinaman who was quietly passing with a basket of clothes on his head; and while the dogs mutilated his flesh, a butcher increased the hilarity of the occasion by knocking some of the Chinaman's teeth down his throat with half a brick. This incident sticks in my memory with a more malevolent tenacity perhaps, on account of the fact that I was in the employ of a San Francisco journal at the time, and was not allowed to publish it because it might offend some of the peculiar element that subscribed for the paper. (M.T.)

"Disgraceful Persecution of a Boy," *The Galaxy*, May 1870

(b)

As I passed along by one of those monster American tea stores in New York, I found a Chinaman sitting before it acting in the capacity of a sign. Everybody that passed by gave him a steady stare as long as their heads would twist over their shoulders without dislocating their necks, and a group bad stopped to stare deliberately.

Is it not a shame that we, who prate so much about civilization and humanity, are content to degrade a fellow-being to such an office as this? Is it not time for reflection when we find ourselves willing to see in such a being matter for frivolous curiosity instead of regret and grave reflection? Here was a poor creature whom hard fortune had exiled from his natural home beyond the seas, and whose troubles ought to have touched these idle strangers that thronged about him; but did it? Apparently not. Men calling themselves superior race, the race of culture and of gentle blood, scanned his quaint Chinese hat with peaked roof and ball on top, and his long queue dangling down his back; his short silken blouse, curiously frogged and figured (and, like the rest of his raiment, rusty, dilapidated, and awkwardly put on); his blue cotton, tight-legged pants, tied close around the ankles; and his clumsy blunt-toed shoes with thick cork soles; and having so scanned him from head to foot, cracked some unseemly joke about his outlandish attire or his melancholy face, and passed on. In my heart I pitied the friendless Mongol. I wondered what was passing behind his sad face, and what distant scene his vacant eye was dreaming of. Were his thoughts with his heart, ten thousand miles away, beyond the billowy wastes of the Pacific? among the rice-fields and the plumy palms of China? under the shadows of remembered mountain peaks, or in groves of bloomy shrubs and strange forest trees unknown to climes like ours? And now and then, rippling among his visions and his dreams, did he hear familiar laughter and half-forgotten voices, and did he catch fitful glimpses of the friendly faces of a bygone time? A cruel fate it is, I said, that is befallen this bronzed wanderer. In order that the group of idlers might be touched at least by the words of the poor fellow, since the appeal of his pauper dress and his dreary exile was lost upon them, I touched him on the shoulder and said:

"Cheer up - don't be downhearted. It is not America that treats you in this way, it is merely one citizen, whose greed of gain has eaten the humanity out of his heart. America has a broader hospitality for the exiled and oppressed. America and Americans are always ready to help the unfortunate. Money shall be raised - you shall go back to China - you shall see your friends again. What wages do they pay you here?"

"Divil a cint but four dollars a week and find meself; but its aisy, barrin' the troublesome furrin clothes that's so expinsive."

The exile remains at his post. The New York tea merchants who need picturesque signs are not likely to run out of Chinamen.

"John Chinaman in New York," *The Galaxy*, September 1870

4

By 1869, the transplanted Philadelphian and author-to-be of Progress and Poverty - *a landmark work in American ethics and economic thought - Henry George had become a well-known newspaperman in the Bay Area: he was editor of the* Oakland Daily Transcript, *a paper representing the views of the local Democratic Party. While editor of the* Transcript, *he had published in the* New York Tribune *a lengthy article featuring economic and racial arguments in favor of Chinese exclusion (a), to which cause he had become increasingly sympathetic. Afterwards, he sent a copy of the article to famed British philosopher and political economist John Stuart Mill for comment. In his reply (b), published by George in the* Transcript, *Mill accepted some of George's postulates, but differed with others, including the matter of whether some people could exclude others from a part of the "earth's surface." In both cases, it is interesting to note how racist notions were so readily accepted by men famous for their concern for the general welfare.*[1]

(a)
THE WAGES QUESTION

It is obvious that Chinese competition must reduce wages, and it would seem just as obvious that, to the extent which it does this, its introduction is to the interest of capital and opposed to the interests of labor. But the advocates, upon the Pacific Coast, of the free introduction of these people, hold that this is not so, and, insisting upon the literal acceptance of the half truth that "the interests of labor and capital are identical," argue that a reduction of wages by this means will be a real benefit to the community at large, by attracting capital and stimulating production, while it will do no harm to the working classes, as the lessening of the cost of production will so reduce prices that the laborer will be able to purchase with his lower wages as much as before. According to them, the saving effected by the use of low-priced Chinese labor is precisely the same as that effected by the use of machinery; and as the introduction of machinery has resulted in increased comfort and employment for all classes, so, they argue, will the introduction of Chinese labor result. For, say they, the occupation of the lower branches of industry by the Chinese will open opportunities for the displaced whites in the higher, giving them employment as foremen, superintendents, clerks, etc., when they lose it as journeymen mechanics.

This, I believe, is a fair statement of the opinions held by a large and powerful class, and inasmuch as they are put forward by the most influential portion of the press, and advocated by many who claim the position of public teachers, they are worth an examination in detail. And as in examining them we touch upon questions which are and would be of general interest, even if there was not a single Chinaman in America or any prospect of one coming here (and for the sake of greater clearness), let us eliminate at first the Chinese and local considerations, and treat the general problem. If a general reduction of wages would, as is claimed, work no hardship to the laborer, because prices would fall in the same proportion, then the converse is true that it would work no benefit to his employer - as his receipts would diminish in the same ratio as his expenses, while the power of his capital would not appreciate, and no increase of production could take place.

If this position is correct, then the knotty labor question is indeed solved; the interests of labor and capital are indeed identical. Provided the movement be general, to raise wages as high and as often as asked would be only an act of empty complaisance on the part of the employers; to submit willingly to any reduction, only cheap courtesy on the part of the employed.

This fallacy rests upon the assumption that all profits, rents, etc., would be reduced by and in the same proportion as the reduction in wages, which is manifestly absurd. Nor, when we speak of a "general reduction of wages" in the sense the term is used in this discussion, we do not mean all wages, but only the wages of manual labor. Wages of superintendence, the professions, etc., would be unchanged, and could only be affected indirectly and after some time, by a reduction in the wages of manual labor.

And, as consumers constitute a larger body than laborers, even if consumers get the whole benefit of the reduction in the cost of production consequent on the lowering of wages, it is evident that the laborer's gain as a consumer would be less than his loss as a laborer. It requires no argument to show that to take $5 a day from five men, and to divide it again between them and two more, would be a losing operation to the five.

But consumers would not necessarily get the benefit of any part of the reduction in cost of production. The whole benefit would at first go to employers in increased profits. Whether any would subsequently come to consumers would depend upon the competition which increased profits caused. The more general the reduction of wages, the longer would it take for this competition to be felt; for if wages sank equally and profits rose equally, there would be no inducement for capital to leave one occupation and seek another, and the fresh accessions of capital to produce competition could only come from abroad or from new savings.

Plainly, when we speak of a reduction of wages in any general and permanent sense, we mean this, if we mean anything - that in the division of the joint production of labor and capital, the share of labor is to be smaller, that of capital larger. This is precisely what the reduction of wages consequent upon the introduction of Chinese labor means....

CHARACTER OF THE CHINESE

The population of our country has been drawn from many different sources; but hitherto, with but one exception these accessions have been of the same race, and though widely differing in language, customs and national characteristics, have been capable of being welded into a homogeneous people. The Mongolians, who are now coming among us on the other side of the continent, differ from our own race by as strongly marked characteristics as do the negroes, while they will not as readily fall into our ways as the negroes. The difference between the two races in this respect is as the difference between an ignorant but docile child, and a grown man, sharp but narrow-minded, opinionated and set in character. The negro when brought to this country was a simple barbarian with nothing to unlearn: the Chinese have a civilization and history of their own; a vanity which causes them to look down on all other races, habits of thought rendered permanent by being stamped upon countless generations. From present appearances we shall have a permanent Chinese population; but a population whose individual components will be constantly changing, at least for a long time to come. A population born in China, expecting to return to China, living here in a little China of its own, and without the slightest attachment to the country - utter heathens, treacherous, sensual, cowardly and cruel. They will bring no women with them (and probably will not for a little while yet) except those for purposes of prostitution; and the children of these, of whom there are some hundreds in California, will exercise upon the whole mass but little perceptible influence, while they will be in all respects as essentially Chinese as though born and reared in China.

To a certain extent the Chinese become quickly Americanized; but this Americanization is only superficial. They learn to buy and sell, to labor according to American modes, just as they discard the umbrella shaped hat, wide drawers and thick paper shoes, for the felt hat, pantaloons and boots; but they retain all their essential habits and modes of thought just as they retain their cues. The Chinaman running a sewing machine, driving a sand cart, or firing up an engine in California, is just as essentially a Chinaman as his brother, who, on the other side of the Pacific, is working in the same way, and with the same implements, as his fathers worked a thousand years ago....

"The Chinese in California," *New York Tribune*, May 1, 1869

(b)

Avignon, France, Oct. 23, 1869.

Dear Sir: - The subject on which you have asked my opinion involves two of the most difficult and embarrassing questions of political morality - the extent and limits of the right of those who have first taken possession of an unoccupied portion of the earth's surface to exclude the remainder of mankind from inhabiting it, and the means which can be legitimately used by the more improved branches of the human species to protect themselves from being hurtfully incroached upon by those of a lower grade in civilization. The Chinese immigration to America raises both these questions. To furnish a general answer to either of them would be a most arduous undertaking.

Concerning the purely economical view of the subject, I entirely agree with you; and it could hardly be better stated and argued than it is in your article in the *New York Tribune*. That the Chinese immigration, if it attains great dimensions, must be economically injurious to the mass of the present population; that it must diminish their wages, and reduce them to a lower stage of physical comfort and well-being, I have no doubt. Nothing can be more fallacious than the attempts to make out that thus to lower wages is the way to raise them, or that there is any compensation, in an economical point of view, to those whose labor is displaced, or who are obliged to work for a greatly reduced remuneration. On general principles this state of things, were it sure to continue, would justify the exclusion of the immigrants, on the ground that, with their habits in respect to population, only a temporary good is done to the Chinese people by admitting part of their surplus numbers, while a permanent harm is done to a more civilized and improved portion of mankind.

But there is also much to be said on the other side. Is it justifiable to assume that the character and habits of the Chinese are unsusceptible of improvement? The institutions of the United States are the most potent means that have yet existed of spreading the most important elements of civilization down to the poorest and most ignorant of the laboring masses. If every Chinese child were compulsorily brought under your school system, or under a still more effective one, if possible, and kept under it for a sufficient number of years, would not the Chinese population be in time raised to the level of the American? I believe, indeed, that hitherto the number of Chinese born in America has not been very great; but so long as this is the case - so long (that is) as the Chinese do not come in families and settle, but those who come are mostly men, and return to their native country, the evil can hardly reach so great a magnitude as to require that it should be put a stop to by force.

One kind of restrictive measure seems to me not only desirable, but absolutely called for: the most stringent laws against introducing Chinese immigrants as coolies, i.e., under contracts binding them to the service of particular persons. All such obligations are a form of compulsory labor, that is, of slavery; and though I know that the legal invalidity of such contracts does not prevent them from being made, I cannot but think that if pains were taken to make it known to the immigrants that such engagements are not legally binding, and especially if it were made a penal offense to enter into them, that mode of immigration would receive a considerable check; and it does not seem probable that any other mode, among so poor a population as the Chinese, can attain such dimensions as to compete very injuriously with American labor. Short of that point, the opportunity given to numerous Chinese of becoming familiar with better and more civilized habits of life, is one of the best chances that can be opened up for the improvement of the Chinese in their own country, and one which it does not seem to me that it would be right to withhold from them. I am, dear sir,

Yours very sincerely,
J.S. Mill

"John Stuart Mill on the Chinese Immigration," *Oakland Daily Transcript*, November 20, 1869

5

One of the nation's leading reformers, a leading advocate of racial equality and the rights of labor, Wendell Phillips supported the Chinese, defending their rights to become citizens, to vote, and to freely emigrate to the United States. In the selections which follow, published in what had been previously known as the National Anti-Slavery Standard, *Phillips struck out hard at business interests who sought to use Chinese workers as a lever to lower the wage standard; while partially accepting certain of the prejudices of many in the contemporary labor movement, he affirmed the humanity of Chinese immigrants and their entitlement to the "protection of our laws."[2]*

We welcome every man of every race to our soil and to the protection of our laws. We welcome every man to the best opportunities of improving himself and making money that our social and political systems afford. Let every oppressed man come; let every poor man come; let every man who wishes to change his residence come - we welcome all; frankly acknowledging the principle that every human being has the right to choose his residence just where he pleases on the planet. Our faith in our political institutions and in our social system is that both can endure all the strain which such immigration will produce. More than this, we believe that our civilization will be perfected only by gathering into itself the patient toil, the content with moderate wages, the cunning hand, the inventive brain, the taste and aspirations, the deep religious sentiment, the rollicking humor and vivid imagination, the profound insight and far-reaching sagacity which mark the different races; each contributing one special trait to the great whole.

But such immigration to be safe and helpful must be spontaneous. It must be the result of individual will obeying the laws of industry and the tendencies of the age. *Immigration of labor is an unmixed good. Importation of human freight is an unmitigated evil.*

This brings us to the question of importing Chinese laborers. The Chinese are a painstaking, industrious, thrifty, inventive, self-respectful, and law-abiding race. They have some pretensions to democratic institutions and moral culture - are a little too much machines; but we shall soon shake that servility out of them. Their coming will be a welcome and valuable addition to the mosaic of our nationality; but, in order to that, they must come spontaneously, of their own free will and motion, as the Irish, Germans, and English have done. If the capital of the country sets to work, by system and wide co-operation, to import them in masses, to disgorge them upon us with unnatural rapidity, - then their coming will be a peril to our political system. and a disastrous check to our social progress.

We lay it down as a fundamental principle, - never to be lost sight of, - that every immigrant of every race must be admitted to citizenship, if he asks for it. The right to be naturalized must not be limited by race, creed, or birthplace. Secondly, every adult here, native or naturalized, must vote. In spite of this, give us time, with only a natural amount of immigration, and we can trust the education and numbers of our native voters to safely absorb and make over the foreign element. Irish and German immigration has been only a ripple on our ocean's breadth; generally speaking, it has only been a healthy stir. But it is easily possible for associated capital to hurry the coming of the Chinese in such masses as will enable these money lords to control the ballot-box by their bond-servants. An extended North Adams can do more than lessen shoemakers' wages; one thousand such Samsons, the associated capital of Massachusetts, can swamp and overwhelm the ballot-box of that State. We hold it to be clearly within the province, and as clearly the duty of legislation, to avert this danger. Capital is too strong now. The public welfare demands that its political power be crippled. Universal suffrage is admissible only on condition of an educated people. We cannot undertake to educate the whole world at once. In detachments, million by million, we can digest the whole human race.

Then as to the influence of such importation on the laboring classes. The Chinaman will make shoes for seventy-five cents a day. The average wage for such work in Massachusetts is two dollars. What will become of the native working-men under such competition? He met similar competition from the Irish immigrants and the German; but it never harmed him. They came in such natural and moderate numbers as to be easily absorbed, without producing any ill-effect on wages. These continued steadily to advance. So will it be in the case of the Chinese, if he be left to come naturally by his individual motion; imported in overwhelming masses by the concerted action of capital, he will crush the labor of America down to a pauper level, for many years to come....

The rate of wages is said to depend upon supply and demand. The rule is sound; but so equivocal that it is worth little. Rate of wages really depends on what the workman *thinks* will buy him the necessities of life....

"Supply and demand," therefore, are to be understood, with a qualification. The "ideas" of the "supply" are a most important element in the calculation. What are the ideas of the "supply"? These regulate his wages. The Chinaman works cheap because he is a barbarian, and seeks gratification of only the lowest, the most inevitable wants. The American demands more because the ages, - because Homer and Plato, Egypt and Rome, Luther and Shakespeare, Cromwell and Washington, the printing-press and the telegraph, the ballot-box and the Bible, - have made him ten times as much a MAN. Bring the Chinese to us slowly, naturally, and we shall soon lift him to the level of the same artificial and civilized wants that we feel. Then capitalist and laborer will be equally helped. Fill our industrial channels with imported millions, and you choke them ruinously. They who seek to flood us, artificially, with barbarous labor, are dragging down the American home to the level of the houseless street-herds of China. If the working-men have not combined to prevent this, it is time they should. When rich men conspire, poor men should combine.

In such combinations, - inevitable and indispensable in the circumstances, - the best minds and hearts of the land are with them. Only let them be sure not to copy the tyranny which makes their opponents weak. Their only strength is an admitted principle, - all men equal, equally free to carve each his own career, and entitled to all the aid his fellows can give. Stand on that unflinchingly; rebuke every threat; avoid all violence; appeal only to discussion and the ballot....

"The Chinese," *National Standard*, July 30, 1870

6

Professor Augustus Layres, author of several pamphlets on the "Chinese question," took issue with the general thrust of testimony presented to the 1876 Congressional Investigation [see Part I]. In the essay below, he emphasized that the Chinese were more law-abiding and honest than others. His line of reasoning ran contrary to the stereotype of Chinese criminality promoted by the Investigation.

The Chinese are not, as it has been charged, a band of criminals and vicious, but on the contrary, a very laborious, frugal, quiet, and law-abiding people. There are no bummers among them, nor drunkards, nor bull-dosers, but with rare exceptions. The testimony of Alfred Clarke, Clerk of the Chief of Police, (an anti-Chinese witness) is very conclusive in this respect. "Prostitution, violation of the cubic air ordinance and gambling are the principal offenses for which arrests are made among the Chinese." But prostitution among the Chinese is no more common than among the other nationalities, as any person who takes a stroll through Dupont, Sacramento, and other streets of San Francisco, either by day or night, can soon discover. The municipal authorities, however, have deemed best to punish the Chinese alone for the infraction of the law.

The Chinese are fast learning both our language and customs, notwithstanding they are slow in adopting them. But why should they adopt them when they see so much bad example of dishonesty, drunkenness, and inhuman persecution against them, for no other reason except because they earn a morsel of bread by prolonged toil, day and night, which those who boast of belonging to the superior race would fain take from their mouths and give to their white families? What right have they who set such barbarous and unchristian examples in this age of freedom and equal rights, to demand social assimilation from the Chinese? Do we, ourselves, wish to assimilate with any people whose practices and doctrines we condemn? If the Chinese are slow in adopting our civilization and Christian religion, not they, but the anti-Chinese crusaders themselves should bear the blame. And for them to appeal to Congress and the American people, and ask the restriction of Chinese immigration, on the ground that they do not assimilate with us, is the climax of impudence!

These men are constantly clamoring against the Chinese immigrants, yet complain because they do not as other immigrants come here to stay and do not conform with our habits and manners. What charming consistency!

However, as this allegation is likely to constitute the main ground for urging a restriction of Chinese immigration, before yielding to its weight, may we be permitted to inquire into the main and perhaps the only real cause of this want of social homogeneity on the part of the Chinese as well as of other foreigners, in order to see whether the blame attaches to them or to our civil government.

A tour of observation through the different colonies settled in our large cities, will disclose the fact that where a considerable people of foreign nationality form as it were a separate community, it is because they have not a sufficient knowledge of the English language. The necessity of a common medium of social intercourse which is afforded by their native tongue draws them together, and by their numbers they find ample supply among themselves for all their wants....

The remedy universally adopted for conquering this aversion of certain foreigners to amalgamation and obtaining a homogeneous nationality is to *impart a free, and if necessary, obligatory education, particularly in the English language, to all the children of the people.*

The same theory applies to the case of the Chinese now under discussion, but with greater force. They too are compelled to live together as a separate people, chiefly because the great majority of them ignore the English language. But are they to blame for this lack of knowledge and want of assimilation? "They evince an eagerness for learning," says Dr. Loomis in his school report, "which is especially commented upon by strangers." They pay their pro-rata of the taxes for the support of public schools; but our benevolent, equitable and just civil government persistently refuses to grant admission to Chinese children into the public schools through prejudice and antipathy of race. And after suffering so great a wrong from the State and the Municipal Government, in violation of our treaty stipulations, shall the Chinese be subjected to a still greater wrong by way of punishment from the Federal Government, restricting their immigration on account of the lack of assimilation of which they are not the cause? Aye, the sense of right and justice is not yet dead in the American people and Congress!

These and other charges being disproved by fact and reason, why should Congress restrict Chinese immigration any more than that of any other nationality? Would not such a discrimination be a gross insult to the Chinese people and Government? Would it not be an act of flagrant injustice which would challenge the condemnation of the whole civilized world? What a sport would monarchical countries make of our boasted freedom, human equality, and independence! How would the enemies of popular government in our midst, who are constantly plotting its destruction, rejoice secretly in their hearts over this first departure from our national policy, successfully followed by us for one hundred years - "to make no discrimination between nations" - they would regard it as the first retrograde step in our career of liberty and civilization, as a tacit denial of one of the cardinal principles of the immortal Declaration of Independence, as the turning point of this great revolution of ideas wrought in this century by the United States of America. Let us fondly hope and pray that Congress will never consent to thus fatally stab our nation!

Both Sides of the Chinese Question, or Critical Analysis of the Evidence for and Against Chinese Immigration, As elicited before the Congressional Commission; Also, A Review of Senator Sargent's Report; with an Appendix, Concerning a Wide-Spread Conspiracy against the Chinese; Respectfully Dedicated to the Friends of Right, Justice, and Humanity, Pamphlet, San Francisco, A.F. Woodbridge, 1877, pp. 22-23

7

> *Joseph C.G. Kennedy spoke before the Senate Foreign Relations Committee in February 1878 in favor of the right of Chinese to settle in the United States. To buttress his stance, he submitted an article demonstrating that, despite the conclusion drawn by the 1876 Congressional Investigation, the presence of Chinese labor had not appreciably depressed wages in California. [Many of the figures used by Kennedy were later employed by Senator George Hoar - see Part I].*

Now, as to the charge that Chinese labor, by its cheapness, degrades white labor to a degree below sustaining points is perfectly preposterous in the light of the fact that nowhere in this great country can men live cheaper than in California; and that other fact, that the wages paid Caucasians on the Pacific coast at the present time are much higher than are paid for similar services anywhere in the Atlantic States. The temporary lull in work, owing to a dry season and the general commercial depression, has created that which the Caucasian attributes to the Chinaman's determination to be ever working at the best wages his industry and fidelity will command.

The Chinese labor doubtless reduces the prices of labor to some extent, but it reduces also the cost of many articles indispensable to the laboring man of other nationalities, and enables him to live well on wages whereon it would, ten years since, have been impossible to exist. The poor man can, at the present prices of labor in California, purchase an entire outfit of clothing, a barrel of flour, a barrel of pork, and a cooking-stove for 25 per cent. less hours of labor than was possible twenty years since. He can in any part of that State live better on one dollar per day than was then possible on five. People talk of their taking away the labor of mechanics, but it is not so; why, even in the matter of boots and shoes, which they are charged with monopolizing, the commercial report of the past year shows that while in 1873 there were 34,667 cases of boots and shoes imported into San Francisco, the cases in the year 1877 numbered 49,094, exporting at the same time 50,000 hides and over 3,000 packages of leather, worth $365,000. They imported last year between three and four million bags, 106,700 boxes of candles, while to Great Britain alone they exported 1,260,000 pounds of tallow, and imported 30,000 boxes of soap.

Such figures, which could be multiplied to a hundred industries, proclaim louder than any hue and cry that there is yet room for labor.

Now, what are prices of labor in California? Let the *San Francisco Bulletin*, of the 9th of February, 1878, tell the story, which it does in the following leading article, which will set at rest the charge that the Chinese, by their low charges for labor, have brought starvation tot the doors of American and European laborers:.....

CARPENTER'S WAGES.

The price paid to carpenter's in California ranges from $3 to $3.50 per day. This is the general rule throughout the city. But there are many cases where unemployed men will work for less, ranging from $2 up to $3 per day. In Providence, Rhode Island, during the past year the wages of carpenters have averaged from $1.50 to $1.75 per day....

MACHINISTS AND BRASS FOUNDERS.

The prices paid machinists in this city range from $3 to $4 per day. The great majority of this class of workmen receive $3.50. Many receive the highest price, $4. The wages of this class of labor is more than 50 per cent. higher here than in the East. In the Eastern States machinists get from $1.75 to $2.50 per day. Brass-founders East receive $3 per day; here $4.50....

WOOLEN-MILL HANDS.

In our woolen-mills common labor is paid $2 per day. Skilled labor averages from $2.50 to $3.50 per day, depending upon the kind of work preferred. In the East, mule-spinners receive as high pay as any of the operatives, and their wages do not average much over $1.50 per day, but here the remuneration is greater. The weavers - girls and women - range from 90 cents to $1.50 per day, the average being about $1. On ordinary work in eastern cotton-mills women will not average much over $22 per month. Boys and girls are paid from 3 to 6 cents per hour, laborers and watchmen 10 to 11 cents....

BOOT AND SHOE MAKERS.

In the boot and shoe manufacturing business California is paying for white labor from 50 to 60 per cent. more than is being paid East. For some kinds of work our manufacturers are paying 65 cents where 30 cents are paid East, and $1 against $62^{1/2}$ cents. Wages here average from $12 to $20 per week, depending upon the kind of work. In the East complaints are made that workmen will average from $5 to $10 only. In Toronto, workmen say that they receive from $4 to $8 per week, and they have struck for higher wages. Leather will average less in price here than East, yet much of the material used by eastern boot and shoe manufacturers is shipped from this coast, manufactured, and sent back to us to be sold at as great, if not greater, profit than can be made on the same articles manufactured here....

NORTHERN AND SOUTHERN LABOR.

Were the prices of every kind of labor on this coast compared with those paid for the same labor, it is probable that our prices would be found to exceed those paid East in nearly, if not every case. In the South labor is much cheaper than in Northern States, laborers working more hours per day at a less price. Gentlemen who have been engaged in cotton manufacturing, both in the South and in New England, affirm that mills in Georgia can be built and equipped at 25 per cent. less cost than at the North, and the class of operatives obtainable is better and cheaper than can be found North. On plantations contracts are made with help for any year at wages varying from $6 to $8 per month, with board, for first-class hands. It is thus seen that we are paying much higher wages than can be obtained in any other part of the country, with the exception of those mining districts that are now being opened up.

Now gentlemen, are you not satisfied that the late turmoil in California was based upon something else than inadequate wages?

Argument of Joseph C.G. Kennedy, Adverse to Legislation By Congress on Treaties Existing: And Reviewing the Report of Mr. Sargent of the Joint Special Committee to Investigate Chinese Immigration, Read Before Committee on Foreign Relations, February 20, 1878, Washington, Government Printing Office, 1878, pp. 29-31

8

Chung Wai Hsin Pao's broadside recalls the sympathetic testimony of Fred Bee and Benjamin Brooks [see part I], claiming that such men represented an important, albeit a minority, segment of California public opinion. There is present in the piece a certain anti-Irish, anti-labor current common to apparently merchant-backed statements and appeals, but Chung Wai Hsin Pao also expressed sympathy for California's white workers. Basing himself on local newspaper reports, he too declared that Chinese competition had not harmed wage scales in the state.

But suppose we admit that the party favoring Chinese immigration in California is largely in the minority! On what grounds, pray, do you, members of the majority, expect from Congress a decision in your favor? On the ground of numerical superiority? We claim it on the ground of truth, right and justice! And do you think that truth has lost any of its power on account of your large vote at the last election? Or do you believe and hope that an honest Congress will turn a deaf ear to prayer of the minority, though backed by right and justice, in abject condescension to a clamorous multitude?

Congress cannot and will not, throw aside the testimony obtained by the Congressional Commission of Inquiry in 1876, by which your charges and allegations were utterly disproved. Men of unimpeachable character, high standing in the community, holding positions of trust, having large interests at stake, ministers of the gospel, missionaries, judges, lawyers and merchants in large number, who have resided in California ten, twenty and thirty years, who have had intercourse with the Chinese most of their time, spoke of facts that came under their actual observation, and affirmed their truth under oath; a testimony of eye-witnesses, so emphatic, so unexceptionable is altogether invincible. The anti-Chinese testimony, on the contrary, was conspicuous for its glaring contradictions and the paucity of its high-order witnesses, few of whom could claim a long residence in the State and large commercial transactions with the Chinese. Police officers, detectives, laborers, reporters of newspapers made up in large measure, the number of those who testified against the Chinese....

But we wish to press this matter still further. If, as you affirm, the people of California are practically a unit on this question, or, if your former testimony taken by the Congressional Committee is unassailable, what need was there of strengthening your position by holding another inquiry into the Chinese question through the friendly services of the Congressional Committee on Labor during a most exciting State canvass? And why were you so afraid to admit the pro-Chinese testimony, that the investigation was brought to a close as soon as it sought a hearing by the Committee through the earnest solicitation of the Rev. Otis Gibson? It is for you to reconcile this action with your boastful declaration that the people of California are unanimously and unalterably opposed to Chinese immigration.

We too sympathize with the white workingman who suffers poverty from crushing opposition or even competition. If, therefore, it were true that the presence of the Chinese in California is a block to the prosperous advancement of our working-classes, we would not raise our voice against this unchristian and inhuman crusade. But it is not....

And shall a class of industrious emigrants, who have assisted in creating new industries, in building railroads, reclaiming swamp lands, opening new agricultural districts, be excluded from our country, driven from cities and towns, as they now propose to do in California, in conformity with Article XIX of the New Constitution, regardless of the existing treaty with China? Who are they that make this infamous demand? For the greater part they are foreigners, a large number of whom came but yesterday from a land of oppression, in abject poverty and ignorance; who have been endowed with political rights and privileges by the excessive magnanimity of the American Government. Yet, incredible as it may appear, they are so selfish, so ungrateful, so insolent, as to demand from the same beneficent government, that it shall refuse to the Chinese even a small share of that hospitality which has been liberally accorded to them; and without stopping to reflect that this is a national question, on which the voice of the other States must also be heard, they insist, even under threats, that Congress shall decide it in their favor, on the vote of California alone! Can impudence and temerity go any farther? They have reached that point where patience on the part of the government ceases to be a virtue. Let the Friends of Truth, Right and Justice take notice of all this.

Chung Wai Hsin Pao, *The Pro-Chinese Minority of California: To the American People, President and Congress. Reply to Governor Irwin's Circular Regarding the Vote of California against Chinese Immigration*, broadside, San Francisco, 1879

9

The following is taken from a pamphlet about a Chinese immigrant (a converted Christian) and his eye-opening and disillusioning experiences in San Francisco and Washington. Reproducing the stereotypical pronunciation of English by Chinese, which was exaggerated and ridiculed in racist fashion, the story's importance lies in its indictment of the political and religious duplicity which facilitated the passage of the Chinese Exclusion Act.

Chapter IV

Chang had been two years in the land of the Christian.

During that period he had seen much, and learned a great deal.

He had reflected on the subject of civilization and Christianity.

His reflections resulted in a more thorough understanding of the term "Christian nation," in contradistinction to the term "heathen nation"; and he reflected the matter down to as fine a distinction between a genuine Christian - a real, Christ loving Christian - and a large majority of people who called themselves Christians, simply because they were not born in China or Africa.

Chang learned, too, that a genuine heathen was less dangerous, less vindictive, less cruel; more honest, more generous, and more helpful to his fellow heathen; that a so-called Christian was merely a heathen born in a land where the Bible is generally read.

Having convinced himself that the theory of religion was the grandest boon to man, a divine revelation and not a magnificent philosophy, he turned his investigations in another direction.

He became wise when he learned to value the precept independently of the practice.

Chang studied the laws of the land and the intent and purpose of the constitution, and the result of his studies led him to demand as a political right for his countrymen those equalities that had been denied them through the mere moral force of a boasted Christianity.

He resolved to test whether the constitutional obligations were as readily ignored by this great Christian nation as are the precepts and obligations of their faith as pronounced in the Bible, the great palladium of the eternal truth of the Christian belief.

Chang started off for Washington.

As he traveled eastward from the great Western States, he branched toward the South and chanced to be present during an election.

We will not tell what he saw, but he came to believe that Christianity and modern civilization displayed itself by different methods in different localities.

He was a witness to scenes of horror and outrage that convinced him that heathenism was not the only excuse for the practice of the methods of Satan by professed followers of Christ.

He learned that certain political exigencies served as an excuse for the good Christian to lay aside the precepts of peace, charity, and good will, and stalk forth, pistol and bowie knife in hand, to slay and kill unoffending human beings.

At length Chang reached Washington, the capital of the great Christian nation, and here again he had another view of the grand developments of modern civilization.

He saw men sitting in conclave as honored law makers, many of them holding their seats as the fruit of fraud, bribery, cheating, violence and murder.

He shuddered, poor lorn heathen that he was! but the fearful facts stared him in the face, as some of the genuine developments of the advanced civilization of the times.

As Chang contemplated these facts, it was no surprise to him that these legislators, with the opening prayer of the chaplain ringing in their ears, deliberately voted away the *common rights of man* from a portion of their fellow beings, and tried to checkmate by legislation the *undoubted purpose of that Supreme God* whom they had, through their chaplain, invited to overrule to His glory the results of their law making.

Chang had been a few weeks in Washington taking observations, when he determined to interview a member of the committee on foreign relations in regard to the prospects of his fellow countrymen.

The member whom Chang chanced to address was a fair type of the average congressman.

There are certainly wiser, and possibly better men, and again there are none in our national Congress.

The gentleman was a Western member, a whole-souled, easy going sort of man, generous as the world goes, and careless in view of the fearful responsibility of living and dying, of record, and final judgment.

The congressman had been spending some hours with a few visitors from his native country, and at the time Chang addressed him was slightly under the influence of "the cup that cheers" and inebriates also.

"Whatee you gotee against Chinee man?" asked our hero.

"Whatee I got-ee gin-ee Chinee man-ee? I got-ee nuttee ginee Chi-nee man-ee," was the honorable member's jocular reply.

"You-ee Chistee manee?"

The congressman smiled and answered frankly:

"I was brought up a Christian, but hang it! I don't live up to my teaching somehow!"

"Wellee, thisee Chistee landee?"

Again the congressman smiled good-naturedly and answered as frankly as before.

"They call it a Christian land, but I must say there are some pretty hard Christians around loose."

"Wellee, you claimee that Chistee sentiment allee wasee goodee?"

"What are you driving at, my friend?"

"I wantee good answer."

The congressman was a keen wit, and saw that the Chinee was a quick-witted, sharp, intelligent representative of his race.

Under the circumstances the gentleman determined to answer this earnest inquirer squarely.

"You have been investigating modern Christianity and civilization, eh?"

"Yes-ee."

"Well, my good friend, the religion of this land appears to be politics! I will tell you that the inducements of religion are the eternal rewards (I mean as men generally take it, judging from their actions), and the inducements in politics are the rewards; and as the rewards of the latter are more immediate, while the Christian's rewards are somewhat indefinite and remote, all classes practice practically under the 'ruling' that a bird in the hand is worth two in the bush!"

"I don't understanee you," said Chang, "you meanee there are not goodee men?"

"Well, never."

"Whatee, nevee?"

"Well, hardly ever!"

"I wasee fraidee you tellee truthee."

Again the congressman smiled, possibly not at the idea of a politician telling the truth, but at the sheer simplicity and honesty of the poor Asiatic.

"I'll tell you, my friend, the fact is men are in no measure more self-deceived than in this matter of religion; and the rule applies almost universally in this Christian land, rising from the man wallowing in the gutter to the clergyman in the pulpit, all profess one thing and practice another; the present rewards of this world are eagerly grasped at, while the remote rewards promised to the Christian are held in reserve. It is one of the practical mottoes of Christianity to 'take in' everything that is good and pleasant; and you will see this exemplified when the politician accepts the office that has been won by fraud at the ballot box, and when the clergyman flits from one pulpit to another, as the greater inducement is offered in the way of salary, like a child who deserts the pursuit of one butterfly when one of more brilliant colors sails before him."

"You notee muchee faithee in Chistee manee?"

"Well, my good friend, I must say that my faith is shaken."

"You votee for the Chinee bill?"

"No, sir! I am a pretty bad cuss, and I winked at a little political dodge that won me my election, but, thank Heaven! the monstrous wrong of *deliberately* legislating against any one class of human beings cannot be laid at my door! and I must say one thing, *that where your countrymen have not yet penetrated in large numbers, I think the whole Christian thought is adverse to the bill!*"

The congressman had a merry twinkle in his eye at this opportunity of stating how the whole sentiment of *disinterested* Christians was magnanimously adverse to the Chinese bill and favorable to Asiatic emigration.

The remark was made in the spirit of the patriot who expressed himself as self-denyingly willing to see his brother-in-law drafted at the time of the great unpleasantness.

Chang spent some time in Washington after his interview with the jocular member of the committee on foreign relations.

He finally sought an interview with several men who had always been recognized as foremost in their advocacy of the rights of the downtrodden and oppressed.

Alas! how the mighty had fallen!

The poor heathen learned a fresh lesson in the intricate windings of "Chistee man's" policy.

Political exigency demanded that a man should bewail the sorrows of an oppressed class.

When advocating these rights their silver-tongued oratory drops as sweet words of sympathy as angel lips might let fall.

The Bible, history and civilization are brought forward as allies to add to the force and matter of their arguments.

Political exigencies on the other hand make it the policy to ignore the rights of the Chinee, and the mighty humanist who pleaded for the rights of the African, spent all his eloquence to rob the Chinaman of the self-same rights....

Chang's adventures in the Christian land finally ended, and returning to China he adopted an American fashion and commenced lecturing throughout the Chinese Empire.

His conclusions were that Christianity was a divine revelation, and that its precepts were emanations worthy the Creator of the Universe, and that no matter how much civilization might owe to Christianity, *the latter owed very little to civilization.*

Space precludes a more extended account of poor Chang's conclusions, but we will state that it was only necessary for him to tell absolute facts to even a heathen audience to understand fully how glorious was Christian precept and how lamentable general Christian practice.

It now remains to see whether a Christian nation will shadow itself under the monstrous iniquity of the infamous - aye, satanic Chinese bill!

Uncle Sam-ee and His Little Chi-nee, New York, Collin, 1879, pp. 24-32

10

Not long before his death, the outstanding abolitionist and humanitarian William Lloyd Garrison contributed the following letter to the New York Tribune *in response to the Chinese exclusion debate in the Senate. He was particularly concerned with the possible - in his view, wrongful - repeal of the Burlingame Treaty, and was especially angered by the collaboration of Republican leaders in so "vulgar" a project. [sons William Lloyd Garrison II and Francis J. Garrison were*

also opposed to exclusion; see the Petition from Massachusetts against
the Geary Act in Part I above; see also the New York Times *report*
of Garrison II's anti-exclusion speech, January 13, 1902].

To the Editor of the *Tribune.*
Sir:

Whatever inevitably tends to the subversion of the fundamental
principles of this Government as set forth in the Declaration of Independence
and the Constitution of the United States, or is sure to add a fresh stain of
caste proscription to the many that have sullied our National character, should
at once arrest the attention, and in some form elicit the indignant protest, of
every lover of his country, every friend of the whole human race; for

"He who allows oppression shares the crime."

A case strikingly in point is pending at this hour in the passage of an
act through Congress, summarily abrogating our present equitable and
advantageous treaty with China, and forbidding under pains and penalties any
vessel from bringing to these shores, at one time, more than fifteen Chinese,
whether as visitors or immigrants, whether the most cultured or the most
ignorant. Only fifteen at the extent! Would sixteen put this Republic in
jeopardy? If so, what assurance have we that fifteen may be safely tolerated?
To "make assurance double sure, and take a bond of fate," why not make the
exclusion complete in all cases? Does not

"One sickly sheep infect the flock,

And poison all the rest?"

True, without counting any of that class (a comparatively small number) now
among us, we have a population of more than forty millions, and rapidly
augmenting by natural increase and immigration from other parts of the
world; popular education is more widely diffused here than in any other land;
the Bible and Christian institutions (at least so recognized) dominate every
State in the Union: we stand as a people on the highest plane yet attained in
regard to industry, skill, invention, enterprise, the enjoyment of a comfortable
subsistence, and the means of improvement; our collective wealth is enormous,
and our resources for its accumulation and distribution, utilized or yet to be
drawn upon, inexhaustible; we have boasted, *ad nauseam usque,* that this is a
land of liberty and equal rights, and asylum for all in other lands who may
wish to better their condition by coming to us; and we have long since
complacently "ciphered out" that, so extended are our national domains, not

less than one thousand millions of people may occupy them without crowding. But, it seems, rich and intelligent and powerful and populous and territorially magnificent as we are, we have all reason to apprehend the most disastrous consequences to our safety and interests, and the stability of our republican institutions, if more than fifteen Chinese are allowed to enter any one of our ports in any single vessel! The sixteenth is more than we are willing or able to bear! Therefore, let him keep his distance. We shall be on the watch for his advent from the Atlantic to the Pacific coast; and if we catch him, we will make our soil too hot for him to stand upon and exact of the daring shipmaster conveying him here the penalty in such case provided.

Really, it is difficult in this case which is the greater, its absurdity or injustice. We have allowed all other peoples to take up their abode with us, notwithstanding their ignorance, destitution, unfortunate training, and difference of race; and they have come by the million - Englishmen, Irishmen, Scotchmen, Frenchmen, Germans, Scandinavians, Italians, Africans, etc., etc.; so that in the aggregate they constitute a formidable portion of the population. We must either drive out these, or keep any more of them seeking a refuge here, or else keep the barrier down and let the Chinese find an equal entrance, and be protected in the enjoyment of equal rights and privileges....

The debate on the question of Chinese immigration in the United States Senate yesterday - to judge from the report of it in this morning's journals - was, with one or two honorable exceptions, most disgraceful to all who participated in it, and displayed a demogogical, partisan rivalry between Republican and Democratic Senators as to who should the most strongly cater to the brutal, persecuting spirit which for the time being is so rampant in California under the leadership of that most ignorant, profane, strike-engendering and besotted declaimer Denis Kearney - himself a foreigner, or of foreign descent, and much more entitled to be in a lunatic asylum than running at large. Of the Senatorial leader of the sham Democracy of this country, Thurman, nothing better could reasonably be expected; but that Senator Blaine, not less conspicuous as a leader in the Republican ranks, should zealously advocate the total repeal of the Burlingame Treaty, in order that an almost total restriction shall be laid upon Chinese immigration, is something more surprising and even more discreditable than in the case of Senator Sargent, of California, who most ignobly conforms to the miserable Chinese "craze" with which that section of the country is infected....

The reasons advanced by Mr. Blaine in opposition to the Chinese were unworthy of his head and heart, and therefore unworthy of the least consideration, being based on contempt of race, a low selfishness, a blind and cowardly fear of consequences, and the gratification for party purposes of a local hatred (in its climax reaching to the diabolical) against a helpless, unoffending, industrious, frugal, and intemperate class of inhabitants. They are such reasons as were formerly urged by some against freely allowing the Irish to emigrate to this country; and against emancipating the Southern slave population; and against labor-saving machinery, as reducing the wages of the laborer, etc., etc. They are not born of reason, or justice, or historical experience. If the proposed measure shall be carried and enforced, the Chinese Government may proclaim non-intercourse with this country, and find as ample justification in so doing....

This is the spirit of caste; black versus white. It is essentially the same everywhere - vulgar, conceited and contemptible. Cannot Senator Blaine be instructed by it? Respectfully yours,

William Lloyd Garrison
Boston, Mass., Feb. 15, 1879
New York Tribune, February 17, 1879

11

The following New York Times *editorial, a comment on the on-going debate in Congress, is of interest for both its sharpness and the fact that a newspaper in San Francisco, heart of the anti-Chinese movement, saw fit to publish it. Former president U.S. Grant did not win the Republican presidential nomination that year; the party platform adopted in convention, with James A. Garfield as standard bearer, endorsed Chinese exclusion.*

There is every reason to believe that within a few days a San Francisco mob will make an attack on the Chinamen. The preparations for this attack are in open progress, and Mr. Dennis Kearney, the eminent California statesman whom Mr. Hayes once honored with a long interview at the White House, is now appealing to his followers to furnish money for erecting a neat and serviceable gallows on the Sand Lots whereon to hang the wretches who are guilty of being Chinamen.[3] As the Mayor of the city is the ally and tool of Kearney, no protection will be given by him to the Chinese, and the fate of these unhappy heathen, in case the anticipated riot takes place, can be easily imagined.

There are a few weak sentimentalists in the Eastern States who would look upon a massacre of the Chinese in San Francisco as a shameful crime. When that event occurs they will denounce Kearney and Kalloch[4] with much energy, and will assert that the American nation has been disgraced. Such people, however, have nothing to do with real politics, and their opinions are of very little consequence.

Practical men are growing tired of the foolish sentimentality which is talked in Eastern cities concerning the Chinese. We are told that because the United States has made a treaty with China guaranteeing protection to Chinese residing in this country, it is a disgraceful breach of faith to permit the San Francisco Chinamen to be persecuted and massacred. Suppose it is. What of it? Can China compel us to keep a treaty, and if not, can we be expected to keep it? The United States has made numerous treaties with our Indian tribes, and violated them whenever the Northwestern voter has desired to seize the land of the Indians. It is one of the fundamental principles of our Government that we are under no obligation to keep treaties made with Indians, since the latter are weak and powerless. We keep treaties made with nations like England and France who are able to resent bad faith and dishonesty on our part, but the Indians can be cheated with impunity. We can apply the same reasoning to the treaty which exists between the United States and China. We can violate it with impunity, since China cannot possibly invade our Coasts with a powerful fleet and batter down our towns. As for pretending that we must keep a treaty because it would be dishonorable to do otherwise, that is mere sentimental nonsense. To tell a Government that has recognized no law of honesty at home in its dealings with weak copper-colored people, that it must be honorable when dealing with weak yellow people, is a waste of breath.

Of course, it would be possible to put an end to lawless persecution of the Chinese provided it were possible to do so, but it so happens that it would be unpopular. Which great political party is foolish enough to risk losing the votes of the Pacific States by undertaking to do justice to the Chinese? What if it is morally right to do justice even to yellow heathen? Politicians do not make a practice of doing right because it is right. They are practical men, and their rule of conduct is to do what will secure votes. It would not pay for any politician or any party to take up the cause of the Chinamen. Votes are not to be obtained in that way. The true way to please the Sand Lot voters is either to openly sympathize with their hatred of the Chinese, or to ignore the whole subject, and after the Chinese have been massacred, to mildly deprecate such irregular action on the part of the impulsive working men in San Francisco.

What, then, is the use of the sentimental talk concerning the poor Chinamen, and the duty of keeping our treaty with China, which we hear from visionary people who know nothing of politics? Dennis Kearney and his followers intend to drive out the Chinamen, and there is no more reason for protecting the Chinese against him than there has been for protecting the Indians against white men who wanted their lands. The question of the right or wrong of the matter is of no consequence, since the motive which governs in our public affairs is a desire to secure votes, not a sentimental desire to do right for the right's sake. The sooner the Chinese are exterminated, the sooner San Francisco will be at peace. If anyone calls this a brutal and shameful doctrine, it may be retorted that such a criticism comes rather late in the day. We have systematically treated the Indians with the same technical injustice with which the Chinese are now threatened, and so long as our people accept quietly the profits of such a policy, it behooves them to remain quiet concerning the persecution of the Chinese and the violation of our treaty obligations with China.

There is precisely one eminent American citizen who has openly shown his contempt for Kearney and his gang - heedless of the votes he might thereby lose. Gen. Grant snubbed Kearney in San Francisco by refusing to see that person when he called at Gen. Grant's hotel. Perhaps Gen. Grant would also have the courage to protect the Chinese, in case he were in a position to do so, but then he is not a professional politician, and disdains to bid for votes by courting demagogues. This is probably one of the reasons why his possible election to the Presidency is regarded by some people as a danger to our institutions. It would probably be a serious danger to Mr. Kearney and his kind, should they undertake to indulge in arson and murder.

"The Chinese Must Go," *New York Times*, February 26, 1880, reprinted in *The California Independent*, March 13, 1880

12

Other materials appearing in the California Independent *suggest its dissent from the prevailing view. The first piece below compares anti-Chinese racism in the United States with anti-Semitic prejudice in newly unified Germany (a); appended to Barton's article was the* Independent's *editorial question, "What has Kearney done with the money he collected for the erection of a gallows on the Sand-lot?" The second article (b) deals with a different angle of the exclusion controversy.*

(a)

We have our crusade against the Chinese, and Germany has her crusade against the Jew. Treitschke[5] and Marr, the Kearney and the Kalloch of the German intellectual sand-lot, are firing the Teutonic heart with a bitter hatred against the descendants of Abraham, that race whose line has its initial away back into the very dimness of the historic, almost coeval with the beginning of that of the Chino-Mongol, and along which, down through the vast ages, has come to us civilization, science, invention, free law and all that to-day make the world grand and historic.

These German agitators of race prejudice bring the charge that the Jews are filling the benches of the universities and the colleges, as well as elbowing the Christians in the fields of finance, speculation and the lighter arts. The result is, the formation of "anti-Semitic Leagues," not unlike our anti-Chinese Ward Clubs of San Francisco, in which the watchword or cry is: "The Jew must go!" Kearney and Kalloch say the Chinese are intemperate, industrious, economical, ingenious and apt in intellectual acquirement, and are therefore proving themselves more than the equal in the race of life with the Irish; hence the cry: "The Chinese must go!"

These virtues, upon which the true civilization and the true grandeur of nations can alone be built, our Sand-lot agitators declare to be a crime with the Chinese; and, standing upon the same plane of thought, the Treitschkes and Marrs of the German Sand-lot declare these very same virtues to be a crime with the Jew. Thus it is, with these new-school reformers, the possession of these virtues in the case of the Chinese and the Jews is a great crime; while, according to their own admission, their absence with others is even also a crime. Surely the logic of the Sand-lot, whether in San Francisco or in Berlin, is beyond the comprehension of the most acute logician.

It is a little singular that just at this point of history a bitter persecution should be inaugurated against two of the oldest and most historic races of mankind - races whom some scholars contend have a common origin, Semitic - races in whom temperance, industry, economy, financial genius and social order have the grandest exemplifications; races who had constructed civilizations, enacted governments, written codes of law, and had given creation to epic and lyric verse, that still enchant and thrill, long before the Aryan, with one exception, had struck his tent on the steppe, or had arisen to the dignity of legal compact, or had an inspiration embodied in language above the monosyllabic.

These are features of these contemporaneous persecutions which have remarkable significance. In the Providence of God, the Chinese have come to us that they may acquire potency of idea preparatory to the opening up of a new and a grander chapter of national history. In the vast womb of the vital and material resources of this people are now lying in embryo; a great empire of progress, an empire whose parallels and longitudes are destined to yet vibrate beneath the giant tread of steam power; whose seas and rivers are yet to stir with the navies of commerce and of war; and whose language shall yet embody the inspirations of Christian law, ethics and poetic sentiment.

The Jews, in the Providence of God, have been deprived of their autonomy and scattered throughout every realm of the sun, that they may dispense among the nations that religious faith which shall save from licentiousness and anarchy; that faith out of which naturally come constitutions and statutes of freedom; and out of which has come that grand empire of Christian law, under whose sublime inspirations humanity is being steadily lifted toward this ideal.

These are, however, views that probably lie far beyond the horizon that bounds the visions of either the German or the American Sand-lot. They are no doubt cypherings as occult in meaning to these persecutors of race as were the finger-tracings of God's angel upon the Babylonian wall to the eyes of the reeling, blasphemous debauchees. And yet they have a meaning, as did those of Babylon, and will, at some time in the future, have interpretation as had those prophecies of utter overthrow upon one hand, and of complete triumph upon the other.

W.H. Barton, "A Historic Parallel," *California Independent*, March 13, 1880

(b)

By common consent, the Press is recognized as the most potential educator of the hour. In the forming of public sentiment, and the moral and intellectual sculpturing of the mind of the masses, no other agent possesses so vast and so effective a power. Hence, its responsibilities reach out into the infinite. The mind that directs the columns of a modern, daily newspaper is clothed with a power that might well cause an angel to hesitate in its assumption. And yet, the men in whose hands this fearful responsibility mainly rests to-day, are men whose sole aim seems to be to gather coin and to oppress the weak and despised. This has vivid illustration in the present newspaper directory of San Francisco. For coin, the Sand-lot is recognized, the demagogue is encouraged, and a helpless community of strangers is denied its natural and international rights. Every immunity of treaty stipulation, every feature of Christian equity, and every principle of the higher law, is violated under the tuitions of our local press. Were we to designate the niche in the ages to which the Press of San Francisco in its moral expression belongs, we should tread backward over long centuries of history to seek for the true and appropriate one; over centuries until our feet touched the boundaries of the far antique, when statutes and customs were written in blood.

"San Francisco Press and the Chinese," *California Independent*, March 6, 1880

13

In 1885-1886, Seattle witnessed violent outbreaks against the Chinese, intended to drive the latter out of the city entirely. The expulsion of the Chinese was indeed accomplished in a number of Western centers during the period: Tacoma (Washington), Eureka (California), Rock Springs (Wyoming), Truckee (California). Persistent force and threats against the Chinese led President Grover Cleveland to dispatch troops to Seattle and to put the city under a state of emergency in February 1886. Earlier, seventeen prominent residents of Seattle were indicted for conspiracy against the government (under the 1875 Civil Rights Act forbidding racial discrimination in public facilities) in the wake of the first attacks. Judge Roger S. Greene, of the Third Judicial District of Washington Territory, opened their trial with a denunciation before the Grand Jury of anti-Chinese persecution.

Major local papers, including the Seattle Daily Call *and the* Post-Intelligencer, *responded with harsh criticism of both the charges and Judge Greene. The* Call *of November 13, 1885 termed his speech a "fanatical address."*[6]

....To attempt to deprive a man of his "life" by force or fright is manifestly an unlawful act. Quite as manifestly unlawful is to try by such means to take away his "liberty." And what shall I say of an attempt against his "pursuit of happiness?" Is it not equally unlawful to try to restrain him by such means in that pursuit? Clearly it is. Very essential to the happiness of a human being is the liberty to see and speak to, and deal with his fellow-men, to employ and be employed, to give and receive mutual attentions and kindnesses, and to form and cultivate the ties of friendship and affection. Any combination for the purpose of denying to any human being these sources of happiness, or any of them, is unlawful. Who the person or persons may be whose life, liberty or pursuit of happiness is thus interfered with, matters not. He may be a laborer or he may be an idler, he may be rich or he may be poor, he may be German, Irish, American, English or Chinese, a citizen, or a sojourner, or a stranger, it makes no difference. There is one law for all, and that which is unlawful as against one, is unlawful against any....

It has been publicly and notoriously charged that the laboring man - I mean the wage laborers of this vicinity - have as a class and with few exceptions entered into unlawful combinations against the Chinese. I cannot believe it. And I believe that anything in recent events in this community that looks that way will yet be otherwise and satisfactorily explained.

If there be any class of able bodied citizens, to whom the laws should be especially dear, and who should specially care to uphold them, it is the wage laborers; and this for many reasons:

1st. Those that labor with their hands for wages though a minority of the population, constitute so considerable a proportion of the voters, and are so unified in interest that they can continually bring to bear on legislation and administration of the laws a greater influence than is ordinarily within the reach of any other class.

2d, Because, as the wise man says, riches are a defence, and the laboring man has not as a rule the defence of riches and is left to the defence secured him by the laws.

3d, Because, as the wise man says again, wisdom is a defence, and the laboring man has not as a rule that leisure or opportunity or inclination for acquisition and application of knowledge, which others possess; and the law is his substitute, the embodied wisdom of the ages.

4th, Because the laborer generally rears a larger family than the man of any other class, and has, therefor, for his family's sake and the future of his children a deeper and more abiding interest than others in the maintenance and permanence of the peace that laws are designed to secure.

I am a Christian, and it follows necessarily that my sympathies are with the "common people," of whom it is written that when my beloved Master was on earth, they "heard him gladly." I am sprung from wage-laboring stock. I myself have worked for wages. My own hands for many years were calloused with toil of a rugged New England farm. That which is for the true interest of the laborer, I regard as my own. And I am glad of the present opportunity to declare my conviction, that the interest of the commonwealth is identical with that of the laborer. He cannot fight against the authority of the commonwealth without fighting against his own interests. His interests are to be wrought out and attained *through the commonwealth and by the exercise of its great and all controlling power or not at all....*

Ladies and Gentlemen, because such are my thoughts and convictions, I am unready, I am unwilling, to believe that workingmen of this district have as a class entered into any conspiracy. Opportunity is now offered to the working class to show that they have no fellowship with such, and that their hearts are loyal and patriotic and that all suspicion to the contrary is mistaken and unjust. It is the plain duty of every law-loving citizen to bring to light and justice every guilty man....Now let the guilty parties, if they are included in your accusations, be fairly tried, and let the result of the trials go out world-wide; and let all those who are looking to our beautiful shores as to a desirable place to live - let them, I say, in simple justice know, before they come, whether there is here a government to protect them, or whether our so-called government is a mockery and a farce....

"Arrested for Conspiracy," *Seattle Daily Call*, November 11, 1885

14

A number of advocates for the rights of the Chinese - like Yan Phou Lee - occasionally criticized other immigrant groups to buttress their contention that the Chinese possessed a higher moral character, and hence should not be kept out of the United States. Thus, their writings might embrace a number of essentially derogatory stereotypes. In Yan Phou Lee's case, however, the argument also included a particularly sharp and biting exposure of racial prejudice against the Chinese.

No nation can afford to let go its high ideals. The founders of the American Republic asserted the principle that all men are created equal, and made this fair land a refuge for the whole world. Its manifest destiny, therefore, is to be the teacher and leader of nations in liberty. Its supremacy should be maintained by good faith and righteous dealing, and not by the display of selfishness and greed. But now, looking at the actions of this generation of Americans in their treatment of other races, who can get rid of the idea that Nation, which Abraham Lincoln said was conceived in liberty, waxed great through oppression, and was really dedicated to the proposition that all men are created to prey on one another?

How far this Republic has departed from its high ideal and reversed its traditionary policy may be seen in the laws passed against the Chinese....

So long as the Chinese served their purpose and did not come into collision with the hoodlum element afterwards imported to California, the people of that State had nothing to complain of regarding them. Why should they, when, at one time, half the revenue of the State was raised out of the Chinese miners? But the time came when wages fell with the cost of living. The loafers became strong enough to have their votes sought after. Their wants were attended to. Their complaints became the motive power of political activity. So many took up the cry against the Chinese that it was declared that no party could succeed on the Pacific coast which did not adopt the hoodlums' cause as its own. Supposing that no party could succeed, would the Union have gone to ruin?

Those who remember events of some thirty-five years ago will see nothing strange in the antagonism of one class of laborers to another. Opposition to the Chinese is identical with the opposition to the free immigration of Europeans, and especially of the Irish; for it was once urged against the trans-Atlantic immigrants that their cheap labor "would degrade, demoralize, and pauperize American labor, and displace intelligent Americans in many branches of employment." There was a bitter conflict, but the sensible view prevailed. For it was found that a greater supply of unskilled labor made it possible for skilled laborers to demand higher wages and more regular employment.

Why is it that the American laborer was soon raised to a higher social and industrial plane, and ceased to fear Irish competition, while the Irish still dread the competition of the Chinese? It is simply because the Irish are industrially inferior to their competitors. They have not the ability to get above competition, like the Americans, and so, perforce, they must dispute with the Chinese for the chance to be hewers of wood and drawers of water.

Such industrial conflicts occur every day, as, for instance, between trade-unionists and scabs, Irish and Germans, Italians who came yesterday and Italians who come to-day. Let them fight it out by lawful means, and let the fittest survive; but you do not take the side of one against the other, - least of all, the side of the strong against the weak. Why, then, take the side of the European immigrants against the Chinese? But you say there are many objections against the latter which cannot be made against the former, and the Chinese stand charged with too many things to make them desirable. Ah, yes! I see. But it is only fair to look into these charges before we pass our judgment. It has been urged:

I. *That the influx of Chinese is a standing menace to Republican institutions upon the Pacific coast and the existence there of Christian civilization.*

That is what I call a severe reflection on Republican institutions and Christian civilization. Republican institutions have withstood the strain of 13,000,000 of the lower classes of Europe, among whom may be found Anarchists, Socialists, Communists, Nihilists, political assassins, and cut-throats; but they cannot endure the assaults of a few hundred thousands of the most peaceable and most easily-governed people in the world!

Christianity must have lost its pristine power, for, having subdued and civilized one-half the world, it is now powerless before the resistance of a handful of Chinese! Surely the Chinese must be angels or devils! If angels, they would go without your bidding. If devils, you would not be able to drive them out....

II. *That the Chinese have a quasi-government among themselves.*

If I deny this, perhaps you will not believe me. Allow me to quote the testimony of a man of irreproachable character, the Rev. Dr. William Speer,[7] who wrote to the *New York Tribune* that the Six Companies, credited with the government of the Chinese colony, were purely benevolent associations, and that he had frequently attended their meetings, and could, moreover, speak from many years' experience as a missionary in China. It is a significant fact that the minister of the Gospel, who knew all about the subject, was not believed before howling, ignorant demagogues. It was laying a premium on ignorance....

IV. *That the Chinese have displaced white laborers by low wages and cheap living, and their presence discourages and retards white immigration to the Pacific States.*

This charge displays so little regard for truth and the principles of political economy that it seems like folly to attempt an answer. But please to remember that it was by the application of Chinese "cheap labor" to the building of the railroads, the reclamation of swamp-lands, to mining, fruit-culture, and manufacturing, that an immense vista of employment was opened up for Caucasians, and that millions now are enabled to live in comfort and luxury where formerly adventurers and desperadoes disputed with wild beasts and wilder men for the possession of the land. Even when the Chinaman's work is menial (and he does it because he must live, and is too honest to steal and too proud to go to the almshouse), he is employed because of the scarcity of such laborers. It is proved that his work enables many to turn their whole attention to something else, so that even the hoodlum may don a clean shirt at least once a month. You may as well run down machinery as to sneer at Chinese cheap labor. Machines live on nothing at all; they have displaced millions of laborers; why not do away with machines?

Besides, are you sure that Chinese laborers would not ask more if they dared, or take more money if they could get it?

It is the Chinese who are constantly displaced by Caucasians. As soon as an industry gets on its feet by the help of Chinese "cheap labor," Chinese workmen are discharged to make room for others....

VII. *The Chinese neither have intercourse with the Caucasians nor will assimilate with them.*

Yes, just think of it! As soon as the ship comes into the harbor, a committee of the citizens get on board to present the Chinaman with the freedom of the city (valued at $5). A big crowd gathers at the wharf to receive him with shouts of joy (and showers of stones). The aristocrats of the place flock to his hotel to pay their respects (and to take away things to remember him by). He is so feted and caressed by Caucasian society that it is a wonder his head is not turned (or twisted off).

In spite of such treatment, the Chinese will keep "themselves to themselves" and snub the American community. Did you know that the Jews accused the Samaritans of refusing to have intercourse with them?

VIII. *The Chinese come and go as pagans.*

Mr. Beecher[8] said in reference to this charge: "We have clubbed them, stoned them, burned their houses, and murdered some of them; yet they refuse to be converted. I do not know any way, except to blow them up with nitro-glycerine, if we are ever to get them to heaven." In spite of these doubtful inducements to become Christians, more than 500 have been admitted to the church....

XI. *That the Chinese bring women of bad character to San Francisco, and that their vices are corrupting the morals of the city.*

How serious a charge this is we cannot realize until we get at all the facts. Just imagine California, the most virtuous of States, and San Francisco, the most immaculate of cities, lying helpless under the upas-tree of Chinese immorality! Have you ever been to San Francisco? Unless you can endure paradise and Eden-like purity, you would better not go there. Why, the Sabbath stillness in that city is simply appalling. The people all go to church, and if you suggest whiskey toddy or a base-ball game on Sunday, they will turn up their eyes, throw up their hands, and pray the Lord to have mercy on you. There are no drunken brawls at any time (except in Chinatown), and it is the policeman's picnic-ground (except in Chinatown). Besides churches, they have numerous temples dedicated to Venus, wherein pious persons work off their surplus devotion. Why is it that these fair vestals wear so little clothing? They are afraid to clog the things of the spirit with the habiliments of sense. Californians are pure, moral, and religious, in all that they do. As for having disreputable houses, or women with loose morals about them, I tell you they are as innocent as lambs. Indeed, Satan could not have made a greater commotion in Eden than the Chinese in California. One would suppose that such a model community would "clean out" those bad Chinese women. But it did not. It deputed a number of special policemen to watch and arrest them, but it seems that these specials had the marvelous power of transmuting their brass into pure gold, and that, in the exercise of that power, they were as blind as bats. If the virtuous community of San Francisco permitted their morals to be corrupted, it is their own fault.

Such are the charges made against the Chinese. Such were the reasons for legislating against them; - and they still have their influence, as is shown by the utterances of labor organs; by the unreasoning prejudice against the Chinese which finds lodgment in the minds of the people; and by the periodical outbreaks and outrages perpetrated against them without arousing the public conscience.

Yan Phou Lee, "The Chinese Must Stay," *North American Review*, Vol. 148, No. 4 (April 1889), pp. 476, 477-478, 478-479, 479-480, 481, 483

15

The Chinese Equal Rights League was formed in September 1892 in New York City, with the chief purpose of combatting those sections of the proposed Geary Act which discriminated against Chinese then living in the United States. Drawing its main initiators from among New York-area Chinese merchants, the League held a mass meeting at Cooper Union some three weeks after its founding, at which Chinese and other opponents of the bill spoke from the podium. According to the introduction to the following resolution and appeal, a thousand supporters who were not Chinese joined two hundred Chinese merchants at the gathering. Of interest, aside from the substantial multiracial attendance, was the coupling of the demand for equal rights for Chinese already here with opposition to the admission of new Chinese immigrants. Ironically, some of those present may have been attracted by an appeal to prejudice.

To the American People, Friends of Humanity: -
We, the members of the Chinese Equal Rights League in the United States, who have adopted this country and its customs in the main, are at this moment engaged in a perilous struggle in which our dearest rights as men and residents are involved. Doubtless the reading public is acquainted with the fact that during the last session of the Fifty-second Congress, a Bill was passed, styled the "Geary Bill" or "Chinese Registration Act," in which the attempt is made to humiliate every Chinaman, regardless of his moral, intellectual and material standing in the community, neither his long residence in the country is considered. By this mean and unjust Act discriminating between foreign residents from different countries has traversed and contraversed the fundamental principles of common law.

As residents of the United States we claim a common manhood with all other nationalities, and believe we should have that manhood recognized according to the principles of common humanity and American freedom. This monstrous and inhuman measure is a blot upon the civilization of the Western World, and is destined to retard the progress already made by the good people of this country in the East in art, science, commerce and religion.

We appeal to the humane, liberty-loving sentiment of the American people, who are lovers of equal rights and even-handed justice, a people from who sprung such illustrious characters as Washington, Jefferson, Clay, Sumner, lastly Lincoln, the citizen of the world, the friend of humanity and the champion of freedom: such illustrious warriors as Sherman, Sheridan, Logan and Grant, whose deeds of valor in the cause of freedom are to be seen in the grand march of American development - a development which merits the emulation of the nations of the earth. Must this growth be retarded simply on account of the doings of a misguided element who have suffered their feelings to control reason, encouraging a prejudice fiendish in its nature and purpose against a class of people who are industrious, law-abiding and honest? Can there be found a more inoffensive class in the body politic? not that we are cowards, but because we believe that mildness and simplicity should be the controling element in the character of a great man as well as in a great race of people. We have and are still paying our portion of government taxation, thereby assisting in supporting the Government, and thereby sharing an equal part in the support of the nation.

We love and admire the Government, and look with joy to her instrumentality in promoting every good and just cause among men, to her unwavering love of human rights, to her glorious efforts for the advancement of human happiness.

We, therefore, appeal for an equal chance in the race of life in this our adopted home - a large number of us have spent almost our entire lives in this country and claim no other but this as ours. Our motto is *"Character and fitness should be the requirement of all who are desirous of becoming citizens of the American Republic."*

We feel keenly the disgrace unjustly and maliciously heaped upon us by a cruel Congress. That for the purpose of prohibiting Chinese immigration more than one hundred thousand honest and respectable Chinese residents should be made to wear the badge of disgrace as ticket-of-leave men in your penitentiaries; that they should be tagged and branded as a whole lot of cattle for the slaughter; that they should be seen upon your streets with tearful eyes and heavy hearts, objects of scorn and public ridicule. No! We do not believe it, that so great a people as the Americans would consent to so small a principle toward a mere handful of defenceless men.

Our interest is here, because our homes, our families and our all are here. America is our home through long residence. Why, then, should we not consider your welfare ours? Chinese immigration, as well as Irish, Italian and other immigration, cannot be stopped by the persecution of our law-abiding citizens in the United States.

Treat us as men, and we will do our duty as men, and will aid you to stop this obnoxious evil that threatens the welfare of this Republic. We do not want any more Chinese here than you do. The scarcer the Chinese here, the better would be our conditions among you.

Appeal of the Chinese Equal Rights League to the People of the United States for Equality of Manhood, pamphlet, Chinese Equal Rights League, New York, 1892, pp. 2-3

16

The pressures of discrimination sometimes produced tragic results.[9]

Ah Bow gave Chinatown a sensation yesterday by hanging himself.

They do not often have a suicide in Mott Street. Opium and old age are the prevailing causes of death in that crooked thoroughfare.

Ah Bow was sick and out of work. Some time ago his brother, Lum Chum, who keeps a restaurant in the basement of 6 Chatham Square, took pity on Ah Bow and gave him a place to sleep and all he wanted to eat.

Although relieved of his necessities, Ah Bow continued to be despondent and would sit by the hour in the dingy little basement, with his arms crossed and his legs drawn up under him, thinking, with his almond eyes half closed, of his wife, his son, and his mother in the far-away Flowery Kingdom.

Lum Chum's restaurant is a great gathering place for the rich men of Chinatown, and as they sat around the sides of the room at night, smoking their long pipes and relating wonderful tales of their luck at fantan, poor little

Ah Bow, with his pinched face, presented a sorrowful contrast to the scene of contentment and good health. Ah Bow said several times he would feel better dead, but his friends did not heed his words.

Yesterday morning Lum Chum stumbled down into the basement half awake and felt his way through the dim light toward the kitchen. As he reached for the knob of the kitchen door, Lum Chum saw something that caused him to shout in astonishment and fright.

Ah Bow, stone dead, with his almond eyes staring wide open, was kneeling on the wooden floor with a double noose around his neck. His fingers were clenched, and the expression of his face was enough to startle a more phlegmatic person than Lum Chum. Ah Bow had hanged himself to a door.

Chu Quam rushed forth from his bunk in terror, followed by the cook. When the latter saw Ah Bow's body he became hysterical.

The news that Ah Bow had hanged himself spread quickly, and two of Lum Chum's superstitious steady boarders hastily packed up their clothes and left the place.

A crowd of Chinamen soon collected at the restaurant. Ah Bow's body was taken to an undertaker's shop in Mott Street, where it was attired in flowered slippers and an elaborate gown. Tuesday Ah Bow will be buried with pomp and ceremony.

"Suicide in Chinatown," *New York Times*, August 21, 1893

17

The persistence of a more tolerant approach to the Chinese living in the Pacific Northwest is reflected in this 1895 editorial in the Seattle Argus.

The amount of time and energy expended by the people of Tacoma in the exclusion of Chinese appears almost ridiculous. Public indignation meetings have been held against the employment by Mr. Riggs of Chinese servants, and the chamber of commerce have coldly, calmly, and dispassionately discussed the awful crisis at several well attended meetings.

Tacoma will be victorious over these two poor friendless heathens, and they will have to "vamoose."

This should be one of the proudest days in Tacoma's history. The heart of every true Tacomaite should swell with pride for his native town where forty thousand valiant men, and women, armed to the teeth, have put to route two poor, inoffensive heathens.

Does it not seem strange, when you come to think about it, that ever since the Chinese were driven by main force from Tacoma, that city, which apparently had everything to its advantage, should have steadily made progress backward, while Seattle, where the leading citizens rose up and prevented this outrage, should have gone the other way with equal rapidity?

The *Argus* has no special love for a Chinaman. But it does believe in giving every human being, no matter how lowly their station, all of the rights which are accorded them by law.

"John and Tacoma," *Seattle Argus*, December 21, 1895

18

Joaquin Miller, a well-known figure and writer on the West Coast, often identified with "labor." Below, he presents a strong, if patronizing, defense of the integrity and skill of Chinese workers, a position he expresses in behalf of "real" workingmen, while taking issue with recent strikes and labor union activity in San Francisco. The year 1901 in fact marked the burgeoning of an "open shop" movement by employers, engendering a variety of responses by workers. San Francisco witnessed a general waterfront strike and the birth of a strong labor-based political party that year; the latter's program included an anti-Asian clause.[10]

....Now a word about the "hordes" that are to "overrun us." Senator Morton estimated that we had about 75,000 Chinese in California. We may have that number now; we may have only half so many, but I think, at one time, we have had at least a quarter of a million. This was when the placer mines were open to all, and the Harvard, Yale, and Princeton graduate shovelled dirt in the same gulch with "John" for gold and went home; and John sold it to his newly-arrived cousin, "on tick," and went home also. Then the cousin worked the claim to the bed-rock and went home, too.

So things went on till the first Pacific railroad was built, and when the last old claim was worked out, as a rule, the Chinaman went home. The quarter million of Chinese, without any restriction at all, had dwindled to about 75,000. Thus much for the "hordes" that are to overrun us. How illogical that the yellow element of the American press should be forever boasting of American valor, and yet constantly warning us to beware of the "hordes of degraded Mongolians that are to overrun us."

One word more about these "degraded" foreigners. They are, all their hundreds of millions of them, the best educated people in the world. They, as a rule, spend just about twice as much time at school as Americans. They, perhaps, learn more than twice as much; but unfortunately for them, their lessons are all of the past. They know little of the present and trust their future entirely to the just precepts of Confucius, however antique and impracticable these may be. A child is taken to school almost as soon as it is big enough to walk, and it stays there ten hours in the day, seven days in the week and ten months in the year. The Empire provides the book. It is all in rhyme, and every line of the one thousand, more or less, is a precept or a proverb, and each precept is in three words or sounds. The very first lesson, or line, ever laid in the hands of these hundreds of millions is simply this:

"Man born good." The second line, or precept, is: "Gem be polished."

....As for the honesty of these people, I appeal to every English merchant or banker, from Pekin to Hong Kong, to answer if he ever heard of a dishonest Chinese merchant or banker. So far from that, not only has every English bank two Chinamen to receive and hand out money, but every bank in Japan has the same. The English will tell you half in jest, that the Japanese is an Oriental Yankee, and does not trust his own people; and they will tell you, half in earnest, that the English bankers employ Chinese to handle their money because they never make mistakes. These people of China have never had anything like a bankrupt law. If a man cannot pay his debts, or some one does not secretly come forward and pay them, at the end of each year, he has "lost his face," and so dies by his own hand. Yet, with all their piteous poverty, they have no such word as "hard times," for everything must be settled up by the end of the year. There can be no extension of time. Confucius forbade it.

Filthy? There are some places in San Francisco, kept for show - I know what I am saying - where "guides" beg to take you at night. Go into these "show" places, opium dens or worse, and you will find that the only persons there, except the keeper, are depraved white men and women. The Chinaman does not go into a "joint" to smoke opium. It is against the law, and he knows how eager the police are to take him in a wrong. Besides that, he is a solitary creature, as a rule. At home, since the British forced opium upon him, he smokes much, but alone.

Of course, we have but an inferior class of Chinese with us, for they are naturally proud and will not come where they are not wanted, except to get bread. But if you care to go to the little Chinese settlement in San Francisco, to shop or to see, go alone. You may learn a little about the real China there. For instance, you will see the man, not the mother, fondling the little one. You will see him stand the little, animated flower-pot on the sidewalk and see it throw its little, silk sleeves around its papa's legs and hug heartily. You will see plenty of heart and not so very much dirt.

If I could only induce our Americans to journey to and through the Orient, instead of going so much to Europe, I am sure they would learn to despise all thought of an Exclusion Act.

The Chinese in the placer mines, where I worked alongside of them for years, always took time, at the end of a day's work, to entirely change their clothes and take a bath. I never knew a Chinese miner who did not. I never knew any other foreign miner who did. In fact, I never knew one of the other foreigners to take a bath of any kind, except by accident. The Chinese are the cleanest people in person in the world, except, perhaps, the English gentlemen who take their daily "dip."

In conclusion, let me say I never saw a drunken Chinaman. I never saw a Chinese beggar. I never knew of a lazy one. I sat as County Judge of Grant County, Oregon, for four years, where the miners had sold out to the Chinese to such an extent that the larger half of the mining properties was Chinese. Yet in all that time there was not one criminal case involving a Chinaman and but one civil one, and in the latter case a white man was finally indicted by his fellow-citizens for perjury.

Be assured, you will find all this wild cry simply sensation, as was the yellow howl of late in San Francisco, where the "laboring man" went on a strike at a time when there was more work than he could do, and at the best wages ever paid in the last three decades of our history. This laboring man struck because other laboring men did not choose to join him and his "beer joints." And nothing came of it, except that many good men were either killed or maimed and millions were wasted. Then the "laboring man" had to go to work alongside of the non-union man or not at all, as he pleased. But this sort of "laboring man" has paralyzed the coast before and will do it again, if he can.

It is but equity that the Chinaman shall come here if we go there. This land is too great and too good to forget equity. I repeat, we need the Chinese quite as much as they need us, and that is much indeed. And I say that, so long as the city of San Francisco, the State of California, and the Federal Government pander to and try to please and appease this ignorant mob of outlaws, who crowd the saloons and in their drunken desperation tear to pieces honest men who want to work but refuse to associate with them, just so long will San Francisco remain a reproach, as it has been all the season past. Bring in the Chinamen, and plenty of them, to help to take their places if they do not want to work. Let us see which is the stronger, a hoodlum mob of San Francisco or the President and the people of the United States.

Bear with me. I am a laboring man. I have never aspired to or attained much beyond hard work. I have built miles of stone wall here, planted thousands and thousands of trees, worked alongside of all sorts of "hands" right here, as all know, for the past fifteen years, all the time when not at work elsewhere, and so it is that I know what a real laboring man is.

I will not venture to advise; but I will say that if the man who really wants to work will keep out of the saloon, and go into the country and get a piece of land and go to work on it, he will soon look at things as I have set them down. He will soon want Chinese "help" for wife and babes, and above all, a Chinese gardener. Or, if he cannot tear himself from the city, let him open a shop, start a factory, and employ Chinese, do almost anything except beg and bully; for that is simply about all that a strike means. This is about all that these missions to the President and these appeals to Congress mean. The so-called "laboring man," who is not one in ten of the real laboring men, simply is a beggar and a bully. He does not want to work. He only wants to get something for nothing.

Joaquin Miller, "The Chinese and the Exclusion Act," *North American Review*, Vol. 173, December 1901, pp. 785-786, 786-789

19

This "Statement," written and prepared by an Irish-American and a Chinese-American, was simultaneously a compilation of materials indicating the status of the Chinese, including discrimination against them, and an argument in favor of fair treatment. The

Statement placed the blame for the anti-Chinese campaign upon organized labor. The following selections are taken from the Summary. Ironically, the pamphlet concludes with a quote from the anti-Chinese Henry George ["Think of the powers now wasted...." See Progress and Poverty, *Volume II, Doubleday, 1898, p. 549]*

We have gathered the facts. It remains to assemble and arrange them in some approach to order. The time is too short to make the mosaic a pleasure to the eye. The careful reader will discern that the material has been gleaned from all sources. We have gone back to the early history of the State and we have culled items from the current issues of the daily newspaper. We have trusted that the mere statement of the facts was all the argument needed to prove the case. We have shown that from the earliest history of the State the Chinaman has been with us. From the day that the three Chinese landed here in 1848, and became the servants in the household of the Pioneer, C.V. Gillespie, to the present time, the Chinese have been an indispensable part of our domestic economy.

We have resurrected a list of the outrages perpetrated upon the Chinese in this State during the last fifty years, which should bring the blush of shame to every American.

I say American, because California alone should not justly bear the blame. She was not responsible for the law as it was interpreted in People v. Hall, in 1854, and in the more famous decision in the Dred Scott case.

During the perpetration of all these outrages the patient and long-suffering Chinaman was our trusted servant, the companion of our children, and the mainstay of the household. And there is hardly an instance on record in which our Yellow Brother sought revenge for his injuries or made reprisals on the defenseless.

In the early history of the State when the few Caucasian laborers who were here could not be relied upon, the Chinese built our railways.

They were indispensable on the farm. Most of our orchards owe their origin and existence to the patient labor of the intelligent Chinaman. Our fruit industry, that amounts to nearly $10,000,000 during the current year, depends upon them for its very existence. They have leveed our swamp lands, and the man who knows what kind of work that is and grudges the hard-earned dollar which the Chinese toiler receives therefor is usually one who is very careful to avoid all such exposure and expenditure of effort himself.

We have shown by the amplest and most indisputable evidence that but for the presence of the Chinese in the early history of our State, it would have been impossible to start and carry on many of our manufacturing industries. The testimony given at nearly all the investigations made by our Labor Commissioners proved that the Chinese were absolutely indispensable to our manufacturing interests.

This is especially true of the cigar, shoe and woolen industries. It has been proved that, immediately after the Geary Act went into effect, the industries which mainly depended upon the labor of the Chinese gradually and steadily declined. And today, with a population nearly three times what we had thirty years ago, we have, for example, fewer white shoemakers than we had in 1869. And a similar fact applies to the cigar industry, the woolen industry and to other industries in a greater or lesser degree.

Our fishing industry, especially deep water fishing, has been dependent upon Chinese labor. And we have Dr. Jordan's emphatic testimony as to their usefulness and necessity in that severe and indispensable occupation.

Speaking of fish, every housewife in San Francisco knows that since the use of steam fishing vessels has been introduced into our waters by a class of foreigners who are eligible to citizenship, the price of fish has been steadily raised, even above that of meat, in some cases. The Italian owners of these improved fishing appliances have formed a "Trust" and have successfully ousted the Chinese fishermen, much to the detriment of the pocket of every American household. Yet, in our blindness and "Yellow" prejudice, we can see no good in "John." We have given him a bad name and we seem resolutely determined to prove that he deserves it.

And this, the cultivation of edible sea weeds, suggests the fact that - a most valuable food-product of our seacoast - is almost wholly neglected. If our prejudice would be allow us to employ the Chinese they would efficiently aid us in gathering this most valuable harvest of the sea.

This *statement* has conclusively proven one important fact: that the present campaign against the Asiatic is wholly the work of the Trade Unions - that the people at large have hardly any interest in it. We have shown how the Secretary of a State Labor Organization can at any time manufacture a semblance of public opinion. For example, the Secretary of the Building Trades Council of California, with its 170 affiliated organizations, can at any time get the newspapers to publish, discuss and seemingly approve the gist of their resolutions.

We have given the reader the very best that can be said against the Chinese, the mouthings of the demagogue and the arguments of the statesmen. We have shown the irrelevancy of their illustrations - the insufficiency of their facts and the incompetency of their conclusions....

We have shown that in this country, at least, there is no danger of population pressing upon the limits of subsistence. But that it is constantly pressing upon the fences of privilege, and the enclosures of franchise; and will continue to do so until the people have sense enough to let down the bars and remove the fences that hinder free access to the natural resources which they enclose.

Yes, that is the solution of the problem; Trust in God - set free the land, the support of all life - adjust transportation and exchange in accordance with modern knowledge and social needs. The force thus set free will revolutionize the conditions of men and hasten the day when the toiler can sit under his own vine and fig tree, with none to molest or make him afraid. With free access to the soil and freedom to exchange its products with all mankind, we need have no fear of over-production; as the gratification of man's desire has always been the incentive to progress. There is no condition conceivable where the cultured demands of humanity can be satisfied. No man has exhausted the inherent resources of an acre of land. Desire is an infinite attribute of mankind. The capacity to satisfy it is finite and limited.

"Think of the powers now wasted; of the infinite fields of knowledge yet to be explored; of the possibilities of which the wondrous inventions of this century give us but a hint. With want destroyed; with greed changed to noble passion; with the fraternity that is born of equality taking the place of the jealousy and fear that now array men against each other; with mental power loosed by conditions that give to the humblest comfort and leisure, and who shall measure the heights to which civilization may soar?

"Words fail the thought! It is the Golden Age of which poets have sung and high-raised seers have told in metaphor. It is the glorious vision which has always haunted man with gleams of fitful splendor. It is what he saw whose eyes were closed as in a trance at Patmos. It is the culmination of Christianity - the city of God on earth, with its walls of jasper and its gates of pearl. It is the reign of the Prince of Peace."

To aid in the attainment of the conditions so eloquently described by the printer-prophet who has given us the antidote to the poison of exclusion acts, I ask the workingmen themselves to extend the same right to the Chinaman that we did to the negro. Let us take from his path all restrictions of treaty and statute. Let us grant to him the rights that we ask for ourselves, and admit him to all the privileges and duties of American citizenship.

Then we may not look with such contempt upon the race that has given to history Confucius, Mencius, Jenghis Khan and Timour.

Patrick Healy and Ng Poon Chew, *A Statement for Non-Exclusion*, San Francisco, 1905, pp. 198-200, 209-210

Notes

1. Alexander Saxton presents an interesting critique of the George-Mill correspondence in *The Indispensable Enemy: Labor and the Anti-Chinese Movement in California*, Berkeley, 1971, pp. 100-103.

2. Chinese exclusion became an issue in New England in 1870. Phillips refers to the Chinese workers brought to North Adams, Massachusetts from San Francisco during a shoeworkers' strike conducted by the Knights of St. Crispin. The union's effort to organize the Chinese fell short, giving way to anti-Chinese hostility. See Ronald Takaki, *Strangers from a Different Shore: A History of Asian Americans*, Boston, 1989, pp. 95-99. Crispin support for exclusion was also manifested in San Francisco: Elmer Clarence Sandmeyer, *The Anti-Chinese Movement in California*, Urbana, 1991 (1939), p. 47.

3. Kearney, leader of the anti-Chinese agitation and of the Workingmen's Party of California, is discussed in Part IV and is well-scrutinized by Saxton; a cogent description is found in Franklin Folsom, *Impatient Armies of the Poor: The Story of Collective Action of the Unemployed*, Niwot, Colorado, 1991, chapter 9.

4. Isaac Kalloch, a minister and former abolitionist, was then mayor of San Francisco. Saxton, pp. 139-152.

5. Heinrich von Treitschke, an extreme German nationalist and anti-Semite, was later to declare the Jews "an element of decomposition." Carleton J.H. Hayes, *A Generation of Materialism, 1871-1900*, New York, 1941, p. 243.

6. Anti-Chinese developments in the Pacific Northwest are traced in Carlos A. Schwantes, *Radical Heritage: Labor, Socialism, and Reform in Washington and British Columbia, 1885-1917*, Seattle, 1979, pp. 22-29, 34-35, 157-159. A pioneering piece is Jules Alexander Karlin, "Anti-Chinese Outbreaks in Seattle, 1885-1886," *Pacific Northwest Quarterly*, Vol. 39, No. 2 (April 1948), pp. 103-129. A revealing analysis of a Pacific Northwest Chinese community can be found in P. Scott Corbett and Nancy Parker Corbett, "The Chinese in Oregon, c. 1870-1880," *Oregon Historical Quarterly*, Vol. 78 (1977), pp. 73-85.

7. See Part III.

8. Henry Ward Beecher, the radical reformer, clergyman, and former abolitionist, endorsed both the rights and the cheap labor of the Chinese in America, a paradox outlined in Saxton, pp. 132-137. A substantial biography of Beecher is Clifford Edward Clark, *Henry Ward Beecher: Spokesman for a Middle-class America*, Urbana, 1978.

9. There is mention here of Chinese in the culinary trades. The rise of Chinese labor in both restaurants and laundries was consequent to its exclusion from other occupations during the middle and late nineteenth century. See Paul C.P. Siu, *The Chinese Laundryman: A Study of Social Isolation*, New York, 1987.

10. A critic notes that while Miller romanticized the American West in his writings, he "championed its oppressed peoples, Mexican and Chinese as well as Indian." Benjamin S. Lawson, *Joaquin Miller*, Boise, 1980, p. 48; Miller defended the Native American resistance to white encroachment in *Unwritten History: Life Amongst the Modocs*, Upper Saddle River, N.J., 1968 (1874). Miller spent the year 1900 in China, covering the Boxer Rebellion for the *San Francisco Examiner*. Harr Wagner, *Joaquin Miller and His Other Self*, San Francisco, 1929, p. 192.

Part III: The Views of the Clergy

The appeals of clergymen for racial justice and fair treatment for Chinese and Japanese immigrants, for an end to their exclusion, form an important component of the movement for Asian rights in the United States. While ministers occasionally employed ethnic or racial stereotypes to make the point that Asians were desirable people to have in the United States, a sufficient body of humanitarian content suffuses the statements and petitions below to register their sentiments as essentially democratic. Several of the churchmen from whom relevant materials are selected became well known precisely for their support of justice for Asians in America.[1]

Among the first was the Reverend William Speer - founder of the Chinese Presbyterian Church in San Francisco in the 1850's and editor of the Chinese-English paper, *The Oriental* [Documents 1a and b]. Some twenty years later, Congregationalist pastor D.A.L. Stone came to the defense of the Chinese during the 1870's in much the same tones as Speer, echoing both the latter's support for basic rights and his paternalism [Document 2]. The contemporary activity and reputation of Otis Gibson [Document 3] places him at the forefront of those ministers urging fair treatment of the Chinese; likewise, he embraced certain of the prejudices common to other clerical supporters of that cause. The same contradictions run through L.T. Chamberlain's 1879 sermon [Document 4].[2] The *California Independent* editorial [Document 5] calls the religious convictions of the persecutors of the Chinese into question. Missionary Esther Baldwin's condemnation of the Chinese Exclusion Act is one of the most articulate on record [Document 6]. The response of the Methodist Episcopal Church to anti-Chinese outbreaks in the 1880's [Document 7] suggests that the views of the more tolerant clergy were not expressed in isolation from the brutal facts of discrimination and violence sanctioned by governmental codification. After opposing the racist drive in Seattle in 1886, local Methodists were treated with contempt by the press [Document 8]. The statement of a Jersey City minister represents the clerical contribution to the campaign against the Geary Act [Document 9].

While most church support for Asians' rights went to the Chinese, appeals for the basic liberties of Japanese in the United States were also heard [Documents 10 and 11]. An editorial from a leading Protestant periodical, written during World War II, summarizes and extends several cogent arguments for the rights of all Asians in America   nearly one hundred years after the first such clerical appeal [Document 12].

1

The Reverend William Speer was an outstanding supporter of the rights of the Chinese during California's early statehood years. He lectured widely (particularly in San Francisco), wrote prolifically, initiated English and other classes for Chinese immigrants. The lecture below embraces many of the key contentions of Protestant clergymen backing the Chinese: that they were honest, gentle, civilized, and educated people, ripe for Christianizing and deserving of better treatment. Of note is Speer's contention that the Chinese may have landed on the American continent before the arrival of Europeans. The second statement (b) rebuts a number of the key charges against Chinese workers, specifically challenging the notion of their degraded character. Both statements appeared in opposition to, and in spite of, one of the earliest waves of anti-Chinese propaganda, which was highlighted by the People vs. Hall *decision [see Part I].*[3]

(a)

Western nations claim to have discovered America some three hundred and sixty years ago. But there is reason at once to presume that it was subjects of the Chinese Empire, either Tartars or Chinese, that at first disturbed its vast solitudes with the sounds of the human voice, and who planted on its soil imperishable monuments of human industry. Place the newly arrived Chinaman and the Indian side by side, and you observe the same complexion. Listen to the tongue of the latter, and while most of the dialects have partaken more of the Tartar original, a Chinese element may also may be traced. For instance, the Otomi language, which covered a wider territory than any other but the Aztec among the nations of the Western part of our continent, is said to exhibit a remarkable affinity to the Chinese, both in its monosyllabic structure and in its general vocabulary.

If it be asked, how the Orientals could have reached this country, a high American authority [Redfield] says: "A knowledge of the winds and currents of the Pacific Ocean will, I am convinced, serve to remove all mystery and all doubt from the once vexed question of the first peopling of its islands from the Asiatic continent, and in spite of the long urged objection of the opposition of the trade-winds. A case is still recent where the wreck of a Japanese junk was drifted the entire distance to the Sandwich islands, with its surviving crew; thus completing nearly half of the great circuit of the winds and currents in the North Pacific. But we shall find an additional means of transport near the Equator, which is afforded in the north-west monsoon of the Indian and Pacific Oceans, and which is found, according to my inquiries, to extend at one portion of the year as far eastward as the Society Islands, or more than half the distance from the Indian Ocean to the coast of South America." Within a few weeks past, we have seen in this city a Japanese merchant, who had recently been rescued from the wreck of a native junk, in which, after nine months, he had been carried to a considerable distance northward of the Sandwich Islands. When we consider the countless fleets of vessels, of every description, that checker the Chinese seas, it would be wonderful if some of them, by the frequent storms and the great current which precipitates the Northern Pacific upon the American coast, were not landed here; and equally wonderful if some, by the great counter current and trade-winds of the tropical zone, did not bear back tidings of the new world....

A...more complete argument might be presented...from a general survey of the Aztec civilization, and a comparison of it with that of the Chinese. The Spanish priest or soldier who crossed the Pacific from the ancient empire of the East to its counterpart in the West, when he walked its fields, might have beheld the same respect paid to agriculture as a profession, the same dependence of government on the products of the soil chiefly for its revenue, and the payment of taxes in kind; also similar modes of irrigation to increase the yield of the earth, and large public granaries in which the excess of the luxuriant harvest was deposited for years of drought and famine. In the place of trade he would have seen the same association of merchants and mechanics into powerful guilds for the protection of their privileges and their prices....In the workshop he would have been delighted by the same dazzling exhibition of fine porcelain, of lacquer work in wood, of cotton cloth, of a species of silk spun from a worm, of precious stones skilfully cut and polished, and of different metals brilliantly enchased. About the abodes of wealth he would have wandered in brilliant gardens, containing collections of plants never excelled by any in Europe, adorned by sparkling pools, and airy pavilions, whose graceful pillars were inscribed with poetic or fanciful quotations....Should he converse with a company of students, their attention to astrology, their use of a hieroglyphic and ideographic system of characters in writing, the amazing resemblance of the calendar, and the principle of the annotation of time, which has been so much remarked by the learned of Europe, nay, even as minute a circumstance as the mode of preserving their books, not in scrolls, but in alternate fanlike folds, would have confirmed his delusion....

How can we interpret coincidences so universal, so minute, and so remarkable, save by the presumption of a common origin to the customs, the arts, and the religious institutions, of the Chinese and Aztec nations? And further, is it not probable from this extraordinary retention of the filial form and feelings, that subsequent to the original colonization there were occasional intercommunications between the separate families? And still again, why should it be thought incredible that the Chinese Fusang is indeed the American California, and that the Oriental discoverers have higher rights and honors, by ten centuries, vested in this soil, than any European nation? - that the people of the East were acquainted with this antipodal continent in the days of the emperor Justinian, before the overthrow of the Roman empire, a thousand years before the flag of Spain or England was lifted upon it by Christopher Columbus or Sebastian Cabot?....

We live in a *portion of our country* seemingly appointed by God as the spot from which the chief influences tending to the civilization and christianization of Eastern Asia shall flow.

Four cities will in time be the great commercial centres of the world - London, New York, San Francisco, Shanghai - the eastern and western gates of the two respective continents. We may declare of this magnificent harbor, with its internal connections, and its advantages incomparable elsewhere on this shore of the continent, as the far-reaching mind of Humboldt observed in respect to the Isthmus of Panama - it is "a point of the globe destined by nature to change the face of the commercial system of nations."

Fellow Citizens of San Francisco and California! It becomes us to reflect upon the responsibility to God and to the human race imposed upon us by our position and relations. In becoming a citizen of this community each individual assumes his share. Each, voluntarily or involuntarily, sensible or insensibly, but daily and unceasingly, is adding his impress to the destinies of remote races. Each ray of influence, whether beneficent or malignant, can no more pause than starlight can pause, ere it impinges on some distant sphere. Let us be earnest, faithful, prudent, forbearing, sincere, honest, patient, generous, in the discharge of our several obligations to that Empire, that like a majestic, but long-sick, and almost-dying queen, reaches her enfeebled arms, lifts her plaintive voice, and turns her longing eyes to us, for sympathy, for counsel, for salvation.

China and California: Their Relations, Past and Present. A Lecture, in continuation of a series in relation to the Chinese People, delivered in the Stockton Street Presbyterian Church, San Francisco, Marvin and Hitchcock, 1853, pamphlet, pp. 4-5, 9, 10, 27

(b)

To obtain a satisfactory view of the Chinese as we find them in California, it will be necessary first to ask, who are these people? and how came they here?

It has been said that they are coolies. By this it is meant they belong to a general degraded caste in their native country. The word "coolie" is sometimes applied to Chinese laboring men, inferior servants, and farm hands, by Europeans. But there is *no caste* in China, any more than in the United States. The mistaken ideas which prevail on this subject have arisen from the confounding the Chinese people and customs with those of India, where the entire social system is widely different. The English newspapers, familiar with Indian usages, and viewing all the nations of the East through the medium of the press in their great colonial presidencies of Bengal, Bombay and Madras, have originated in Great Britain and America gross mistakes in regard to the other countries of whose trade the East India Company held also a long monopoly. The Hindustani word "coolie," is one of those inflicted upon the

Chinese, in whose language it has no equivalent, and who have no caste or class whom it represents. It would be justly held degrading to style an English laborer of whatever occupation, in China, a "coolie," and it is not right to attach to Chinese the odium of a social debasement which is peculiar to another country, to other institutions, and to another and most dissimilar people. Their emigrants are just what any other people are: laborers, cooks, boatmen, farmers, carpenters, stone masons, bricklayers, shop-keepers, book-binders, weavers, tea-packers, gardeners, and just what an equal number from any other land might be expected to present in the variety of their occupations. Some, that speak English best, have been scholars in missionary schools, or employees about foreign *hongs*. Here and there is a literary man, though rarely seen, and his accomplishments unappreciated. Then, there is an abundance of the vilest classes - the gambler, the infamous female, and others, who prey upon the fortunate, the unwary, or the wanton of their own countrymen.

An Humble Plea, Addressed to the Legislature of California, In Behalf of the Immigrants From the Empire of China to this State, San Francisco, published at the office of *The Oriental*, 1856, pamphlet, pp. 5-6

2

>   *In the sermon excerpted below, the Congregationalist minister D.A.L. Stone challenged a number of anti-Chinese arguments. At the time Stone gave his sermon, a particularly bitter anti-Chinese campaign was just beginning.*

This is Not a Californian, but an American Question.

In this special relation of ours to the subject, we are in danger of taking narrow views of it. Such views, just so far as they lack breadth, must lack soundness and completeness. We must remember that this is not a Californian question, but an American question. It will be an unwarrantable assumption for us to speak for the whole country. It is not for New York to say who shall land at Castle Garden, nor for San Francisco to say who shall have entrance at the Golden Gate. This grand sea-portal is not city property, like the entrance to a park - it belongs to the nation and the Continent. What affects us, in this matter, has its weight, and ought to have, in setting the national policy; but there will be other weights to be cast also into the balances. If we would grasp the elements of a conclusion that shall stand as right and just in all impartial judgment...we must consider the question, not in the narrow, sectional view, as representatives of American civilization, and as advocates of the best human progress.

It is a large problem. It includes many and weighty conditions. It is to be calmly and carefully surveyed on all sides. It cannot be solved simply by appeal to the sentiment of philanthropy and by the "glittering generalities" of spread-eagle oratory on the one side, nor by an appeal to class-prejudice and the rant of political partisanship on the other. We cannot safely commit it to the passions of the hour, and the clamors of selfishness and jealousy. Nothing less than the ablest and wisest practical statesmanship can cope with it.

I do not assume to speak with the comprehension, or in the name of such statesmanship; but I approach the subject as an inquirer - well convinced on some points, and on others waiting for clearer light.

Shall the Chinese Receive an American Welcome.

For the purposes of this discussion we may divide the question into two parts: Shall the Chinese immigration, properly regulated, be welcomed? And, How shall these strangers be treated as they are found in the midst of us?

Under the first inquiry, we stand at the outset face to face with the great American idea of opening this free and broad land as a refuge and a shelter to all who would seek its shores. We have stood within our magnificent domain, and feeling that we had room enough for all, and that we possessed the happiest and freest form of government of any nation on earth, we have said in the hearing of all the families of men, "Lift up your heads, oh ye gates, and be ye lifted up ye asylum doors, that whosoever will may enter in!" We have called to the oppressed of every land, the downtrodden of old world kingdoms, the millions under despotic rule, all who labored much and gathered little, to whom hope and progress and daily bread were denied, ground to the earth with burdensome taxation, wearing the yoke of aristocratic institutions, famishing and forlorn, with neither free limb, nor free speech, nor free thought, and only the rigors of an iron lot clasping them fast - "come

hither and you shall find a home, and the heritage extended to every dweller
on American soil, life, liberty and the pursuit of happiness." This has been our
attitude and our boast. We have turned all hopeless eyes toward this country.
We have drawn millions of fettered feet within our borders. We have asked
no such questions as these: What is your birth? What is your nationality?
What is your religion? We have only asked, will you come in as good subjects,
under our laws? This, I say, has been the American idea. Must we modify and
restrict this welcome? Must we change this policy? Has the time come when
we must make special rules, establish exceptions, and stand on guard? If a
restrictive legislation is to be inaugurated, how far shall it extend? Shall it
apply to one race, or more than one? If new conditions are imposed in one
direction, what answer shall be given to the next demand in some other
direction? Is there to be an endless debate of class with class, as to the right
of a home under the American flag, and is our political arena to be clouded,
henceforth, with the dust of angry combatants on these new issues? You see
the question thus opened has a wild and perilous outlook. Once begin this
controversy and it may reach other interests and other fortunes than those
originally involved. It may set up new tests on the Atlantic, as well as on the
Pacific strand, for no man can fix bounds to its range....

Can we Assimilate the Chinese Element?

Shall we say, then, that we will receive as helpers and fellow laborers...all that
come, provided it is such a type of life as we can digest and assimilate? I do
not object to the sentiment of this qualification. I believe it is sound and true.
On this point, then it is not the incoming of members that raises any question,
but the quality, the kind. Indeed the whole foreign immigration, compared
with the Chinese, is at least as ten to one. And against this mass of the nine-
tenths, neither labor nor capital makes any protest. But the Chinese element,
it is maintained, is an element by itself. It is isolated and clannish. It does not
blend with other elements. In blood and religion, and social life, it keeps itself
separate and distinct. Can it ever be digested, assimilated and Americanized?
This is a very grave inquiry. But I think it ought to be said in truth and
fairness that the Chinese are scarcely more clannish that the Irish. In domestic
and social alliances our friends of the Emerald Isle keep mostly to themselves.
If they touch other races in our national fellowship without chafing, and
collision, they do not amalgamate with them and cease to be Irish. Every

where they are easily discriminated, by feature and speech and social relations. And if there begin to be exception to this rule, it has been a long process to bring about such a change. Even with the powerful helps of common schools, political privilege and political co-working, the Irish are still mainly a distinctive class in our population. And I need not tell you that in the matter of schools, they are increasingly anxious to be still more separate and distinct. But we do not make these facts a ground of objection to their free welcome.

It is too soon to say that we cannot to the same extent assimilate the Asian element. The experiment is new. The obstacles are novel. The influence of our institutions has not had time to produce effects....

How Shall we Treat Those who are With Us.

And now as to the treatment of those who are found on our soil. We are not left to the freedom of our own prejudices and passions. We are bound by international obligation and law. We may not transcend the stipulations into which our Government has voluntarily entered. Any infraction of these rules is not simply inhuman - it is falsehood, treachery, bad faith, treason.

If your people in China had been hounded by the brutality which has in so many instances persecuted and maltreated these foreigners in this community, the Pacific waters would have been white with the foam of our avenging fleets, and our remonstrance would have been uttered in thunders at the cannon's mouth.

The municipal regulations just proposed here as applying to these strangers, are of the nature of discriminating persecution, a violation of the acts of the supreme government of this land, an outrage upon common humanity and common decency. We may talk of "imported barbarism" - this is home barbarism of the most unmixed and blackest shade.

The tone in which the question has been discussed by portions of the public press, though in words deprecating such issue, is fitted to inflame the passions of the people, to stimulate violence, and to incite riot and bloodshed. Every lover of good order, of the tranquility and good name and prosperity of this city, and of human rights, should frown upon and denounce such incendiary agitation.

The Christian View.

I have not yet spoken of the distinctively Christian view, and I have only room to glance at it in closing. The great Chinese empire is by covenant, and promise, a part of His inheritance who shall reign from the river unto the ends of the earth. The representatives of this race are brought hither in providence, not simply to be at school under the social and civil institutions of our American civilization, but under the enlightning and transforming power of Christian nurture and the Gospel of grace and salvation....But for the realization of so great a hope our Christianity must be just, humane, hospitable, and true to the common brotherhood of man. We cannot, as Christians, commend our faith to those whom, as American citizens, we despise, reject and abuse.

"The Chinese Question," *San Francisco Daily Alta*, June 16, 1873

3

A Methodist Episcopal minister, Otis Gibson spoke and wrote widely on the Chinese; his testimony was a highlight of the 1876 Congressional Investigation [see Part I]. His massive book, The Chinese in America, *is a key primary source in tracing ministerial support for the rights of the Chinese: for his part in mobilizing such support, Gibson was burned in effigy during the 1876 pogroms. Interestingly, at one point in the excerpts below, he draws a condemnatory parallel between contemporary anti-Chinese attitudes and the infamous Dred Scott decision of 1857. Although he was a consistent foe of relevant federal and state policies of discrimination, Gibson's stance included anti-Catholic, anti-Irish dimensions; stereotypical representations of Irish-American speech appear in the book.[4]*

It is a humiliating fact that the greatest enthusiasm is often manifested upon issues where ignorance, bigotry, prejudice and selfishness play the principal parts. The history of the "Anti-Chinese Crusade" in California, during this Centennial year of American independence; the grounds upon which it has been waged; the character and spirit of its leaders and active agents; the methods of the campaign, the willful misrepresentations made concerning helpless and defenseless strangers who have come to us by special invitation; the criminal perversion of testimony given under oath; the ill-concealed effort to blacken the character of Protestant Missions and missionaries, in order to make a case against the Chinamen; the proud arrogance and assumption of superior virtue and morality by a class of men, many of whom, in daily life and practice, fall far below the average Chinaman - all these things conspire to cause a blush of shame on the cheek of every intelligent Christian citizen who understands the case, whenever the subject is mentioned.

Indeed, the whole discussion of this question, so far as these political demagogues are concerned, has been so puerile, so utterly destitute of logic and sound argument, - in its spirit and intent so subversive of the fundamental principles of liberty upon which the whole fabric of our government is built, - so blind to patent facts, so utterly regardless of truth, honor, and justice, that it requires no ordinary patience to arrange the shameful facts in hand, and write out an impartial sketch of its history.

In the Spring of the present year (1876), two facts conspired to give certain political aspirants a coveted occasion to inaugurate a bitter and wide-spread Anti-Chinese agitation. First, the decision of the Supreme Court of the United States, that the State legislations of California, prohibiting the importation of lewd Chinese women was unconstitutional. Second, the fact that an unusually large number of Chinese immigrants were arriving each month, with *rumors* that multitudes more were only waiting an opportunity to come. These two facts furnished an immediate occasion, and fresh material for an appeal to the selfishness, bigotry, and race prejudices of the people, in order to excite their hostility against the Chinese, and thereby secure their adherence to the political school of the agitators and lift them into office. The result has been that, for political purposes alone, the leaders of both political parties, and the secular press generally, have declared war upon the Chinamen. The press has deprecated the constant, violent assaults and abuses heaped upon the Chinamen, not because of the injustice and brutality of such conduct, but simply on the low, selfish ground that these acts of violence would injure the Anti-Chinese cause in the Eastern States. And before the Commissioners appointed by the municipal government of San Francisco could reach Washington, with the address and resolutions of the famous Anti-Chinese Mass-meeting of April 5th, a California Senator, Mr. A.A. Sargent, had anticipated all they had to say in a speech before the Senate, May 2, 1876.

A large portion of the press of California devoted itself to fanning the flames of excitement. The people were daily treated to editorials and correspondence setting forth in exaggerated and highly colored phrases the vices and crimes of the Chinese people, the ruin caused by Chinese cheap labor, and the tremendous impending evils of further Chinese immigration. All the existing evils which affect the morals of our own people were charged upon the Chinese. All the sufferings of the poor and wretched were the results of Chinese immigration. The very vices and crimes of our hoodlum element were traced to the presence and competition of Chinese labor. The people were admonished to remember that China had a population of four hundred millions, an alien race, incapable of assimilating with and attaining to our higher forms of civilization, and that a constant stream from such a source would soon overrun and devastate the whole land. With admirable sophistry and flattery it was maintained that a "European after being in this country a few years, becomes as good a citizen, and as patriotic as a native born; a Chinaman never." (But the *fact* is, *some* Europeans make bad citizens, some Chinamen make good ones.) The working classes were easily made the dupes and tools of the demagogues. They were made to believe that if the Chinese were removed out of the way, thousands of white laborers, more than now, would immediately find employment at greatly increased wages. The Chinese laboring men were all called coolie slaves, and for a white man to be a common laborer beside a servile class, was disgraceful in the extreme, and utterly repugnant to the noble instincts of the intelligent yeomanry of this free land....

What then are the evils and dangers of this Chinese immigration greater and more fearful than the evils and dangers of our European, that in order to put a stop to it, a departure from first principles is required, and a radical change in the policy and usages of our Government demanded?

We have seen that Chinese cheap labor is not the evil, for Chinese labor on the Pacific Coast to-day is as well paid as is the same kind of labor in the Atlantic States. It is not a lack of industry and frugality on the part of the Chinese, nor a lack of commercial enterprise and commercial honesty, nor yet the absence of brain or muscle power, their competitors themselves being the judges. It is not that "they fill our prisons, our almshouses and our hospitals." The immigration from Europe, according to official statistics, enjoys largely the monopoly of the privileges of those institutions. It is not because the Chinese do not "pay promptly their debts, their rents, and their taxes." Where, then, shall the answer be found? Is it that they have not adopted our fashions of dress? They might perhaps ask what is the constitutional fashion of dress in this country? Is it that they eat rice, pork and vegetables, instead of bread and cheese, beef and potatoes? Is it that they drink tea instead of whiskey and beer? Is it that they cut some of their hair shorter, and some of it longer than the average American? Is it that they can not speak the English language? Neither do the Germans, and the Germans are quite as persistent in retaining their native tongue in this country as the Chinese are in retaining theirs. Is it, that the Chinese do not attend our public schools and try to learn our language and our civilization? The fact is, that though taxed to support these schools, the Chinese are peremptorily refused admission to their privileges. At great public expense, a part of which is borne by the Chinese, we teach the European immigrants our language, and even go so far as to perfect them in their own language. But we give to the Chinese among us, no such opportunity to cultivate their minds and improve their condition, and yet we feat their competition.

Is the danger to be found in the fact that the Chinese do not, to any extent, observe our national Sabbath-day and its institutions? There are many, perhaps a majority of the intelligent citizens of this Christian Republic, who firmly believe that European immigration is more dangerous in this respect than the Chinese, more destructive of the morals and virtue of our people, more subversive of the civil and religious liberties of which we boast....

A great deal has been said, in Congress and out of Congress, by the Anti-Chinese memorialists and by the Anti-Chinese clubs of California, about the importance of the repeal or modification of the Burlingame treaty with China, in order to check the immigration of the Chinese to this country.

Strangely enough, it seems to be the prevailing opinion that without special treaty stipulation, providing for their coming and for their protection while here, the Chinese would have no right to come to this country to live; and if they should come without such treaty stipulations they would have no right, under the Constitution, to claim for their lives and property the equal protections of our laws, or, in other words, "no rights which white men would be bound to respect." Such an idea is a monstrous libel upon the principles, the policy, and usages of this nation. That such opinions should prevail among the Chinese themselves is quite natural; for, according to long-established laws and customs in China, without special treaty provisions the people of other countries may not enter China, and, if entering without such treaty permission, they may not claim for their lives and property the protection of the Chinese Government.

But the laws, the policy, and the Constitution of these United States are upon a different basis altogether. For one hundred years, from the beginning until now, the doors of this country, on the east and on the west, on the north and on the south, have been opened alike to all comers, from all lands, without any distinction of race, color, language, or previous condition in life. No treaty is required with any foreign government in order that its subjects may have the right to come to this country to live. That matter, so far as our Government is concerned, is left entirely to the voluntary choice of the individual. No passport is demanded at American ports of the foreigner who comes to travel over this broad land; none from the immigrant comes to make his home in this New World.

Modify or abrogate and repeal the Burlingame treaty as we please, the Chinese would still have just the same right to come here, to live here, and to claim for their lives and property the protection of our laws while here, that the Germans or French or Irish or the people of any other nation have. The Burlingame treaty was dictated, as all our treaties with China have been dictated by our Government, for our benefit, not for the benefit of the Chinese. In giving a tardy consent to the terms of these treaties, the Chinese have been obliged to depart from their settled policy, to violate long-cherished principles, and to overthrow established customs. But the terms of these treaties, requiring such concessions on the part of the Chinese Government, require no concessions whatever on the part of our Government. Our treaties secure for Americans in China rights and privileges which they could not claim without such treaty stipulations; but these treaties secure to the Chinese in America no single right or privilege which they could not claim under our Constitution without the existence of any treaty whatever. It is very plain, then, that the repeal of the Burlingame treaty will not prevent Chinese immigration, because that treaty did not give them the right to come. It simply stated their natural and inalienable right to come if they so desired, and it made a few regulations respecting the details of their coming....

...It is plainly evident that the right of the Chinese to immigrate to this country is not found in the stipulations of the Burlingame treaty, but that right is found in the fundamental principles our Government, which are enumerated in that treaty as the basis of its stipulations; principles new to the Chinese, but with us as old as our national existence. *To prohibit the Chinese from coming to this country requires not so much a modification of treaties as it requires a marked departure from the broad principles upon which our Government is established, and which have been our boast and glory for a hundred years.*

Is the cause sufficient to require such a sacrifice? Is the Government ready to make the departure? Can not our Government regulate her own ships and ports, rather than trample under foot eternal principles?

If, as a sanitary measure, no vessel from a foreign port should be permitted at a single entry to land more than two hundred passengers upon our shores the cause would be fully met, threatening dangers from beyond either sea would be in a measure averted, and American-born people would have a little better opportunity than they now enjoy to manage their own affairs and preserve and regulate their own cherished institutions.

The Chinese in America, Cincinnati, Hitchcock and Walden, 1877, pp. 293-296, 365-367, 369-373

4

Preaching in his Norwich, Connecticut church in 1879 (while Congress debated an exclusion bill that President Rutherford B. Hayes would later veto), the Reverend L.T. Chamberlain questioned the ethics of discrimination in a nation allegedly founded on principles of liberty. His sermon included the point that while many felt the Chinese presence bred poverty in San Francisco, destitution was ironically widespread in communities where no Chinese lived at all. Chamberlain echoes Speer's salute to Chinese civilization, defends cheap labor, pays tribute to the contribution of Chinese workers, and expresses hope for their conversion to Christianity.

Ah, do you comprehend the greatness of the issue? Do you begin to realize how this is a thing in which the world is more than a spectator, and humanity more than an incidental participant? Does it dawn on you, that, *prima facie*, the case is against the Republic? I will utter not one word in prejudgment of the issue. I can understand that the act might be justifiable. I can imagine that circumstances might warrant the extent of the severity. It were possible that the seeming injustice should prove to be the truest Christian wisdom. Yet this, my friends, is already clear; that the justifying reasons must be singularly urgent, must be supremely weighty, or the case will go against the western nation. From some source there must be brought considerations of most exceptional moment, or the Christian will be shamed in contrast with the Pagan. Yet the decree has been pronounced. We will search with care for the grounds on which it may be upheld....

But, there must - one would say - be the reason somewhere, for the act before us; for Congress is not composed of either the demented or the wholly depraved. I cling to my faith in the general wisdom and integrity of our national legislature. I cannot readily believe that either party in Washington is predominantly corrupt. And, moreover, this Chinese legislation is supported by both parties, or at least by their distinguished leaders. May it not be, then, that the reason of the action taken is in the character of the emigrants themselves? Certainly one might surmise that they were infectious persons, that they contaminated the common air, or that they were corrupters of the popular morals! And that is not far from the allegation actually made. It is avowed by the supporters of the proscription, that the Chinese emigrant is uncleanly and immoral, to a degree of which the Anglo-Saxon mind cannot conceive; that he lives like the beast, and sets at naught every dictate of decency and health. And that statement is not simply by the low ruffians of the streets and sand-flats, it is repeated by many of the true and good. We must, accordingly, give it weight. If it is warranted, the case requires swift remedial treatment. It may require even the severity of excision, of absolute removal. But you will note one comprehensive, signal fact which, by somewhat and at once, rebuts the sweeping charge! It is universally admitted, - mark it, *universally* admitted - that the Chinaman is peaceable, patient, frugal, sober, industrious, apt at learning, successful in traffic, skilled in the arts requiring delicacy of manipulation, capable of great physical endurance, and especially fitted for resisting malarias. Do you suppose that such qualities are consistent with the abysmal pollution, the nameless, inconceivable beastliness in which the Chinaman is said to wallow? Do you not know that his vices must be somewhat less than are alleged? Do you think that such creatures of foulness physical and moral, could possibly excel as makers of cigars, boxes, sashes, doors, blinds, boots, shoes, bags, even ladies' and children's wear, and clothing generally? Would they excel in placer-mining, farming, fishing, gardening, fruit-picking, peddling, laundrying, and domestic service? And I have only named, word for word, the things which their enemies say they are monopolizing to-day on the Pacific coast! Do you imagine that the men who, when Sacramento was menaced by a flood, faced the danger and raised the levee which saved the city[5]; the men who climbed the perilous heights of the Sierra Nevada, and over ravines and through the living rock gave the Pacific rail-road its path from the centre to the sea; do you imagine, I say, that those men are beneath our conception in moral and social degradation?

You may well shudder at what is the unquestionable condition of the Chinese quarter in San Francisco, but you may shudder also, and as well, at the condition of quarters in which their asserted superiors alone are found. Herded like beasts, - a thing appalling and really unthinkable to the pure, immaculate Anglo-Saxon mind? Why I read but five days ago, of enormous, filthy, immoral, overcrowded, malarious, pestilential tenement-blocks in the very metropolis of America, containing each more than two thousand tenants, and not a Chinaman among them! Moreover, if San Francisco has within her municipality, as we are told, the "feculence and foulness of Sodom and Gomorrah," it is certainly her own shame as well as that of the Chinese which is attested. She has ample power to regulate the general conditions under which her inhabitants shall live. As she herself claims virtue and Christian wisdom, why doesn't she apply the ready remedy, instead of aspersing a whole race? Tell here, please, that she flaunts her own disgrace, when she testifies of her Chinese burrowing in the ground, and disregarding the common rules of civilized life. If such are the facts, she ought herself to be indicted for criminal, shameful neglect. The probable truth is that the average Chinaman in the United States, is of something like the average decency of his class!....

You know that hate begets hate. Do you think that with protection abrogated or surrendered, and proscription enacted, the Chinese will continue their past attention to our message from Christ? They will perceive, none more surely, that the word is gainsaid by deed. They may perhaps be tolerant in their own domain, and shame us by their forbearance, but their hearts must needs be hardened. They will be apt to turn, I think, from that Christ whose followers appear so unscrupulous, to that Confucius who taught them respect for pledges as one of the first principles of life. It were not, in justice, to be resented by us, should they take occasion to expel all our missionaries, as well as to close up their ports to our trade.

Let this hostile act become our veritable law, and the cause of Christ in China, so far as we are concerned with it, is apparently stricken to death. Aye, though it is prevented from becoming law, how shall we repair even the present loss? Who will restore that confidence which is so sensitive to wounds?....

Anti-Chinese Legislation: A Sermon Preached in the Broadway Church, Norwich, Conn., March 2, 1879, by the pastor, Rev. L.T. Chamberlain, pamphlet, pp. 4-5, 9-11, 22

5

Opening with a line from the distinguished scholar and Unitarian minister Samuel Johnson, the following editorial from the California Independent *[from which other material may be found in Part II], casts doubt on the religious integrity of Christian opponents of the Chinese.*

Johnson, author of *Oriental Religions*, says: "It became necessary for the Chino-Mongol to plant foot upon the soil of California to learn all the possibilities of cruelty." That this is a truth, no man who has witnessed the daily persecutions of the Chinese among us, can for a moment conscientiously dispute. In all the history of the attrition of races so bloody, so cruel as is that which records the persecution of the Chino-Mongol in California. It is a tragedy of race; that must take its place beside that which has left so deep its scars upon the heart of the Jew. No other people but that of Israel has drank so deeply at the hands of the Christian (?) of the bitter cup of sorrow. This is the one great blot - the one great moral eclipse that rests upon our State history. No deluge of waters, no cyclone of fire can ever remove this dark stain upon our escutcheon. Nothing but the blood of the Atonement can relieve us in our individuality from this supreme sin of cruelty. And yet, it is in the heart of men who bow at Christian (?) altars that this barbarism has its inspiration.

Assumed worshippers of Christ first lead in this great crusade against a helpless race. Then follows the political demagogue who loves office and its emoluments more than principle or country, and next follows the instinctively cruel whose abnormal nature only pulsates with joyous fervor, when it riots in the suffering and the blood of some defenseless creature of God.

But let us wait, we whose hearts have gone out in sympathy towards this dark skinned race whose barks by the favoring gales of Divine Providence have been cast upon our shores, and we shall at some time of the future be able to rejoice in an act of emancipation, paralleled only be that which gave the rights of common manhood to 3,000,000 of American bondmen.

"Chinese Persecution," *California Independent*, March 6, 1880

6

> In the excerpts below, Esther E. Baldwin excoriates the Chinese exclusion process. She spent nearly twenty years in missionary work in China. Though part of the material is fairly standard proselytizing and reflective of anti-Irish and anti-working class prejudices, Baldwin takes issue with key components of anti-Chinese racism.

I here *assert*, fearless of any counter-statement *capable of proof*, that the Chinese to-day are the most industrious, quiet, honest, sober, patient, and forbearing (oh, how forbearing!) immigrants in this land. And how have they been treated? If they go into the streets, they are insulted; if they stay at home, they are not exempt. Newspapers vie with each other in libelling them;

even Christian men, through party rule, unite with hoodlums in the cry "Away with them!" They have been compelled to pay their taxes over and over again; are taxed for our schools, and not allowed to attend them. They have been beaten and killed, and no one has redressed their wrongs; nay, more, officers whose business it was to protect have stood by and said, "It is only a Chinaman!"....

California has been the breeding-place for anti-Chinese agents. Not content with brutalizing its own people, and disgracing itself, and the rest of our country, before the heathen as well as civilized world, it has sent out its agents along the coast to hawk its lies, and incite to murder and robbery, until "Kearneyites" and "sand-lots" at once suggested their native locality. The Chinese at first were not only welcomed, but invited, to California. The European immigrant demanded four and five dollars a day for work; but when the Chinaman came, by invitation, he was willing to work for two and three dollars a day. This was his sin at first, and persecution at once commenced; and when prices, by a fair competition, levelled to a somewhat reasonable rate, but by no means to "cheap labor" (for still wages were high comparable with those in the East), so that industries formerly impossible could be carried on, enriching the State, this hatred of the Chinese only increased. They had dared to compete, and successfully, with the European laborer, and so were never forgiven. The politician, wanting the votes of those ruling laborers, joined in the cry; and soon official silence, or sanction, made all manner of wrong possible....

When members of our churches *talk* temperance, and *vote* rum; when they talk justice, and vote oppression; when they talk for the enforcement of the law, and *silently* see its violation, - it certainly is clearly duty for pastors affectionately but earnestly to find the moral courage to speak out the truth. Such men declaim against *political* sermons; but, if the Christian voters of this land recognized the momentous responsibility of holding the ballot, such sermons would not be needed. But when principle goes down before party even in the church, then it surely becomes duty for the shepherds of the flock to call back the wandering sheep to the fold of safety. Moral courage with the loving spirit of Christ must win all but the *determined* sinner.

For our own safety as a nation, we need to be on the alert, and relax not the strict holding to the principles of justice and righteousness upon which this nation was founded. As things are, *even a woman needs only common-sense* and foresight to dread the future. It may seem a thing so small as to be unworthy the serious consideration of our voters, that Chinamen are insulted in our streets, the laundrymen's windows broken; Yung Ley Teep, on his way to a mission Sabbath school, killed on the street in New York City; years of persecution, oppression, robbery, and murder in California and on the Pacific Coast, and fearful massacres, crime added to crime, and each growing greater, and adding a blacker page to our nation's history. But in the meanwhile these are *educators* downward, and "strikes" and "dynamite" and communism are of near relation to what we have already had and permitted. The mass of the voters on the Pacific Coast looked serenely on Kearneyism as long as only the stranger from China suffered; but presently it began to be labor against capital, and this looked wonderfully like communism; and then "Committees of Safety" felt it necessary to take a stand for capital if not for men. The same element that persecutes and murders the Chinese is just the very element to make this nation wail in revolution and blood. National crime receives national penalty, and justly. God waited long for us to right the oppressed of this land; but the end of waiting came, and we had our baptism of blood from north to south, from east to west. And can it be possible that the very same generation can forget so soon? The same righteous Judge is on the throne, and again he will reckon with us. May he who cares for the four hundred million souls which he made in China not deal our to our sixty millions all the judgments we deserve for failing so terribly in duty, and in recognition of the exceeding great blessings we have received from his hand, and our corresponding duty toward others less favored!....

Must the Chinese Go?: An Examination of the Chinese Question, by Mrs. S.L. Baldwin, Eighteen Years a Missionary in China, New York, H.B. Elkins, 1890 [originally published in 1881], pp. 31-32, 33, 68-69

7

New York Methodists petitioned Congress for justice for the Chinese in 1886, incurring the wrath of Oregon's Senator John H. Mitchell, who took umbrage at the meddling of "Eastern men" in the

affairs of Western states and territories, but who nevertheless read their
appeal into the record of senatorial debate.

The New York Annual Conference of the Methodist Episcopal
Church, composed of 280 ministers and representing 44, 266 church members,
beg leave to present to your honorable body their respectful petition showing:

1. That the treaty of 1881 between the United States and China, in
which China gave her consent to the restriction of Chinese laborers to this
country provided that "Chinese laborers who are now in the United States
shall be allowed to come and go of their own free will and accord, and shall
be accorded all the rights, privileges, immunities, and exemptions which are
accorded to the citizens and the subjects of the most favored nation." Said
treaty also contained the following solemn pledge on the part of our
Government: "If Chinese laborers, or Chinese of any other class, now either
temporarily or permanently residing in the territory of the United States meet
with ill treatment at the hands of any other persons the Government of the
United States will exert all its power to devise measures for their protection
and to secure to them the same rights, privileges, immunities, and exemptions
as may be enjoyed by the citizens or subjects of the most favored nation, and
to which they are already entitled by treaty."

2. That most flagrant and grievous outrages have been perpetrated
upon the Chinese in Wyoming and Washington Territories and in the States
of Oregon and California, and in many places in that portion of our country
the purpose is still openly expressed of driving out the Chinese inhabitants.[6]

3. That in the course of these outrages not only has much property
belonging to Chinese residents been destroyed, but many persons have been
put to death.

4. That the failure to keep our treaty obligations and the inhuman
and brutal massacres which have been perpetrated upon these strangers in our
midst have disgraced our country in the eyes of the civilized world and subject
us to the just judgments of a righteous God.

5. That the safety of our citizens in China is imperiled by these
frequent and unredressed wrongs to Chinese subjects in the United States; and
that we have no right to expect that the people of a heathen country will be
more careful of the rights of American merchants and missionaries than the

people of this Christian country are of the rights of the Chinese in our land.

6. That it is imperatively necessary that immediate measures of the most stringent character be taken for the protection of the lives and property of the Chinese in this country, and the spirit of persecution and lawlessness so rife in some regions be sternly rebuked and prompt and efficient punishment be visited upon lawbreakers.

We therefore petition your honorable body to enact, without delay, such measures as will enable the officers of the law to suppress all efforts to persecute and drive out the Chinese and secure to them, wherever they may be in our wide domain, the same protection afforded to all other persons in "life, liberty, and the pursuit of happiness."

And for this your petitioners will ever pray.

John Hipple Mitchell, *The Chinese Problem. The People of the Pacific states and territories defended against gross misrepresentations of their position and action on the Chinese question.* Speech in the Senate of the United States, Wednesday, April 28, 1886, pamphlet, pages 3-4

8

Methodist appeals rang forth under particularly volatile circumstances. The following resolution of an association of ministers, made during the height of anti-Chinese violence in the Pacific Northwest, is a case in point; it was paired with an editorial blast by the newspaper in which it appeared.[7]

Resolved, That we regard the efforts now being made to drive, either by force or fright, inoffensive and law-abiding Chinese residents from the country as cruel, brutal, un-American and un-Christian. We earnestly call upon our people to do all in their power to protect these persecuted people from further violence, and to lose no opportunity of manifesting to these heathen strangers a true Christian spirit. We greatly desire that in this time of persecution these people shall be made to know that the church is their refuge and Christians their truest defenders.

"That Resolution," *Seattle Daily Call*, November 16, 1885

9

Clergymen were among those opposed to the Geary Act, as the newspaper report here illustrates.

The Rev. M.L. Gates, minister of Grace Methodist Episcopal Church, Jersey City Heights, devoted the prelude to his sermon yesterday to the Geary act. He said in part:

"The Geary act is the most farcical of all farcical acts that the last farcical session of the National farcical Congress enacted. When this law was passed, American statesmanship in both parties reached the lowest dregs of the political pot.

"Why discriminate against the Chinese?" he asked. "The claim is made that 'John' is here only and solely for mercenary purposes; that he is impervious to all influences of morality and patriotism, and that he does not assimilate the spirit of Americanism.

"Who can blame him? The terms of the treaty of 1868 preclude him from taking part in our national or municipal affairs. He is here as a foreigner, not as a citizen. How can we expect him to absorb the spirit of a patriotism from the influences of which he is excluded by law?

"But he is a heathen; he practices his idolatries among us, and they are contaminating American morals. I ask, however, Are the Chinese the only heathen population we have? We welcome foreigners that are just as abominably heathen in their nature and customs as the Mongolians ever dared to be. We not only allow such ones entrance without restriction, but grant them the sacred right of franchise and give them rule while they are still under native customs and instincts. If you deport 'John' why do you not deport the Mormons? Those heathen are protected by our flag and have as much power in the making of our laws as any of us have."

When Mr. Gates had ended his sermon resolutions were passed denouncing the Geary act as a disgrace to the Nation and the treatment of the Chinese as involved in the provisions of the act a disgrace to civilization and contrary to the genius of American liberty.

"Calls it Discrimination: The Rev. M.L. Gates of Jersey City Heights Denounces the Geary Law," *New York Times*, May 29, 1893

10

> *Issued during the height of anti-Japanese agitation and legislation, this pamphlet by the Reverend U.G. Murphy of Seattle was inserted into the record of the Congressional Investigation of 1920 [see Part I], as a supplement to Murphy's testimony. Murphy published and distributed the pamphlet himself. The text essentially challenges a host of anti-Japanese notions. Significantly, Murphy's main points were endorsed by the Seattle Ministerial Union.*[8]

An Old Issue. An anti-Japanese agitation is nothing new in California, the Hearst papers have been engaged in it for many years. Recently, however, the Scripp papers of the coast and also the Sacramento "*Bee*" have been specializing in anti-Japanese propaganda, several anti-Japanese societies have been formed, and probably at no time since the original trouble began in California in 1906 has there been so much feeling against the Japanese. So far as the Northwest is concerned, however, anti-Japanese propaganda is new, no newspaper having made it a business to keep before its readers intended to create ill-feeling toward the Japanese until the Seattle "*Star*," and other Scripps papers, took up the matter.

Exaggerations. Persons at all familiar with the real situation have readily realized that the papers and individuals engaged in this tirade against the Japanese have made a practice of grossly exaggerating the facts in the case.

False Statements. That deliberate falsifying has been indulged in to a great extent is also very apparent. The writer made a partial list of the more gross falsehoods published by the local Scripp paper, the "*Star*," and mailed them to the editor, who assured me over the phone that the article would probably be published. It was not published, however.

A Few Selections. In order that the extent to which the anti-Japanese agitators have gone in the attempt to stir up hostility against Japan and the Japanese may be appreciated, a few of the more glaring misrepresentations are given and the facts bearing on the matter shown....

"Coming in Large Numbers." It is being stated that Japan is violating the "Gentlemen's Agreement" in granting passports to large numbers of immigrants, and that, especially during the war, hordes of Japanese entered the U.S. It is even stated that Japan has "sent" large numbers over the Mexican border. To show the intentional misrepresentation it is only necessary to call attention to the fact that the entrances only are given. Little, or nothing is said about the departures. In a letter received from Mr. Caminetti, Commissioner General of Immigration, the following is given as covering Japanese arrivals and departures from the United States for the fiscal year ending June 30, 1919. Arrivals, immigrants, 7,543; departures, 1,849. Non-immigrants, arrivals, 3,416; departures, 5,874. Total arrivals, 10,959; total departures, 7,723. Excess of arrivals over departures, 3,326. Remember this increase of arrivals over departures is accounted for entirely by the wives and children of men already here. In other words, all this row is over a few thousand women and children. But this is not all. Remember, Japanese die, just as other people do. The time may come when the anti-Japanese crowd will discover that the Japanese have some kind of secret way of dodging death entirely, but at the present time the death rate is rather above average. Deduct then at least 1,500 as the loss caused by death during the past year, and you have about 1,700 as the net increase in the Japanese population of the U.S. for the year. This is the size of the "menace." One wonders if it does not also indicate the size of the men who have discovered this "menace"....

"Displacing Americans." Only in the sense that every man is a competitor with every man who engages in the same occupation, are the Japanese competitors. That Americans have moved away from localities because Japanese have entered it is true, but it is also true that such happened principally because of a feeling of race prejudice on the part of Americans. Those who have lived among Asiatics, both in Asia and in this country, have found them good neighbors. The claim made by Mr. Freeman of the Veteran's Welfare Commission, that the Japanese have interfered with placing returned soldiers in occupations, is an absolute untruth, according to Mr. Goodwin, former director of the Commission. There is no evidence that Japanese have interfered in any way with any American getting a job. Hotels and apartment houses are being run by Japanese, but any man with the necessary money may purchase them at any time. That some Japanese have speculated in leases is probably true, but will any one claim that they alone do this? Why overlook the sins of others and center on the few Japanese?....

"Japanese Colonies." It is unfortunate that aliens in many cases have congregated in certain districts. Italian towns, Jewish sections, China-towns, and Japanese communities are all a mistake. But who runs this country, anyway? Who is responsible for this unfortunate and even dangerous phase of American life? In the case of the Oriental, he has often been compelled to live in or near the slums. Until we cease to be sinners in this matter, it ill behooves us to criticise the alien. Some arrangement should be made by which no community would ever have a majority of aliens in it. Our schools should never have a majority of aliens. But that is up to the American people. The immigrant will fall in line, and in most cases, gladly do so. Certainly the Asiatic would do so....

A Whole Set of False Statements. It has been loudly proclaimed that the Japanese are gobbling up the best land. It is claimed that they own nearly all the best farm land near Seattle. As a matter of fact, the Japanese own only a few hundred acres in the state of Washington, and 30,000 acres in California.

When the agitation was on in California to secure the anti-Asiatic land law, it was claimed that the Japanese were buying and leasing everything in sight. An investigation committee, appointed by the legislature, found that they, at that time, owned about 11,000 acres. Inasmuch as California has about 300,000,000 acres of farm land, the gobbling was not very evident. This may be the reason why the committee never published the result of its findings. The ostensible reason was that the legislature did not provide funds for the publication. This committee found that leases for 20,294 acres were recorded. In some way the committee, however, claims to have discovered that most of the leases were not recorded and that altogether 115,000 acres were at that time, 1909, leased by the Japanese. Even granting this, still the total is only two-fifths of one per cent of the farm land of the state. There are communities where the Japanese are congregating too fast, but so far as ousting the Americans or creating a menace, the claim is ridiculous.

The statement that King County, Washington, has 9,000 cows and that the White River Valley has 6,000 of these and that the Japanese own 85 per cent of this 6,000, should be placed alongside of the facts. There are 25,000 milch cows in the county, and the Japanese own 3,000.

It has been stated that the Japanese operate 47 per cent of the hotels in Seattle. There are 1,350 hotels, lodging houses and apartment houses in Seattle. The Japanese operate 328 of these, or 23 per cent.

It has been loudly proclaimed that the births of children to Japanese parents in Placer County, California, was twice that of the whites in 1918. The Board of Health reports, whites 266, Japanese 91.

Big headlines in the Scripps papers claimed that U.S. Railroad Administrator Hines had ordered that Japanese be not employed in railroad work, as they were interfering with the placing of returned soldiers. No such order was issued, and a note from the department states that an investigation had proven that Japanese men were in no way interfering with the employment of white men, and that there was a shortage of labor for railroad work everywhere.

In an attempt to foster opposition to the Japanese, the Washington Advertising Brokerage Co. of Seattle claims that 186 retail grocery stores are operated by the Japanese in Seattle. The correct number is 49. This is about as near the truth as any of the attacks on the Japanese....

No One Proposes Increase in Asiatic Immigration. China is not fighting the exclusion of laborers, though all intelligent Chinese resent the inhuman manner in which this law is applied. At this writing Asiatics in the detention quarters in San Francisco are being treated like beasts. The Japanese government has recognized the inadvisability of permitting laborers to come to the United States as long as there is serious objection to them, no matter on what grounds this objection may be based, hence her offer to put on the restriction from here side. There is nowhere on earth today any kind of international agreement that is being better observed than the "Gentlemen's Agreement," from Japan's side. As for our side, as much cannot be said. It was generally understood that if Japan would prevent the coming of laborers to the United States, anti-Japanese agitation would cease and no discrimination would be enforced against the children of Japanese parents as to school attendance. In spite of this the lower house of the California legislature passed a bill at the last session intended to segregate children of Japanese in schools. The measure was killed in the Senate, however, at the urgent request of the American delegate at the Paris Conference.

Long before Germany scrapped her treaty with Belgium, the United States did the same thing with her treaty with China. From the Asiatic standpoint, the heathen are not all on their side of the Pacific. Still, no one is proposing any increase in Asiatic immigration. However, an increasing number of America's best thinkers are insisting that Asiatic students be admitted to the United States, on limited passports. And Americans are getting tired of being singled out as the only nation that has a "color scheme" for its basis of naturalization. We are beginning to see the reasonableness of relying on standards, and not on the color of a man's face.

Simple Question. The whole matter is not complex at all. Just simply apply the spirit of Christianity, the true American spirit, to our dealings with Asiatics and there is no question that cannot be readily solved. That this nation, and all component parts of it, must always be predominantly white is not being questioned, cannot be questioned. But we must act in a just and humane manner toward all here who are not classed as whites.

The Anti-Japanese Agitation, Seattle, 1920, pp. 2, 3-4, 7-8, 9-10, 11-13

11

President Calvin Coolidge was the recipient of the following protest against exclusion laws from the General Conference of the Methodist Church in 1924. The Reverend H.B. Johnson, a delegate from California, made the proposal to contact the President.

We recognize that the question of immigration is, and must be one of domestic policy; but we also recognize that it is far-reaching in its implications. We do not plead for the wide-open door policy of immigration, but recognize that some kind of a restriction of immigration from all countries is a national necessity....

As Christians, we cannot countenance racial prejudice and discrimination, but insist that when this great nation speaks, through its legislation, it must be in a manner which will commend itself to the thinking and conscience of the nations of the world regardless of color or previous condition.

We confidently depend upon you to use your influence as President in so adjusting the recent immigration enactment as to prevent the calamity that is sure to follow the consummation of such legislation.

"Methodists Asked to Back Japanese," *New York Times*, May 7, 1924

12

During World War II, The Christian Century, *a prominent Protestant periodical, called for repeal of all anti-Asian immigration laws. The editorial is reflective of liberal sentiment among the Protestant churches. The Chinese exclusion laws were indeed repealed at the end of 1943.*[9]

Behind the loud professions of noble purposes with which we are fighting the war in the Pacific there leers a grinning death's head. It is the racial injustice which we have done to the Asian billion. We are fighting, so we have declared, to uphold justice and to thwart tyranny. We criticize our British allies because they have been laggard, as we think, in serving this great cause by granting liberty to India and handing back Hongkong and Kowloon to China. Yet on our American statute books we perpetuate a great wrong against all Asiatic peoples, and the one step we could take of our own free will to do immediate justice to China and India and the Philippines and Indonesia we resolutely refuse to take. We are all for a new deal for Asia - so long as somebody else does the dealing. But let someone suggest, "How about doing justice to yellow and brown peoples in American immigration and naturalization laws?" and our answer is "Sh-h-h! Sh-h-h! Remember the California vote!"

Here and there a few signs of stirring conscience begin to appear. Small church groups, even on the Pacific coast, begin to murmur among themselves that perhaps something ought to be done about Chinese exclusion. A few of the bolder groups have adopted resolutions suggesting as much. To be sure, they speak cautiously. Let a Pacific coast labor leader or a Legion commander loose a blast and many of the well meaning scuttle for cover. Yet there is discernible a rising sentiment in favor of undoing the injustice done the Chinese in the exclusion law of 1882. China, standing off the Japanese after almost six years of war, is popular among us just now. A growing number of Americans think that good political sense, as well as fair dealing, requires us to do something more than cheer China's name in Congress, clap when Chiang Kai-shek's picture appears in the newsreels, return extra-territorial rights we can no longer exercise, give Chinese military missions the run-around, and murmur "So sorry" when the matter of lend-lease is mentioned. Yes, we say, let justice be done China! Let China be given the same quota rights under our immigration laws that we grant the peoples of Europe and Africa.

But justice for the peoples of Asia requires more than that permission be given 105 Chinese a year to enter the United States under an immigration quota. Justice requires that *all* racial stigmas shall be removed from our immigration laws. it involves putting *all* Asiatic peoples on the same quota basis which we apply to others. It means we have got to stop saying, "If you are a white man or a black man you are fit to enter this country, but if you are a brown man or a yellow man you are on a lower level, unfit for our society, and we will keep you out." But that is not all. Justice not only requires dropping all racial discrimination from our immigration laws; it equally requires that naturalization shall be opened to all thus found admittable. The Christian conscience will not rest while American law says, "Because your skin is brown or yellow, you cannot become an American citizen." This is an injustice to the people of India which the people of the United States can right without waiting to see what Britain is going to do for India. It is injustice to the people of Indonesia which we can right without waiting to see what Holland is going to do. It is an injustice to the people of Korea which we can right without waiting to see what Japan is going to do.

Racial discrimination, now embedded in the immigration and naturalization laws of the United States, presents us with a test of our political statesmanship and of our national morals. It is a test of our political statesmanship because as long as this injustice endures we cannot count on the support of the thousand million people of Asia and its adjacent islands. It is a test of our national moral because it offers a means whereby the whole world can find out how much reality there is in our high-sounding international professions....

What, then, should be done? The answer is plain. Let the conscience of Christian America speak! In church schools, in church societies, in church councils, in all manner of gatherings where the mind of American Christianity is brought to bear on the affairs of the nation, let this issue be raised, studied and action demanded. As an act of justice too long delayed Congress should be asked to repeal the provisions of existing statutes which write a color bar into our immigration and naturalization laws, to enact legislation extending the quota principle of the immigration laws to all Asiatics and to make eligible for citizenship any person permitted to enter the country without regard to race, color or place of birth. For those Christians and churches that want to bear a part in building a more just postwar world order, here is one place where the struggle for that order can be begun today and right in our own national back yard.

"Drop the Asiatic Color Bar," *The Christian Century*, February 17, 1943

Notes

1. Despite its perseverance, clerical support for free immigration and fair treatment never characterized the view of the clergy as a whole in the late nineteenth century. The more typical endorsement of exclusion is exemplified by the Reverend David M. Utter, "The Chinese Must Go," *The Unitarian Review and Religious Magazine*, Vol. 12, No. 1 (July 1879), pp. 48-56. Utter pondered: "And why should it be supposed to be a Christian duty to attempt to forward the Kingdom of God by means of taking a bad strain into our national life, when we might, if we needed it, have that vastly superior blood which would come from Germany and Sweden, is a great mystery." (p. 55).
    Clerical dissent called into question the imposing legacy of church-sponsored racism. Many Protestant churches brought to anti-Asian chauvinism the experience of having previously justified African-American oppression with, among other ostensibly biblically-rooted arguments, the "Curse of Ham," which consigned to servitude the apparent descendants of an offender named in the Book of Genesis (9:24, 25). The story, commented W.E.B. DuBois, became "the basis of an astounding literature which has today only a psychological interest. It is sufficient to remember that for several centuries leaders of the Christian Church gravely defended Negro slavery and oppression as the rightful curse of God upon the descendants of a son who had been disrespectful to his drunken father!" DuBois, *The Negro* (1915), New

York, 1970, p. 11.

2. A superior guide to the Christian clergy's attitude to the Chinese is Robert Seager II, "Some Denominational Reactions to Chinese Immigration to California, 1856-1892," *Pacific Historical Review*, Vol. 28 (February 1959), pp. 49-66.

3. Michael L. Stahler supplies good background in "William Speer: Champion of California's Chinese," *Journal of Presbyterian History*, Vol. 48 (1970), pp. 113-129. See also Seager II, pp. 49-50.

4. For an analysis of the anti-Catholic and anti-labor inclination of certain pro-Chinese Protestants, see Seager II, pp. 52, 55-59. Gibson was a missionary in China from 1854 to 1865, He became a national Methodist leader. Following the 1882 Chinese Exclusion Act, Gibson suspended his free immigration position in favor of a proposal for drastically limited Chinese settlement. Seager II, pp. 54-55, 63.

5. Levee construction in the Sacramento delta is described fully in Sucheng Chan, *This Bittersweet Soil: The Chinese in California Agriculture, 1860-1910*, Berkeley, 1986.

6. The reference is to the efforts to expel the Chinese from those areas in the 1880's. They were driven out of Eureka, California in early 1885 and from Tacoma, Washington in 1886. An 1885 dispute between white and Chinese miners ignited an attack on the latter, leaving 28 dead. Alexander Saxton, *The Indispensable Enemy: Labor and the Anti-Chinese Movement in California*, Berkeley, 1971, pp. 201-207.

7. "Why do these over-jealous pastors lean so heavily toward the heathen horde?" the *Daily Call* asked editorially on November 16, 1885: "For the paltry pittance derived from the Chinese mission school."

8. Murphy's pamphlet went through two editions. Some 5000 were circulated, including nearly 1000 by Japanese organizations. U.S. House of Representatives, Committee on Immigration and Naturalization, *Hearings on Japanese Immigration*, 66th Congress, 2nd Session, Part I, July 12, 13, and 14, 1920, Washington, 1921, p. 1316. The San Francisco Congregationalist minister James L. Gordon wrote a pamphlet along the same lines: *Justice to the Japanese*, San Francisco, 192?.

9. Wartime liberal sentiment for repeal of exclusion laws was not necessarily matched by as broad an outcry against the evacuation of Japanese Americans from the West Coast; opposition to the latter policy is reflected in Part VI. Though the demand for repeal elicited anti-racist endorsement from the outset, it was possible for some supporters of repeal to accept Japanese American relocation. Theoretically, the military need justifying relocation made sympathy with China, chief victim of imperial Japan and a U.S. ally, compatible with an undemocratic act calculated to facilitate Allied victory. Nevertheless, the views of the *Christian Century* remained more consistently democratic, as did the pro-repeal stance of such liberal publications as *The Nation*, *The New Republic*, and *Asia and the Americas*. For the latter see the signed editorial, January 1943 issue, p. 4 and the articles under "Repeal Exclusion Laws Now," June 1943, p. 322. *New Republic* pieces in this vein include Bruno Lasker, "End Exclusion Now," May 24, 1943 and "Chinese Exclusion," editorial, September 6, 1943. The House of Representatives approved repeal in October 1943, the Senate a month later: President Roosevelt signed the repeal measure on December 17. The process is documented in Fred W. Riggs, *Pressures on Congress: A Study of the Repeal of Chinese Exclusion*, Westport, 1972 (1950).

Part IV: The Labor Movement

The section which follows documents the trend which supported the organization of Asian workers and the strengthening of working-class solidarity. The view represented here veered from the main attitude of organized labor during the late nineteenth century and most of the twentieth.

Of special interest is the statement taken from the Colored National Labor Union [Document 1], which itself emerged in response to the neglect of Black workers by most unions in the years following the Civil War. *Woodhull & Claflin's Weekly* provides the source for an early socialist statement on Chinese immigration [Document 2]. "For the sake of the white working men of California," H.C. Bennett [Document 3] defended the rights of the Chinese, Jews, and African-Americans in 1870. During the late 1870's, the *Labor Standard*, a weekly edited by prominent labor figure and socialist J.P. McDonnell, debated the Chinese question [Documents 4a-d]; so too did *The Socialist*, a paper published in Detroit [Document 5]. Despite the participation of the Knights of Labor in anti-Chinese activities in the 1870's and 1880's, some dissent from that position was expressed [Documents 6a and b].

A former slave and industrial worker, African-American pastor George Washington Woodbey was one of the few early twentieth-century socialists to back the immigration of Asians to, and their rights in, the United States [Document 7]. Occasionally, in the early 1900's, miners' unions endeavored to organize Asian workers [Documents 8a-c]; that this was accomplished at Rock Springs, Wyoming, scene of much late nineteenth-century anti-Chinese violence, is noteworthy. In sharp contrast to most other labor organizations, the Industrial Workers of the World (founded in 1905) [Document 9] established an approach to unionizing Asian workers in the West and the Pacific Northwest (including Canada) [Documents 10a-c].

Central labor bodies, such as the Seattle Central Labor Council, occasionally adopted a more embracing concept of union membership [Document 11]; while these positions were not general or binding, they point to the recurrent challenge to the prevailing restrictive practice. Samuel Gompers and other American Federation of Labor spokesmen generally confined their support for labor organization among Asians to those who did not live here [Documents 12a and b].

Not unlike the IWW, the Congress of Industrial Organizations encouraged the participation of Asians alongside workers of other races during the Great Depression. An important contribution to the work of the CIO in this connection was made by Communists like Karl Yoneda [Document 13]. Significantly, the International Longshoremen's and Warehousemen's Union on the Pacific Coast and in Hawaii was one of the few organizations that stood by its Japanese members in face of the legal harassment and mass evacuation following Pearl Harbor [Document 14]. Document 15 shows a trend emerging within the AFL during World War II against the Chinese Exclusion Act.

1

The Colored National Labor Union was an important player on the post-Civil War labor scene, bringing the particular problems and demands of African-American workers before the labor movement as a whole. It worked to pressure organized labor, particularly the National Labor Union (headed by the pioneering leader William Sylvis) to take the specific conditions of Black workers more seriously: this entailed demonstrating to the NLU the importance to Black workers of the Republican Party, Radical Reconstruction, and civil rights (and the relevance of these issues to white laborers), as well as encouraging African-American workers to organize on their own. At its founding, the CNLU appealed for unity of all workers: native and foreign-born whites, African-Americans, and Chinese.[1]

With us, too, numbers count and we know the maxim, "in union there is strength," has its significance in the affairs of labor, no less than in politics. Hence, our industrial movement, emancipating itself from every national and partial sentiment, broadens and deepens its foundations, so as to rear theron a superstructure, capacious enough to accommodate at the altar of a common interest, the Irish, the Negro, and the German laborer; to which so far from being excluded, the "poor white" native of the South, struggling out of moral and pecuniary death, into life, "real and earnest," the white mechanic and laborer of the North, so long ill taught and advised, that his true interest is gained by hatred and abuse of the laborer of African descent, as well as the Chinaman, whom designing persons partially enslaving would make in the plantation service of the South the rival and competitor of the former slave class of this country, having with us one and the same interest, are all united, earnestly urged to join us in our movement, and thus aid in the protection and conservation of their and our interests.

National Anti-Slavery Standard, December 18, 1869

2

Woodhull and Claflin's Weekly, *a journal of the late nineteenth-century women's suffrage movement - the pages of which also devoted much attention to the achievement of sexual equality, to free love, and to spiritualism - supported labor causes and socialism. Tennessee Claflin and Victoria Woodhull were associated with the International Working Men's Association for a brief period in the early 1870's; they were leaders of that Association in New York City, until their Section was expelled for what were perceived as erroneous and muddled views. The editors' consistent humanitarianism clearly placed them in opposition to the Chinese exclusion trend in the labor movement.*[2]

The Chinese question is a matter of supreme interest just now. The politician, the conservative thinker, the man of progress, the capitalist and the workman are all interested in the proposal to introduce a new labor element whose supply is practically inexhaustible. We have already said, and we repeat that we think the apprehension of injury to working interests exaggerated....The colored people of the South numbered four millions at the commencement of the war, one-tenth of the whole population. What has been the effect on Northern labor of their enfranchisement and their liberty to go throughout the States?

We are no advocates for the importation of Chinese. We are opposed to any plan of servile labor, and the renewal, under any name, of those class and color relations which have already done us so much mischief. Coolie importation, under labor contracts made in China, has succeeded nowhere. It has been a perpetual misery to the wretched coolie, as witness the horrors of the Chincha Islands; it has been a failure, as witness the British coolie system in the West Indies....But it is the servile labor, not the free labor, which would be the vice in a system of coolie importation.

In China the labor of the operator is so valueless that fifty cents a day would be a very large price. He simply could not live in this country on Chinese wages. It is easy enough to make contracts for labor: whether those contracts could be enforced and compulsory labor exacted is very doubtful. There is law to punish the omissions of duty; but there is no law which can compel performance. It may well be doubted whether contractors and importers of coolie labor would find it pay in our free communities. The Chinese would soon find their value and would insist on it.

But as the Chinaman in his own country is patient, ingenious and thrifty, it is more than possible that we might gain by their presence among us as free laborers. They have done well in California. The numbers in which they could arrive are absurdly overstated. From Liverpool to New York costs twenty dollars. From Canton or Foo Chow to New York could not cost at the lowest computation less than seventy-five - when is a Chinaman on his dime a day wages to save up seventy-five dollars? The arrivals from Europe at the twenty dollar rate do not amount to five thousand a week of all ages; at seventy-five it probably would not reach one-third of that number. Place this ratio against the actual population of the United States and it will be seen how long it would take to bring down wages. It is true this is a crude and perfunctory comparison, but it will serve - other elements are to be taken into consideration - to obtain a fair approximation of probabilities.

The sum of the whole matter is that the Chinese should be welcomed if they bring brains, capital, industry; that in this country there can be no let or bar to immigration. On the other hand, there should be no pauper immigration, nothing that should subject our workers to depressing competition, and no slavery under another name.

"Labor and Capital: Chinese Labor," *Woodhull and Claflin's Weekly*, July 9, 1870

3

Few in labor's ranks were as articulate in defending the Chinese from persecution as H.C. Bennett. The following remarks were made several years before anti-Chinese riots broke out in San Francisco, with full involvement of many unions and workers' organizations. Bennett took the "unpopular side" of the argument, and though he supported the need for cheap Chinese labor, he generally rejected the racist precepts held by the opponents of Chinese rights. Significant is his charge that the contention over the Chinese was a diversion for the labor movement, "a decoy, to draw attention from the real evil."[3]

The assertion that the Chinese are an inferior race of men is not a new cry to raise against a people held in subjection. It is as old as the history of man. The Assyrians, Greeks, Romans, Persians, Egyptians, Normans, Scandinavians, Russians and Spaniards have all maintained this doctrine. But what a refutation of the principle is presented when it is examined by the clear light of history.

The ancient nations have been nearly blotted out of existence. The remnants and monuments of them that remain are preserved in the persons of the races, once held in subjection by them.

The Britons were held for centuries as an inferior race by their Danish, Norman and Roman conquerors. Today they are among the foremost races on earth, in energy, enterprise and intelligence. The Irish were for centuries held as an inferior race by their Saxon rulers - "the hereditary bondsmen," as their great leader, Daniel O'Connell, used to call them - here, on this soil consecrated to freedom, exhibit capabilities for improvement unsurpassed by the immigrants from any other country. Yet less than a century ago, the Irish in England - aye in Ireland, on the beautiful green sod of their native land - were despised and hated by the English as much, or more than the Irish hate and despise the Chinese. During the reign of

Georges, the III and IV, the Parliament, press and pulpit of England and Ireland, resounded with the assertion that the Celtic was inferior to the Saxon race. It is not more than twenty years ago that the cry resounded through the length of this great republic of, "Down with the Irish, America for the Americans!" and similar party cries. From Maine to California, the know-nothing party denounced the Irish just as the Irish here denounce the Chinese, and on a platform, made up of prejudice and hatred, elected a president, Congress and several State legislatures in hostility to the Irish, because they apprehended danger from their influx. The great state of Massachusetts, which has profited more by the labors of Irish men and women in its factories and workshops, than any other State in the Union, passed a law making it necessary for an Irishman to have resided in the country 21 years before he' could be naturalized.

Even in this golden State of California we had a know-nothing governor and legislature, who lost their power through attempting to proscribe Irishmen, because they were foreigners, and their religious belief was considered dangerous to republicanism. The very same men who are now leading the Irishmen against the Chinese, were the leaders of the know-nothing party. It is the nature of such men to look upon all foreigners as their inferiors, while, in truth, they are themselves the very lowest types of American manhood....

The number of Chinese in this State, as stated by the other side, is greatly exaggerated. There are not over thirty-eight thousand of them in the State. Langley's directory gives eight thousand as the number in this city. The anti-coolieites say there are twenty-five thousand in this city and one hundred thousand of them in this State....

That we can ever drive them out of this State is an impossibility. That matter is not left in our hands, for as the Bible tells us, in 26 verse of 17 chapter of Acts:

"God hath made of one blood all nations of men, for to dwell on all the face of the earth, and hath determined the times, before appointed, and the bounds of their habitation."

In conclusion, I will endeavor to prove that it is not the Chinese who have caused the lessened demand for white labor, about which are so many complaints, but the white laborers have brought this upon themselves. I have already demonstrated that the Chinese do not enter into competition with white mechanics. Now I will show you the policy of the white man:

According to the last published statement of the savings banks in this city, they held twenty-eight millions eight hundred ninety-seven thousand six hundred and forty-five dollars on deposit, chiefly the savings of the working classes. It is this immense amount of money drawn out of the channels of trade and productive industry that has become a drag chain on the wheels of progress. This money being used exclusively for the purposes of speculation, the working men have thus been furnishing the money lenders the means to stop production. So long as money earns more for speculative purposes than it does in manufacturing or for developing the resources of the State, so long may we expect to see every department of business stagnant, except that of usury. Speculators who make their hundreds of thousands of dollars annually, employ but little labor. They money locked up in the savings banks is sufficient to set every department of business in active motion. But so long as it returns twelve per cent. to depositors, it is not likely to be employed in manufactures. We cannot have the money and the marbles too. The depositors in the savings banks cannot expect to keep up interest to four times the rate in England, and three times the rate in New York, and expect labor to be in demand at high rates of wages.

Money may be borrowed to any extent in London for manufacturing purposes, at two and a half to three per cent. per annum. The banks of New York are overflowing with money which cannot be loaned at four to six per cent. per annum, because it is too dear. While here in San Francisco, no manufacturer, farmer, or other person engaged in productive industry, can obtain a dollar at less rental than twelve, from that to twenty-four per cent.

We are all insane if we think we can successfully compete with Eastern or European manufacturers, while our labor and capital are from fifty to one hundred per cent. dearer than theirs.

This, the real cause of the stagnation in the demand for labor, is never fairly explained to the working men. The poor Chinese are set up as a decoy, to draw attention from the real evil. It is the cheap labor of the Chinese that keeps the few factories we have in operation. Even the co-operative mills and factories owned by white working men, have to employ Chinese labor to cheapen the costs of their products.

In discussing the question of Chinese labor, I have purposely avoided any reference to the Japanese, because they are not included in the charges made against the Chinese. But if heathenism, color, the place of nativity, race, language, industry and ingenuity, and cheapness of labor, are objections, they will apply with additional force against the Japanese.

H.C. Bennett, *Chinese Labor: A Lecture, Delivered before the San Francisco Mechanics' Society, in reply to the Hon. F.M. Pixley*, San Francisco, May 1870, pamphlet, pp. 13-15, 38, 39-40

4

J.P. McDonnell's Labor Standard *was an important voice of the labor and socialist movements during the 1870's and 1880's. McDonnell, a nationalist organizer in his native Ireland and a supporter of labor causes, had been secretary to Karl Marx. Emigration to the United States brought no diminution in his activity, as he joined the Workingmen's Party of the United States upon its founding in 1876 and put his newspaper at the service of that party. In 1877, the* Standard's *coverage of the great wave of railroad and other strikes earned McDonnell deep respect in the labor movement. After the Workingmen's Party fell victim to factional dispute, McDonnell's espousal of socialism and labor's rights continued; he moved the* Standard *to Paterson, New Jersey, where it advanced the demands of that city's silk workers. While there, he helped organize the International Labor Union, an organization based among unskilled textile workers. So popular was McDonnell that he was named to key labor-related state posts in New Jersey in the 1880's and 1890's.[4] Editorially (b), the* Labor Standard *appears to have supported the rights of the Chinese, in contrast to the majority of labor papers. McDonnell's emphasis on solidarity evoked both sympathetic and hostile letters (a,c,d).*

(a)

San Francisco, May 23, 1878

Editor, LABOR STANDARD

The working force in this city are very much divided; the great mass knowing of no evil as yet but that "the Chinese must go." This cry is their prayer, their text, and their all. Anything that does not embrace this sweeping quack remedy for all the ills of mankind, is subject to severe treatment. Nevertheless in view of all the bulldozing on the part of a set of men who claim the right of free speech only for themselves - not having attained the self-culture to grant the same privilege to others - the most advanced thinking portion of the working class have determined to stand resolute on their own right and have demanded free speech and a fair hearing. There would be no doubt of victory if the workingmen were, as a whole, capable of reasoning in an intelligent manner for themselves; but as the element endorsing Kearney is to a great extent composed only of that selfishly educated class who don't see their way beyond a riot, it is evident that the better and deeper thinking class of workingmen will never unite until this would-be Caesar, Kearney, is removed from all control in the workingmen's movements.

It is only right that our brothers in the East should know who this Kearney is. He is no more than a presumptuous highbinder, seeking only to gain popularity at the expense of others. In fact he is known amongst his former companions in the teaming fraternity as one of the most exacting and tyrannical of masters to his employees. To use their own language, "he treated them like dogs." Does or can the leopard change his spots, and would it not necessitate a change of *his* whole nature and blood?

I know Kearney to have been and to be an open antagonist to education beyond the necessary acquirements to make pliant slaves of future toiling generations. He has always been an enemy to the prosperity of a Lyceum for the object of mutual self-culture. To show the hollowness of this self-styled humanitarian, who combines hypocritical pretences with the most arrogant Caesarism, I will give a couple of instances. Referring to the needs of education, when the subject was before the Lyceum for self-culture he took the ground that (to use his own words) "all this high fallutin education was only fit to make scoundrels of men. What needed they more than to know how to read, write and figure so as to be able to make a living *and money*. The more you educate them the greater the rascals you make of them. He said he was born in the bogs of Ireland, and that his only means to education was that

he had to drive a donkey for a living. He said *he learned how* to put away
something for a rainy day, and if he didn't make much he knew how to
content himself with bread and water. "See what I am now," said he, "I am
making my $300 a month, and have $2000 to $3000 in the bank!!" This was
before his *debut* as a sand lot *reformer*, and before he had lost this same
money in stock speculations, as he subsequently stated in one of the first sand
lot meetings, when he took the opportunity of pretending to seek to vindicate
the depositors who become such heavy losers by the Duncan Bank swindle....

This is the "labor chief of the West," who has got into notoriety by
striking the cord that appeals to the feelings of the masses - "the Chinese must
go." We want no Caesarism. The working people must accomplish their own
emancipation. They will not allow themselves to be led blindfolded by any
man, but above all by a man with such a character as Kearney. The men we
want for leaders must have records beyond reproach.

And in conclusion allow me to say that we want not an anti-Chinese
but a labor movement, and that the present anti-Chinese movement - no
matter what may be the honesty of its rank and file - has *sub-rosa* more to do
with railroad men and capitalists than with labor. Time will write its history.

"The Anti-Chinese Movement - Important Statements, Letter from a Trades
Unionist," *Labor Standard*, June 23, 1878

(b)

The cry that the "Chinese must go" is both narrow and unjust. It
represents no broad or universal principle. It is merely a repetition of the cry
that was raised years ago by native Americans against the immigration of
Irishmen, Englishmen, Germans and others from European nations. It now ill
becomes those, against whom this cry was raised in past years, to raise a
similar tocsin against a class of foreigners who have been degraded by ages of
oppression.

The "Know Nothing" movement had its REAL origin in the dread of
native workmen that they would be undersold in the labor market by the
cheap labor of Great Britain, Germany, and other European countries. The
American workingmen were accustomed to wear better clothes, live in better
habitations, eat better food, and consequently received better wages than the

kingmen of Europe. For these reasons they dreaded the immigration of Europeans, whose habits were not so independent, and whose style of living was so inferior, because they saw clearly that the newcomers would be satisfied with a rate of wages that would provide them with the class of living they had been accustomed to. The feeling at the bottom of the "Know Nothing" movement IN ITS EARLY DAYS was certainly a general one against low wages, and if it had raised the cry:

No low wages -

No cheap labor!

instead of sounding the intolerant, silly, and shameful cry against Irishmen, Englishmen, Germans and all other "foreigners," it would have accomplished incalculable good. As it was it fell into the hands of infamous, scheming politicians, who pandered to the worst prejudices of the masses by raising a cry against men of various religious faiths and foreign nationalities. This policy suited them; it raised them to prominence and office, and allowed what they IN THEIR HEARTS desired; the onward march of low wages.

In our day we must commit no such blunders. We have certainly a right to protest, and use every available means against the capitalistic combinations through which thousands of poor and ill-fed beings are imported to this country from China, Italy and elsewhere, but we have no right to raise a cry against any class of human beings because of their nationality. The workingmen of England have given us an example in this respect which we would do well to follow. Instead of raising a cry throughout all England against the American Chinese who have been brought over there to cut down wages, the workingmen have distinctly stated that they welcome workingmen from all nations, and that their warfare is only against the system of low wages and all those who support it.

Let us do in like manner. Let us organize and raise our voices against low wages and long hours. Let us use our organized power against the capitalistic combinations which carry on a slave trade between this country and China and elsewhere, by importing thousands for the purpose of reducing wages in America. Let our first stand be against those rich and intelligent thieves who strive to perpetuate and establish a system of overwork and starvation-pay. And then against all those, whether they be Chinese or American, Irish or English, French or German, Spanish or Italian who refuse to cooperate for their good and ours, and that of the whole human family.

We must not forget that in Pennsylvania, and other States, where there are no Chinese, there is absolutely a worse state of affairs than exists even in China, and furthermore that America is now doing unto England, what China has been doing unto America.

We favor every effort against the conspiracy of the rich to import cheap labor from Europe and Asia, but we warn the workingmen that no action but International Labor action, and no cry but that of high wages and short hours will lead us into the promised land of peace, plenty and happiness.

"The Chinese Must Go," editorial, *Labor Standard*, June 30, 1878

(c)

San Francisco.
Editor, LABOR STANDARD:

....The labor movement here has been and is yet a progressive one. It began with the watchword "The Chinese Must Go," when it was started up again last year it is true: but although that question remains still unsettled, the W.P. of Cal. has become something more than an Anti-Chinese movement....The W.P. of Cal. is a progressive party, and has proven itself to be so from its inception, and so have its prominent leaders recorded themselves as progressive men and friends of their class whose rights they have defended and asserted. Some of them have brought sacrifices which have won for them the admiration of every honest man - workers and employers. And they have so far proven to have no selfish motives, which shows a virtue totally lacking in their opponents. The cry of Caesarism raised against them is not worthy of men claiming to be trades unionists or friends of labor. It is not heard on this coast from any other source than from our enemies, members of the fraternity of Shoddies, aristocrats, monopolists and all other parasites and vermin which constitute the plagues from which the working class is suffering everywhere. Or it hails from that rule or ruin faction who are crowding in the ranks of labor, the pliant tools of our opponents who are hired to sow dissension and break up all honest, earnest efforts of the masses to emancipate themselves. Such are our worst enemies: they are the wolves in sheep skins, treacherous and cunning in their ways, pretending to work for principles. In trying to accomplish their work of ruin they do not hesitate at any means to accomplish their diabolical ends. The cry is also heard from another few, and I regret it. They are good men who mean well; they feel deeply the existing wrongs and are enthusiastic to have their remedies applied, anxious to have their views adopted, so much so that they surround themselves with a sort of claim to infallibility, and the assumption of such a position completely unfits them to lead the masses; they become repulsive instead of attractive because they are so far ahead of the people that the people cannot see or understand them. For their own good and the cause they champion they ought to be often silent rather than speak or write, but they have no control over themselves, and must have a party of their own based upon their own principles.

....It is said that the people's will is God's will; if that is so it has been affirmed again in the late uprising here. Some of our old labor men found themselves in the position of the old Jewish leader Moses, they could see the promised land from a distance but were not permitted to enter; their power was broken. And some are dead to the masses, because they have wavered in the true faith. Yet I hope their day of resurrection will come again, and they can hasten it by studying the people, so that they will understand each other and direct their actions in the right course. That is why the present leaders have been so far successful. They understand the masses, their capacity and desires, they know they could only get their ear on the Chinese question, and they gave them all they wanted. They are gorged with that now, and are ready to listen to other questions. The leaders are now improving their opportunities by introducing other questions, and circumstances force them on. They are very fast getting the unthinking ones to an understanding of their rights and wrongs, and show them their power which they can wield in united action....

In conclusion I would like to give you as a friend my humble advice, to other party papers as well, if I could. It is this: I would not in the future notice anything calculated to injure or defame the good name of the W.P. of California or any of its leaders. There is but one W.P. here that has a good name or commands any respect, and that is the one of which Kearney is President and Wellock Vice-President; the other is dead numerically and morally....

"The Anti-Chinese Movement," Letter from August Mayer, *Labor Standard*, August 11, 1878

(d)

San Francisco, July 26th 1878.
Editor, LABOR STANDARD:

I was requested by the Cigar Makers' Union of the Pacific coast to send you a few lines in regard to the Editorial which appeared in No. 8 headed, *The Chinese Must go* and to inform you that it is not merely a repetition of the cry that was raised a few years ago by the native Americans against European foreigners, but that the Irishman, German, Englishman with the Americans all stand together shoulder to shoulder to the cry of *the Chinese must go.*

The article was looked upon by all our Trades Unions and workingmen as greatly unjust to the California Workingmens Party.

The Cigar Makers' Union here is doing good work, our numbers are increasing and we are making it warm for the Chinese. One firm advertises for fifty good cigar makers and is expecting them from the East because all those that are here are at work. Hoping you will do us and the workingmen's Party of California justice in the future.

Yours fraternally,
William Wolz, Cor. Sec.,
of the Cigar Makers' Union of the Pacific Coast[5]

"From the San Francisco Cigar Makers," Letter from William Wolz, Cigar Makers' Union of the Pacific Coast, *Labor Standard*, August 11, 1878

5

Also tied to the early socialist trend was The Socialist, *published in Detroit by Joseph Labadie, a printer and former master workman in the Knights of Labor, and Judson Grenell, also a printer. Labadie, the paper's leading figure, clearly inherited the Knights' anti-*

Chinese attitude, though he occasionally published contrary opinions on the subject. Like the Labor Standard, The Socialist *was connected with the Workingmen's Party in the late 1870's. For the most part, the paper supported exclusion of Chinese workers from labor unions and from the USA in general.* The Socialist *reprinted in full the vociferously anti-Asian "Appeal of the California Workingmen's Party." The appearance of B.E.G. Jewett's particularly sharp condemnation of the anti-Chinese sentiment within the labor movement was exceptional.*[6]

To the Editor of THE SOCIALIST

Sir, - Your kindly publication of squibs of one who has spent time and property, and lost situation after situation, in the dissemination of Socialistic ideas and furtherance of kindred aims, encourages me to hope that you will publish the following little suggestion and criticism: In the first place, then, I criticise by *suggesting* that your truly worthy and able paper cease to combat the Chinaman as a class, for what has the duties of the Mikados for the last one thousand years been but to make of them debauched, degraded, greedy, selfish serfs? And what are the wealth-monger Mikados of America doing but making of their own race a set of menials who *"will work lower than a Chinaman?"*

The Chinaman coming here of his own accord and at his own expense of accumulated earnings, has as much right here as you or I or any German, Russ, Switzer, Frank, Turk, Pole, Irish or Ethiopian in the land; and true Socialism demands that as air, land and water are eternally free to the whole race *who wish to live,* they shall NOT be debarred that privilege. For if they are ignorant, vile or needy, it is our duty as first occupants in this land to instruct in intellectual and moral duties and give them the means of performing them as, if we were in their land, it would be their duty to do unto us. What we want to fight is, not the Chinese nor any other imported *stock,* be they Durham bulls or Spanish mules - be they men, women or babies, but we want to fight the *importers,* persons, who, ministering to their own greed, to the lust of the flesh and the pride of life, sell (or *contract*) into bondage the *labor* of others, and drive still others into deeper degradation and poverty. Let our pacific coast friends fight the wealth mongers, and not their slaves, and they will have not only justice but right on their side. Not say: "the Chinese must go," but that "the oppressors, money-mongers, Sharons *et. al.* must go." Let our Labor literature, which is worth more to us now than trade unions or political *sorties*, be supported, and my word for it, there is a better day coming for both the Californians and the Chinese - for New York and the Irish [,] New Jersey and the "skeeters" - than we can now imagine, for a true co-operation will become universal when there shall be no Rockdale dwarflets nor anti-railroad Grangerisms, for it will tell us what to fight and how to fight.

"The Chinese Question," Letter from B.E.G. Jewett, *The Socialist*, May 4, 1878

6

The Knights of Labor, an organization for which cooperation among all who labored was a basic premise, ironically took a consistently hostile view of the Chinese workers in the United States. Officials, members, and leading bodies sanctioned, and often participated in violent attacks in Western states and territories during the 1880's. The mid- and latter parts of that decade marked the high point in the Order's history: thereafter, it declined steadily. There were many issues of contention within the organization; surely, the issue of the Chinese was not primary among them. The disagreements which broke out over the implications of an anti-Chinese resolution at a labor convention in San Francisco suggest, however, that some members of the Knights dissented from the use of force against the Chinese. The executive board of the Knights' District Assembly, believing that the resolution incited physical attack, withdrew from the convention. The San Francisco Alta was probably not incorrect in inferring from this action that the District Assembly preferred a more peaceful expulsion of the Chinese.[7]

(a)

At the conclusion of the Labor Convention on Wednesday, a somewhat startling denouement occurred in the shape of a withdrawal from the Convention of the Executive Board of the District Assembly of Knights of Labor. According to the statements of the members of the Board, the sudden action was inspired by the passage by the Convention of a resolution calling for the expulsion of the Chinese within sixty days. An ALTA reporter visited the Secretary of the Board last evening, and ascertained that discontent has been brewing since the first night of the Convention. In the first place the Board claims to discountenance any violent or incendiary language used in the framing of resolutions....

"Labor Dissensions: A Resolution Causes a Split in the Convention," *San Francisco Daily Alta*, December 4, 1885

(b)

The Knights of Labor represent the strongest and wisest federation of labor ever organized here or elsewhere. The ALTA has had frequent occasion to endorse their levelness of head and coolness of procedure....

In the labor convention now in session in this city, the difference between this organization and the labor that will not organize unless in a mob, has been made apparent.

It has appeared in the discussion of the Chinese question. The convention, by a vote of 60 to 47, has passed this resolution:

While this Convention distinctly recognizes that the Chinese are not the cause of hard times and that the settlement of the Chinese question will not settle the labor question, yet considering their bad moral habits, their low grades of development, their filth, their vices, their race differences with the Caucasian, and their status as willing slaves.

Resolved, That we demand their complete removal from all parts of the Pacific Coast, and especially that they be removed from San Francisco within sixty days.

Sixty men propose to move 40,000 Chinese out of this city in sixty days! How are they going to do it? It cannot be done by lawful means....Unless the resolution is a piece of criminal brag and buncombe, of chatter and vaporing, it means the use of violent measures which will bear heavily upon San Francisco for years to come....

After the labor convention passed this resolution given above, the

Knights of Labor withdrew, and reassembling elsewhere passed this action:

The Executive Board of the District Assembly of the Knights of Labor, having deliberately considered the policy as adopted by the convention assembled in Metropolitan Hall, feel it the duty of the members to withdraw the assembly from the convention. The committee recognize this fact, that the prosperity of the State, as well as the nation, depends upon the perfect security of person and property. With this view, we cannot endorse anything that tends toward violence, and therefore withdraw from the convention.

That action passes the limits of expediency; it is supremely higher than politics; it is statesmanship. The prosperity of the State depends upon the perfect security of person and property, and these statesmen in leather aprons and overalls, Knights of Labor who deserve the title, for they do labor, have set to all men here and abroad a most distinguished example. Present resentments would be served by violating the rights of person and property in the case of the Chinese. There is no doubt about that. If to-morrow every Chinese person in this city were gashed in the throat and their property destroyed, there would go up by few audible protests against the enormity of such an act. That this is so invests the action of the Knights of Labor with a peculiar dignity. They refuse to violate the law against murder and arson for the benefit of labor, so called, because and for the reason worthy of statesmen, the law violated in that way becomes at once a less potent protector of the persons and property of those who violate it, and all others....

San Francisco Daily Alta, editorial, December 4, 1885

7

Most socialists, like others in the labor movement, opposed the emigration of Asians to the United States; exceptions have been suggested in materials appearing in this section. By the early twentieth century, U.S. imperialism was well advanced along the road of overseas subjugation and interference, carrying with it new assumptions of racial supremacy. Many in the labor movement (including Samuel Gompers of the American Federation of Labor) and many socialists supported these notions, which became ammunition in the debate among labor organizations.[8] *Indeed, some of the most vehement arguments against unionization of Japanese and Chinese workers were published by the AFL in the early 1900's. The views of the Reverend George Washington Woodbey, an African-American socialist minister, differed dramatically with the prevailing attitude of labor organizations during the early 1900's. Himself a resident of California, still the base of anti-Asian agitation, Woodbey had been born a slave in Tennessee in 1854. His career in social activism included long service for the Republican Party in the Midwest (he was ordained in Kansas and lived for years in that and neighboring states), prior to joining the Socialist Party. His speech at that Party's 1908 convention - made in the course of debate on the report of the Resolutions committee - reflects a conception of the human family totally at variance with prevailing winds stirring his fellow members. The convention proceedings in fact indicate that, following his remarks, Woodbey was roundly denounced.*[9]

It is generally supposed that the western people, those living on the Pacific slope, are almost as a unit, opposed to Oriental immigration. I am not saying that those living on the western slope oppose them, but where Oriental immigration comes to the western coast it is supposed that the people of the west are in favor of their exclusion. I am in favor of throwing the entire world open to the inhabitants of the world. (Applause.) There are no foreigners, and cannot be, unless some person came down from Mars, or Jupiter, or some place. I stand on the declaration of Thomas Paine when he said "The world is my country." (Applause.) It would be a curious state of affairs for immigrants or the descendants of immigrants from Europe themselves to get control of affairs in this country, and then say to the Oriental immigrants that they should not come here. So far as making this a mere matter of race, I disagree decidedly with the committee, that we need any kind of a committee to decide this matter from a scientific standpoint. We know what we think upon the question of race now as well as we would know two years from now or any other time.

And so far as reducing the standard of living is concerned, the standard of living will be reduced anyhow. You know as well as I do that either the laborer will be brought to the job or the job will be taken to the laborer. Understand? We will either have to produce things as cheap as they can be produced upon foreign soil or the means of production will be carried to the Orient and there the thing will be done. The natural tendency of capitalism is to reduce the standard of living; the standard of living will be reduced anyhow.

Now, listen: It seems to me if we take any stand opposed to any sort of immigration that we are simply playing the old pettifogging trick of the Democrats and Republicans, and will gain nothing by it. (Applause.) I believe it is opposed, as I understand, to the principles of international Socialism. I do not pretend to say that the international Socialist organization takes square ground as to what we should say on the question, but to me Socialism is based, if anything, upon the Brotherhood of Man. This stand that we take in opposition to any sort of immigration is opposed to the very spirit of the Brotherhood of Man. I hope, therefore, that all that part of the committee's report which imposes a restriction on immigration will be stricken out by the convention. It ought to be done; in good faith it ought to be done, because, in the first place, the Socialists are organized in Japan; they are getting organized in China; they will soon be operating in every civilized nation on earth. And are the Socialists of this country to say to the Socialists of Germany, or the Socialists of Sweden, Norway, Japan, China, or any other country, that they are not to go anywhere on the face of the earth? It seems to me absurd to take that position. Therefore, I hope and move that any sort of restriction of immigration will be stricken out of the committee's resolution. (Applause.)

Proceedings of the National Convention of the Socialist Party, 1908, p. 106

8

Unions of miners were basic to organized labor's attitude toward organization of Asian workers.[10] The issue of exclusion in California dates to the Gold Rush, to the matter of excluding or subordinating Chinese workers. Later, miners' organizations (in both the hard rock and coal regions) occasionally developed and practiced forms of interracial solidarity encompassing Chinese workers. This was true of both the United Mine Workers (founded 1890) and the Western Federation of Miners (founded 1893). Influenced by the Knights of Labor and structured on an industry-wide basis, the UMW tended to diverge from the white-only precepts held by the American Federation of Labor, of which it became part: in particular, the UMW organized widely among African-American workers, making the union one of the few interracial ones in the country during the period of the institutionalization of segregation. The Western Federation of Miners lay outside the AFL, increasingly resentful of the latter's craft divisions and conservatism: consequently, the WFM contributed to the forming of the militant Industrial Workers of the World in 1905. The WFM below assesses quite positively the UMW's efforts to reach beyond the ranks of white miners (a), and makes a point of including an appeal for labor unity in an anti-war statement (b). A UMW correspondent reports on organizing among Chinese and Japanese miners (c).

(a)

Delegates from District No. 22 of the United Mine Workers met in Denver on Monday, July 8th and were in session during the past week, and in all probability will not finish their labors until towards the close of the present week. The convention is made up of forty-two delegates representing 9,000 men who are employed in the coal mines of Wyoming. During the past few months the national organization of the United Mine Workers has concentrated its efforts in organizing the mines that are operated by the Union Pacific Coal Company. This great coal corporation of the West opposed every effort upon the part of the organizers, but was gradually forced to succumb to the determined persistency of men who had resolved that the slaves of the Union Pacific should be brought together. The present convention in Denver demonstrates that the United Mine Workers has succeeded in organizing the coal mines of Wyoming, and the fact that two delegates in convention are Japs, representing the Asiatic race, is further proof that the time has come when race and creed prejudice must be banished from the councils of organized labor. The brown and yellow man are here and are competitors in the labor market for jobs, and organized labor cannot afford to build any barriers of prejudice that will keep such men outside the pales of unionism. We are pleased to point out the fact that the United Mine Workers has brought the Jap and Chinese under the banner of the organization, for the reason that the acceptance of the Asiatic in such a powerful organization numerically as the United Mine Workers of America will have much to do with opening the doors of other labor unions to the races from the Orient. That the officials of the United Mine Workers are guarding zealously the interests of the membership and are not asleep was shown when two delegates in the convention were unmasked and exposed as Judas Iscariots in the employ of the Pinkerton agency. Fred J. Benzer, "operator" No. 20, and Olaf E. Erickson, "operator" No. 21, of Rock Springs, Wyoming, were uncovered as traitors and will no longer be able to conceal their treason from their fellowmen. These two human reptiles are no longer valuable to a detective agency nor will they be longer welcome among honest men in the Rocky Mountains.

"The United Mine Workers in Convention at Denver," editorial, *The Miner's Magazine,* July 18, 1907

(b)

....If a war ensues between Japan and the United States, it is but fair that those who are responsible for the quarrel, shall do the fighting. We trust that the working class of this country will not be swept off its feet by appeals to patriotism. The laboring people should remember that the same element in this nation that secures injunctions from judiciaries to subjugate labor and who are able to hire uniformed soldiers to shoot down strikers, when in rebellion against the tyranny of exploiters, belong to that privileged class who will be responsible for the conflict between the United States and Japan. No workingman of this country has any personal quarrel with the brown men of the Orient. He should remember that collective murder in war is no more moral than individual murder through personal differences. When the working class of every nation shall refuse to shoulder the rifle to murder at the bidding of the moneyed power of nations, there shall be no more war.[11]

"Shall there be War?," editorial, *The Miner's Magazine*, July 18, 1907

(c)

Rock Springs, Wyo., Sept. 8, 1908
Editor, Mine Workers' Union:

I think this is the first time in all my life that I ever attempted to break into print, but I feel that the Labor Day celebration in Rock Springs should not be passed by without comment for the reason that I will venture to say that on all the North American continent there was not such another celebration as this one. There have been larger celebrations, no doubt, but never one that afforded a more practical demonstration of the benefits to be derived from being thoroughly organized. The parade started at 10 o'clock a.m., headed by the Rock Springs baseball members of some trades union as well as being members of the musicians' union. Next came the carriages, first with the mayor and chief of police of Rock Springs, followed by the members of the Trades and Labor Council and the members of the city council, followed by the carriage containing District President Thomas Gibson, master of ceremonies, and your humble servant, followed by all the local unions in this vicinity. Nearly every trades union in the country was well represented. The line was well over a mile and a half long, with about two thousand men in line, but what impressed me most was the large number of Chinese and Japanese members of our locals that were in line displaying their buttons, badges and banners with the greatest pride imaginable. It appears that District 22 has practically settled the Oriental question. Apparently they have arrived at the conclusion that it is necessary to do one of three things with the Oriental, either get like them, make them like us, or get rid of them. It was impossible to get rid of them - they did not want to become like them, so they decided to make them as much like us as possible, to the extent of giving them at least an equal opportunity with the white man, so much so that the Chinese or Japanese now get $3.10 to $3.40 per day of eight hours for the same work they were formerly paid from $1.25 to $1.60 per day of ten hours.

This thing of being "shown" works with a great many more people than are bounded by the geographical lines of Missouri. It has brought the Oriental into the local union, he is fast becoming acquainted with Americans and their methods and with the principles of trades unionism and they don't hesitate to express their reference for the new order of things as against the dark age order that exists in the country from which they came. I believe the credit of administering the first trades union obligation to Chinese or Japs belongs to Thomas Gibson, district president of District 22. I do not know whether the "old man" gave the obligation in Chinese or Japanese or not, but they understand it and are living up to it. Another thing, they never make a kick about an assessment, no matter how great it is. They realize that had it not been for the U.M.W. of A. they would still be only be getting the old wage of $1.25 to $1.60 per day, and so long as the Oriental is a factor in the production of coal, or for that matter any other commodity, we are compelled to give them consideration, for it is as certain as death or a mortgage that if the trades unionist does not use them the employer will, and I here and now take off my hat to the officers and members of District 22 for having settled the Oriental question (as far as it was possible for a trades union to settle it), settled too, not because of laws, but in spite of them....

"Labor Day at Rock Springs," Letter to the Editor from W.H. McCluskey, *United Mine Workers' Journal*, September 16, 1909

9

The Industrial Workers of the World did not hesitate to organize Chinese, Japanese, and other Asian workers. Dedicated to industrial unionism, as well as to the notion that unions were society's most trustworthy conductors in every sense, the IWW particularly worked among the unskilled and immigrant workers, those most neglected (if not despised) by the leadership of the American Federation of Labor. In the process, the IWW led a number of important strikes that were unique in the degree of rank-and-file involvement and spirit, and in the national attention they received. Consequently, management and government viewed the IWW with hostility and suspicion, and treated the organization accordingly.

The IWW's emphasis on labor solidarity remained nonetheless consistent, and influenced others in locales where large numbers of Asians labored by the side of workers of other nationalities. (Significant among the joint actions of Asians and others was the strike of Japanese and Mexican-American sugar beet workers in

Oxnard, California in 1903.) In expressing confidence that Chinese and Japanese laborers can be organized - and will make outstanding "industrialists" or protagonists of industrial unionism - the following document represents the IWW's basic view of Asian workers.[12]

The Oriental exclusion question has received so much attention and caused us so much discussion, especially on the Pacific coast, that it is well for us to look for the cause of all this agitation.

So far as is known, the Industrial Workers of the World is the only organization that has ever done any organizing among the Japanese and Chinese in this country. Consequently, a short article from the industrial standpoint of practical experience among these people will be of interest to the readers of THE BULLETIN, as well as educational to a great many so-called American socialists, who claim to be socialists because of a scientific understanding of economics, and yet declare for the exclusion of these people from "our" shores....

JAPANESE AND CHINESE ARE PROMPT WITH PAYMENT OF DUES.

In organizing among the Japanese working men, but little difference is found to that among other nationalities, excepting their shrewdness and honesty to stick with the organization, after having taken the pledge. The first lecture from an industrial working-class standpoint, delivered to them, was before the Japanese Literary Society of Seattle, composed of about six hundred members. This society, of course, is not composed of all working men. It is the Japanese middle class, principally, and it is on this point that the exclusion fight hinges. A few members were secured, and from time to time more were secured, but the old story of lack of finances sufficient to employ a Japanese organizer and place him in the field, is why the work was not carried on successfully.

None of the Japanese or Chinese who become members fail to realize their duty as to paying their dues and keeping in good standing. This cannot be said, truthfully, of all the "whites." The Japanese and Chinese can be organized as rapidly as any other nationality, and when once pledged to stand with you, no fear or doubt need to be entertained as to them, during labor trouble. But some one will say, Why organize them when we can keep them out of this country? The workers cannot keep them out, because the working class does not compose the organized or dominant part of society. The organized part of society that controls today is the employing class, and it is at their will and desire that exclusion or admittance will be regulated....

EXCLUSION IS IN THE INTEREST OF THE MIDDLE CLASS.

At this point let us see why all this agitation. The greater number of the Orientals that have been coming to this country for some time are small business men. In fact, they are pretty much the "Jew Merchant" of the Orient, and when they enter the business field, their shrewdness, coupled with their keen perception of criminal commercialism, spells ruin to all competitors. The little American cock-roacher sees the handwriting on the wall. I have not the space here to quote the many instances repeatedly published by the capitalist papers as to the closing of a "Jap" restaurant because of its being so filthy, etc.; of the "pure food inspector" finding the milk diluted, etc., etc. But the truth of all this is the shifting economic position of the little bourgeois American who secures this persecution in behalf of his own material interest. But the Japanese soon learn this, and then they become equal to the occasion. These people are entering every business of the middle class, and our little American cock-roach merchant sees his finish, unless he can create some disturbance of some kind, and thereby drag the working class into a middle-class fight. This dodge has been worked on the wage slaves many times by the bourgeois, but it remains to be seen whether the dastardly trick can be turned by this dying class in the twentieth century....

COLD FACTS FOR CONSIDERATION BY THE WORKING CLASS.

1. They are here.

2. Thousands of them are wage workers.

3. They have the same commodity to sell as other workers - labor power.

4. They are as anxious as you, to get as much as possible. This is proven by the fact that they have come to this country. For what? To better their conditions.

Granting that the above four statements are facts, and no one dare deny them - then what is the problem that confronts us? The Industrial Organization of these people. To say that "you can't organize them" is a misstatement. We have proven that they can be organized. Had our efforts proven futile among them, then there would be a hook to hang the agitation on for their exclusion. But such is not the case. They can be organized as rapidly, if not more so, than any other nationality on earth. We of the Industrial Workers of the World have organized Japanese and Chinese, and the United Mine Workers of America have organized Japanese in the coal fields of Wyoming. This is proof that they can be organized....

A FEW COMPARISONS OF JAPANESE AND "WHITE" WORKERS.

The Japanese possess the quality of "stick" that is necessary in a wage worker to make a good industrialist. At Port Blakely, where "white" men are driven like Mexican peons in a lumber mill, many Japanese are employed. The Japanese decided to ask for a raise of 20 cents per day. One morning they all rolled up their blankets ready to leave camp if their demands were not granted. The 20 cent raise was granted. This gave the Japanese an average of seven cents per day more than the "white" workmen.

At the Tidewater mill, Tacoma, the Japanese and many "whites" were working for $1.75 per day. The Japanese went on strike for $2 per day. They won. The "whites" hung their heads and held their jobs at $1.75. In a few weeks after the Japanese won, they said: "If we can get the American workers to come with us we can win $2.25 per day." But the "white" workers were satisfied with $1.75 while the Japanese received $2. Their knowledge of the labor field and how to win is illustrated ion the labor report issued by the commissioner of labor of the state of California.

WHAT THE LABOR COMMISSIONER OF CALIFORNIA
HAS TO SAY.

He says that the Japanese do not strike, but that they work on, whatever the condition may be, until all idle labor is out of the field, and then, just when the crop is ripest, when the work must be done, they walk out, making a demand for better wages or shorter hours without any mercy for the employer whatsoever. In other words, they eliminate the scab before they strike.

The labor commissioner of California is quite correct, and it is that very qualification in the Japanese that will make one of the best industrialists ever known. While there are many Japanese working for less than Americans are, there are thousands of Americans working for less than Japanese.

I might cite you, too, many instances similar to the above, but it is not necessary. A few serve as proof. In the above general review of the Japanese, the same holds true of Chinese workers also. In many places along the coast, Chinese may be found drawing better wages than the "whites," and repeatedly in the fish canneries are found Chinese foremen with "white" women and girls working under them. All this complicated mess can only be adjusted by industrial organization and administration....

FAILING TO EXCLUDE, WHAT IS THE PROBLEM BEFORE US?

What is the problem, then, that confronts the worker?

1. The working class, disorganized as they are, cannot force the exclusion of any foreigner from American shores, against the material interest of the employing or capitalist class.

2. If the Japanese be excluded from this country, it will be because of a middle class commercial demand, and the ignorance of the working class will serve only as a dragnet to pull the wage slave, once more, into the cob-webs of middle-class interests.

3. Granting that the Japanese are excluded, the American worker still stands in the world's market to sell his labor power at a price that his employer may manufacture and sell goods at a profit, and compete in the world's market.

Certainly any worker should see the problem that he is confronted with, and to set up or continue an agitation of exclusion is only to blur the facts to be dealt with, from the proletarian standpoint....

In conclusion, let us say that the Industrial Workers of the World will follow this brief review of the Oriental problem with a pamphlet, as soon as sufficient statistics and data can be secured, to show conclusively that there is only one correct and scientific position to be taken on this question, and that is the Industrial Organization of the wage slaves of the world, regardless of race, creed or color. Understanding this, the speaker may appear before an audience and truthfully and scientifically conclude his address with the words: "Workers of the world, unite," without placing his foot in his mouth.

J.H. Walsh, "Japanese and Chinese Exclusion or Industrial Organization, Which?", *Industrial Union Bulletin*, April 11, 1908

10

*Further exposition of the IWW's position and experience
follows. Relevant material is included from a general strike of some
twenty crafts in Vancouver, British Columbia. The Pacific Northwest
of the United States and the area of Canada just to the north share
certain labor traditions, including the popularity of the IWW in the
early twentieth century.[13] Despite the differences between the two
countries, certain common conditions obtained, due in no small part
to the domination of the region by large American corporations and
their Canadian subsidiaries, often through interlocking directorates
generally based in the United States. Asian immigration, and attendant
labor controversies involving multiethnic cooperation, have been part
of Canadian history. There was a Chinese exclusion movement in
Canada, as well as a contrary effort to include Asian immigrants in
united working class activity.*

(a)

The Spokane division of the porters' union (A.F. of L.) held a
meeting April 13 to talk over the invasion of the Japanese. According to the
"Labor World," "vigorous efforts will be made to eradicate the brown men
from industrial competition" - which efforts will have "the support of
organized labor in general." The Industrial Workers of the World have the
largest labor organization in Spokane or in any part of the country around. It
must be understood that the I.W.W. will turn down any effort at
discrimination against our Japanese fellow workers. Are we not correct when
we say that the trades unions foster a state of affairs which allows one set of
workers to be pitted against another set of workers in the same industry;
thereby helping to defeat one another? This is the same old game of "divide
and conquer" on the part of employers and those labor unions which are
influenced by prejudice on account of race, nation or language. If the workers
controlled the U.S. government, or had at present anything to say as to
whether the Japanese were "desirable citizens," it might be interesting for
workingmen to take up the study of comparative ethnology; but the Japanese
are here in the United States by the will of the industrial masters; being here,

the matter should be dealt with as is best for the working class. Now it is not supposed that the members of the porters' union, for instance, would exterminate the Japanese by murder outright, but would be more humane (?) by letting the Japanese starve to death - providing the Japanese could be so far educated into the A.F. of L. principles as to be willing tamely to starve to death. The Japanese are here, they will not starve to death, and they will work as long as the boss will hire them. This being the case, what does the A.F. of L. man expect to gain by antagonizing these men, the Japanese, who are, it will be admitted, not lacking in brains? From all appearances, the porters' union is not so strong as to refuse help - even from a Japanese! Will any man explain just why, as long as the Japanese are here, it would not be better to unite with them to fight the common enemy, the master, than to waste time, energy and strength in fighting another group of workers simply on account of their color - to the huge delight of the employer? If the porters' union were but half as class conscious as the average Japanese worker, there would be better wages and better conditions for the porter than the wretched ones they are now forced to submit to. The Labor Commissioner of California says that in his long experience, the Japanese is the "most merciless" with his employer of any of the help in the California ranches, and bewails the mistake the employers of California made in getting Japanese who will exact everything possible, if they have but half a chance. Can as much be said of the porters' union - that they are "merciless" with the Spokane employers? Hardly! American or Japanese, Italian or Austrian, Swede or Irishman, German or Frenchman; do the employers quarrel among themselves on account of nationality? Not much! They are too wise.

Let the porter count his miserable pay on Saturday night; look at the wretched working conditions he puts up with, and then consider his comfortable, well-fed employer, and then turning to his Japanese fellow-worker, ask himself if it would not be wiser for him to unite with the Japanese to wring more wages and shorter hours from their common robber - the employer!

"Silly Race Prejudice," editorial, *Industrial Worker*, April 22, 1909

(b)

To Industrial Worker, Spokane, Wash.

Vancouver, B.C., June 5th, 1911

Vancouver in throes of a General Strike. Chinese carpenters are striking and craft bricklayers working. Monster mass meeting held Saturday night; 5,000 present. I got the floor and explained that I.W.W. would and must assist in every strike against the boss. I explained how to strike by giving no notice, call of every workers, and refuse to haul or feed scabs or troops. Explained Swedish general strike and strikes in France, Sabotage, fallacy of politics, power on the job and how to get the eight-hour day by refusing to work longer. One great Industrial Union taken with great applause and enthusiasm. Notify all workers to keep away from Vancouver, B.C.

Telegram, Joseph S. Biscay to *Industrial Worker*, June 5, 1911, in *Industrial Worker*, June 8, 1911

(c)

The strike situation in the building industry in Vancouver, B.C., remains unchanged. The bricklayers is the only craft working. They seem to be more numerous than the open scabs. The structural workers have tied up completely their line of work; the same in most other lines. Much was looked for from the street car men and electricians and power men, but they are standing loyal with the bosses when it's in their power to win the strike in one hour, if they would only act. There is considerable feeling against the street car men who are working. Recently several Chinamen stopped on the street in the middle of the car tracks, a car came along and stopped, the motorman opened the vestibule window and called for the Chinks to get out of the way. "Go long, you dlam scab, me union man," was the startling answer he got. It must be remembered that the Chinese carpenters are out with the others. That seems to be the sentiment....

J.S. Biscay, "The Vancouver Strike: Chinese Union Men Curse Scabs. Crafts Are Sticking Together," *Industrial Worker*, June 22, 1911

11

Among the city labor bodies supportive of unionization of Asians in the early 1900's was the Seattle Central Labor Council. Its sympathy for that cause has already been alluded to [Part I]. The Council was committed to industrial and united forms of labor organization, leading a mammoth general strike in 1919.[14]

The Central Labor Council at its weekly meeting last night went on record as favoring the admission of Japanese to all labor unions affiliated with the American Federation of Labor. The action was taken following the reading of a communication from the Journeymen Barbers' International Union acknowledging the receipt of a copy of the resolution the council adopted a few weeks ago, urging that the international admit women barbers to its ranks. In the letter Jacob Fisher, general secretary-treasurer of the international, presumably in sarcasm, wrote:

"I would be pleased to hear from your council as to whether they favor admission of Japanese barbers to membership in our organization, as well as into unions of all other trades."

I.W. Buck, of the local Barbers' Union, moved that the secretary write in answer that the council favored "the organization of all workers in every craft."

The motion was carried without opposition.

"Central Council Would Admit Japanese Unions," *Seattle Daily Times*, May 28, 1914

12

Holding a deep interest in the labor movement abroad, including Japan (a), Samuel Gompers nevertheless made little effort to unionize the millions of unskilled immigrants who hailed from the countries he observed so closely. The hopes of the socialist Call (b), while satisfied to a degree by the decisions of local bodies, were neither met by the AFL nationally nor supported by most leading American Socialists.

(a)

There ought to be no misapprehension in regard to the development of the labor movement in Japan. Like the human, the aggregation of association of humans cannot escape the pitfalls and errors that are common attributes of the human. The movement of labor to seek redress for wrongs, improvement of the material, economic, industrial conditions, may take on various forms and usually does, particularly according to the national and racial, as well as industrial circumstances.

Any organized effort of the workers which is antagonized on the part of governmental authority, is likely to develop into secret effort, and hence so-called radical and oftentimes impractical, so far as the attainment of any tangible results are concerned, except as it manifests antagonism to constituted authority....

My idea of what the governmental attitude should be is to accord freedom of the right of organization, freedom to the right of expression, freedom to exercise the normal activities of the human being...; to hold in principle that which is legal for any one person to do is not illegal when done by two or more persons, but the act in itself must be held to be either legal or illegal; that it is no more illegal for two or more persons to do a legal act than it is for any one person to do it; that is, the right by associated effort to agree to perform labor or to withhold labor, to give patronage or to withhold patronage....

I do not underestimate the difficulties in the way of a government to change its policy so that the full freedom to exercise these activities can be tolerated or permitted or sanctioned by law or by governmental agents.

But I say this from my experience and observation, not only in America, but of a study as well as observation of the history of the development of the organized labor movement in every country on the face of the globe, wherever such an effort has been made, and it holds good wherever it is undertaken, wherever it has developed and grown.

If those in authority in Japan can and will take that position, it will make more for the growth of the development of the Japanese people and the Japanese government and their taking their place among the advanced nations of the world; it will prove an incentive and impulse in no more effective way.

"The Rights of the Japanese Working People and the Attitude of the Japanese Government Toward Them." A Statement by Samuel Gompers President of the American Federation of Labor, to Reverend Doctor Sidney L. Gulick, December 17, 1914, enclosed in Gompers to Gulick, February 24, 1915, *Samuel Gompers Letter-Books*, Library of Congress

(b)

....On the Pacific coast the Japanese have been set up as bogies before the eyes of the American people for years. William Randolph Hearst still is at it. But he now plays almost a lone hand, and the time is not far hence, it appears, when he will play an entirely lone hand - and when that time comes maybe that game won't pay anymore.

Workers in the East used to be told that the workers in the West didn't want the Jap - that the Jap represented a menace to American living standards; and perhaps he did. But the people who told those stories weren't interested in solving the problem, and they either knew where the cards were stacked and falsified, or didn't know and blundered.

Where Antagonism Started.

Race antagonism, you will learn, if you seek the right authorities - and they are here in Baltimore now - didn't begin with the working people, but was planted in them by the common foes of the workers of all races.

Capitalists like race feuds. They foster them everywhere. They have done it in the colonial sections of almost all countries. They went a long way with it on the Pacific coast. And the game is about up....

And now to the hopeful signs of coming sanity. When the California Federation of Labor held its recent convention it listened to a Japanese who delivered a fraternal address. It went further and accepted an invitation from the Japanese Friendly Society - the national labor organization of Japan - to send California union delegates to the jubilee convention in Japan. And it went the great additional step which broke all precedent and appointed a committee to study the problem of ORGANIZING THE JAPANESE WORKERS IN AMERICA.

How to Solve Question.

The California labor organization thinks it has put its finger on the key that will unlock the secret of a successful meeting of the race question that has been the Golden State's most delicate one....

The trade unions reason it out this way: The trouble has been that the Jap will work cheaper. That is why he was a menace to American standards. If he is organized like the Americans he cannot work cheaper and cannot be a menace. The California unions don't care a fig about the color of skin. It is a question of wages and bread and butter.

Whatever of prejudiced talk there has been about the race question as an actual race question has been the result of agitation that grew up around and outside of the real issue. It has been an economic issue. The unions out there think that now, at any rate. And they hope that the investigation to be made during the coming year will be the means of ending forever the Japanese question....

So it is necessary to solve the Japanese problem. Labor knows this, and feels that it alone can produce the solution. It believes that organization on this side of the ocean will help; that organization on the other side will help; that organization on both sides will enable workingmen of both nations to settle every difference to the satisfaction of the workingmen of both nations.

It will be many years before California will consent to let down the bars, and it may be more than one year before the California Federation of Labor will find its ways clear to issue charters to Japanese unions. But the start has been made - a start toward true settlement of one of America's greatest problems.

Chester Wright, "Labor Moves to Solve Jap Problem Soon: Delegates to AFL Convention Will Try to Unionize Nipponese Workers," *New York Call*, November 19, 1916

13

Much of the impetus for uniting Asian and other workers in unions and strikes during the first half of the twentieth century came from labor forces kept outside the ranks of the American Federation of Labor, despite attempts by some to become part of the AFL at various moments. Aside from the IWW, other non-AFL organizations endeavored to bring Chinese, Japanese, and other Asians into unions with other nationalities. An important group in this regard was the Communist Party, which helped unionize Asian workers before, during, and after the Great Depression, urging the AFL to drop its exclusion policies and giving assistance to unaffiliated unions when the Federation's leaders were unwilling to modify their approach. That the Communists were able to help the labor movement record important successes in unionizing Asian workers, organizing the unemployed and promoting multiracial unity, is due in no small part to the activity of Asian Americans who joined that Party and earned respect as sincere trade unionists.

A case in point is Karl Yoneda, a Kibei - born in the USA, educated in Japan. A laborer and union organizer on the West Coast, he served as editor of Rodo Shimbun, *a Japanese language paper issued by the Communist Party. He helped found the AFL's Cannery Workers, which subsequently adhered to the Congress of Industrial Organizations. He was also a member of the International Longshoremen's and Warehousemen's Union. Yoneda's Papers, at UCLA's Asian American Studies Center, contain a wealth of material on Asian workers and unionism. At its founding convention in 1992, the Asian Pacific American Labor Alliance recognized and honored Yoneda's contributions to the labor movement.[15] The following is an excerpt from Yoneda's writings on Japanese-American labor.*

I decided to join and volunteered to be an organizer for the Agricultural Workers Organizing Committee of Southern California (AWOCSC) established by the Los Angeles Japanese Labor Association in the spring of 1927; also on May 1st became a member of the Communist Party using the name Karl Hama, in both organizations. All organizers were either Issei (Japan born) or Kibei (U.S. born but raised in Japan). We signed up over a thousand workers among Mexican, Filipino and Japanese strawberry, tomato and bean pickers and conducted strikes for 25 to 35 cents pay and union recognition....

We found during organizing drives that Japanese were last to sign-up, in contrast to quick responses from Mexican and Filipino laborers. Our successes filled us with enthusiasm, though we realized that more Japanese were behind picket lines - in other words scabbing where strikes occurred. AWOCSC efforts continued till 1929, when the militant Agricultural Workers Industrial Union of the Trade Union Unity League (AWIU-TUUL) emerged in California taking in all farm workers regardless of race, color, creed or nationality.[16] Its membership switched to the new union, later Japanese Sections were established to meet the need for Japanese language material.

Imperial Valley, one of California's most fertile areas, had over 10,000 farm workers - 7,000 Mexicans, 1,000 Japanese, several hundred Filipinos and 1,000 others - employed there in 1930. In January the AWIU sent ten organizers, including Tetsuji Horiuchi, Issei, and Danny Roxas, Filipino, in the valley to start the union. They raised five demands:

25 cents per hour pay; Doing away with all labor contractors;

Elimination of piecework; Improvement of labor camps;

Recognition of camp (union) committees,

at the same time appealing to workers to walk off if growers rejected them, which many did but once again most of these were from small farms.

However, 400 members of the all white AFL shed workers took advantage of the strike situation and shut down a packing house after their demands of $1.00 per hour for lettuce packers and 75 cents for trimmers were turned down....

Seventeen million unemployed were looking for jobs and food during the massive U.S. economic crisis which began in 1929. The Socialist Party had collapsed ideologically many years before, the IWW was no longer an active force, AFL leaders were collaborating with employers by betraying those who dared to strike and [were] not interested in the unemployed. The Communist Party was the only organization which helped to establish National Unemployed Council branches encompassing unemployed workers from all industries....

In '31 and '32, due to prevailing unbearable working conditions such as low pay, long hours, indiscriminate firing and poor housing on California farms where only Japanese were hired, more than 20 strikes, led by the AWIU Japanese Section, were conducted in Chico, Lodi, Walnut Grove, Fresno, Visalia, Bakersfield down to Stanton and San Gabriel Valley among strawberry, raspberry, pea, peach, asparagus, grape and lettuce pickers.

Significantly, these strikes were always supported by their fellow union members who helped "man" the picket lines, strike kitchens, etc.....

AWIU Japanese Sections in Sacramento, Stockton and Los Angeles acted as coordinators of union activities between all farm workers. During 1933, more than 15 AWIU strikes were recorded. In a round figure there were 35,000 Mexican, Filipino, Japanese, Negro, white, small number of Korean and East Indian participants. Over 100 strike leaders were arrested; among them were a Korean and five Kibei organizers. At the Martin Ranch in Visalia, where 250 Japanese grape pickers went on strike for higher pay, I, along with the Korean and seven others, were picked up by a dozen or so deputies and told by the sheriff "Get out of town or go to jail."

Karl Yoneda, *A Partial History of California Japanese Farm Workers*, Southwest Labor Studies Conference, University of California-Berkeley, March 17-18, 1978, pp. 11-12, 13, 14

14

The International Longshoremen's and Warehousemen's Union, the Pacific Coast-based dock and transport union which arose in the course of the 1934 San Francisco General Strike, stressed multiracial cooperation from the first; the ILWU always included Japanese, Chinese, Filipino, and other Asian workers, along with white and African-American workers. A portion of an editorial from the period of World War II puts the union's views in a nutshell.[17]

Race hatred is like an insidious poison gas. Some people don't recognize it until it is too late. "I have nothing against Negroes, but -" or "I don't dislike Scandinavians, but -" are danger signals. Behind the "but" lies ignorance, blind prejudice, and smoldering violence. The "but" means that we have absorbed and been twisted by slanders, false rumors, radio jokes and innuendoes that dress races or nationalities or particular groups with fancied characteristics. The Jew is always grasping and rich. The Negro is shuffling, lazy and dishonest. The Scotchman is tight. The Scandinavian is a "squarehead" and stubborn. The Englishman lacks wit. The Irishman always wants to fight. The Frenchman is queer. These are lies. These are lies we hear at the movies, over the radio, in the news columns and fragments of conversation and we repeat them in what we think is a harmless way. But then along comes an incident. We get mad at somebody for something. The "something" won't magnify to the proportions we would like. So we get mad at the person for being whatever he is and there leaps to mind all the slanders and fictions we ever heard about his race or nationality, or even his church. Then we nurse a grudge, not alone against the offender, but against all people of his kind.

People are people, and you can't hate some people without hating all people - including yourself.

Lincoln said that God must have loved the common people or he wouldn't have made so many of them. Then he must also have loved the colored people, for three-quarters of the people on earth are colored. The white people in our land who would turn the war into a race conflict might ponder that. As for the rest of us, we had better begin to ponder the source of race hatred and its meaning to us. To find the source, look for the profit. Look for the man or men who turn race hatred into dollars and cents in their pockets. They are the exploiting employers. By keeping one group oppressed and outcast, they have a reservoir to play against another.

How well we know that in the ILWU! In 1934 and 1936, when we were in decisive struggles on the waterfront and in the warehouses for decent conditions, we frustrated scabherding by the employers by standing together, white, Negro, Chinese, Philippino and all. We left no outcasts to nurse resentments and become strikebreakers.

On this we cannot now stand still or lean upon the past. Our movement must go either forward or backward, backward to fink days, shapeups and kickbacks on the waterfront, low pay and drudgery and insecurity in the warehouses and plants, or forward toward ever better conditions, decency and security on the job and abundance and happiness in the home. More than anything else such progress depends upon our ability to cement unity among ourselves and make it ever and ever stronger.

"Poison Gas from Berlin," editorial, *The Dispatcher*, December 31, 1943

15

> *The CIO generally took a more favorable view of working*
> *class cooperation than the AFL. But within organized labor as a*
> *whole, including the AFL and state labor bodies affiliated with it, there*
> *was an overall broadening of organizing vision in the 1930's and*
> *1940's. This bore witness both to the impact of the CIO on the labor*
> *movement and to the egalitarian influence of the war against Italy,*
> *Germany, and Japan. The article below refers to a state federation's*
> *defiance of AFL policy during the Second World War and goes on*
> *record for repeal of the Chinese Exclusion Act.*[18]

As the convention of the State Federation of Labor adjourned today, President Thomas A. Murray told the members that while organized labor, conscious of the fact that "democracy is fighting for its life" would make all the sacrifices necessary to hasten eventual victory over the Axis powers, it did not intend to become a doormat for "reaction."

Mr. Murray declared that labor would oppose that "reactionary grouping in industry and in public life which is aiming to sabotage the workers' morale and the war effort itself by destroying the political, social and economic rights which serve to distinguish us from fascist countries."

In line with this declaration the convention adopted a series of recommendations for social legislation and instructed its legislative committee to fight for their enactment....

At a late pre-adjournment session lasting until midnight last night, the convention adopted resolutions condemning race riots and demanding stern action by the authorities to suppress them, and voted for modification of the Chinese Exclusion Act so as to permit the admission of Chinese to this country on a quota basis, on a par with immigrants from other countries. The latter action showed disagreement with the recent stand taken by the executive council of the AFL opposing modification of the act. Under the modification proposed 105 Chinese would be admitted to this country annually....

Joseph Shaplen, "Hold Labor Gains, Murray Insists," *New York Times*, August 27, 1943

Notes

1. For primary materials tracing the CNLU's formation, see Philip S. Foner and Ronald L. Lewis, ed., *The Black Worker During the Era of the National Labor Union*, Phila., 1974, parts I and II passim. See also Foner, *Organized Labor and the Black Worker, 1619-1981*, New York, 1981, chapter 3.

2. Claflin and Woodhull were sisters. A biography of Woodhull by Philip S. Foner is forthcoming. Previous studies include Johanna Johnston, *Mrs. Satan: The Incredible Saga of Victoria C. Woodhull*, New York, 1967; M.M. Marberry, *Vicky: A Biography of Victoria C. Woodhull*, New York, 1967; Emmanie Sachs, *The Terrible Siren: Victoria Woodhull (1838-1927)*, New York, 1928. The dispute with the International Working Men's Association may be traceable in part to the belittling of women and of women's issues by male IWMA leaders. See Foner and Brewster Chamberlain, eds., *Friedrich Sorge's Labor Movement in the United States* Westport, 1977, pp. 158-160, 335. The IWMA became a constituent founder of the Workingmen's Party in 1876.

3. Sources of the anti-Chinese issue as a labor problem in California's early statehood are explored in Rodman Paul, "The Origin of the Chinese Issue in California," *Mississippi Valley Historical Review*, Vol. 25, No. 2 (September 1938), pp. 181-196, and Ralph Mann, "Community Change and Caucasian Attitudes Toward the Chinese: The Case of Two California Mining Towns, 1850-1870," in Milton Cantor, ed., *American Working Class Culture: Explorations in American Labor and Social History*, Westport, 1979, pp. 397-422.

4. McDonnell's background and development are sketched in Herbert G. Gutman, *Work, Culture, and Society in Industrializing America*, New York, 1976, pp. 260-293. The proceedings of the first Congress of the Workingmen's Party are in Foner, ed., *The Formation of the Workingmen's Party of the United States*, New York, 1976. The Party's early years are outlined by Morris Hillquit, *History of Socialism in the United States*, New York, 1909, pp. 190-209. A pictorial history of the Kearney-led organization constitutes "The Workingmen's Party of California, 1877-1882," *California Historical Society Quarterly*, Vol. 55 (1976), pp. 58-71.

5. The San Francisco Cigar Makers' local was notoriously anti-Chinese in the late nineteenth century. Patricia A. Cooper, *Once a Cigar Maker: Men, Women, and Work Culture in American Cigar Factories, 1900-1919*, Urbana, 1987, p. 25.

6. For an assessment of Detroit socialists, see Richard Jules Oestreicher, *Solidarity and Fragmentation: Working People and Class Consciousness in Detroit, 1875-1900*, Urbana, 1986, chapter 3 passim.

7. Studies of the Knights include Leon Fink, *Workingmen's Democracy: the Knights of Labor and American Politics*, Urbana, 1983; Oestricher, *Solidarity and Fragmentation*; Melton McLaurin, *The Knights of Labor in the South*, Westport, 1973. See also Foner, *History of the Labor Movement in the United States*, Vol. 1, New York, 1947, chapters 21-25 passim. Consistent with the prevailingly hostile policy of the Order, former Grand Master Workman Terence Powderley enforced exclusion laws with a vengeance during his tenure as head of the U.S. Bureau of Immigration. Delber L. McKee, "The Chinese Must Go! Commissioner General Powderley and Chinese Immigration, 1897-1902," *Pennsylvania History*, Vol. 44 (1977), pp. 37-51.

8. Morris Hillquit and other leading Socialists were emphatically anti-Asian. Sally M. Miller, "Americans and the Second International," *Proceeding of the American Philosophical Society*, Vol. 120, No. 5 (October 1976), p. 384.

9. Information on and writings by Woodbey are in Philip S. Foner, ed., *Black Socialist Preacher: The Teachings of Reverend George Washington Woodbey and His Disciple Reverend G.W. Slater, Jr.*, San Francisco, 1983. For other data on African-Americans and socialist movements, see Gutman, "Peter H. Clark: Pioneer Negro Socialist," *Journal of Negro Education*, Vol. 34 (1965), pp. 413-424, and especially Foner, *American Socialism and Black Americans: From the Age of Jackson to World War II*, Westport, 1977.

10. For Asians in the mining labor force, see Alexander Saxton, *The Indispensable Enemy: Labor and the Anti-Chinese Movement in California*, Berkeley, 1971, pp. 3-10; Ronald Takaki, *Strangers from a Different Shore: A History of Asian Americans*, Boston, 1989, pp. 80-87. The hardships of Chinese miners in a region outside the main arenas of anti-Chinese agitation are described in Larry D. Quinn, "Chink Chink Chinaman: The Beginning of Nativism in Montana," *Pacific Northwest Quarterly*, Vol. 58, No. 2 (April 1967), pp. 82-89. A superb study of Asian coal miners and the UMW is Yuji Ichioka, "Asian Immigrant Coal Miners and the United Mine Workers of America: Race and Class at Rock Springs, Wyoming, 1907," *Amerasia Journal*, Vol. 6, No. 2 (Fall 1979), pp. 1-23.

11. The rivalry between the two burgeoning imperial powers was exacerbated by discrimination against Japanese in the United States.

12. Histories include Melvyn Dubofsky, *We Shall Be All: A History of the IWW*, Chicago, 1969; Foner, *History of the Labor Movement in the United States (Vol. 4): The Industrial Workers of the World, 1905-1917*, New York, 1965. Tomas Almaguer discusses the beet workers' strike in "Racial Domination and Class Conflict in Capitalist Agriculture: The Oxnard Sugar Beet Workers' Strike of 1903," *Labor History*, Vol. 25 (1984), pp. 325-349.

13. See Carlos A. Schwantes, *Radical Heritage: Labor, Socialism, and Reform in Washington and British Columbia, 1885-1917*, Seattle, 1979. Schwantes indicates that labor solidarity in British Columbia faced stronger obstacles than in Washington in the early twentieth century. Vancouver witnessed vigilante attacks on Asian immigrants in 1907. Schwantes, pp. 157-158. For the IWW in Spokane, Washington, see Schwantes, chapter 12. The Japanese in Canada, chiefly in British Columbia, were evacuated and relocated during World War II: see Part VI of the present volume.

14. The Council is described in Harvey O'Connor, *Revolution in Seattle: A Memoir*, New York, 1964, and Schwantes, pp. 140, 156-160, 207.

15. "Solidarity Starts Cycle for APALA," *AFL-CIO News*, May 11, 1992.

16. The Trade Union Unity League was a grouping of industrial unions initiated by the Communist Party. (It was disbanded during the labor organizing drives which followed the passing of the National Recovery Act [1933], including the famed Section 7A, which sanctioned the right of collective bargaining. See Bruce Minton and John Stuart, *Men Who Lead Labor*, New York, 1937, pp. 19, 62, 79, 100.) For a close examination of such a union, see Bruce Nelson, *Workers on the Waterfront: Seamen, Longshoremen, and Unionism in the 1930's*, Urbana, 1988, chapter 3 passim. An outstanding source on Asians and American radicalism is H.M. Lai's "Historical Survey of Organizations of the Left among the Chinese in America," *Asian America* Vol. 4, No. 3 (Fall 1972), pp. 10-20.

17. Nelson (p. 259-260) demonstrates the ILWU's and National Maritime Union's opposition to racism, in contrast to the Sailor's Union of the Pacific, which was unwaveringly hostile to Asian and Black workers (p. 49) The ILWU and NMU were led by Communist and other left-wing unionists. For the ILWU's multiracial organizing in Hawaii, see Charles P. Larrowe, *Harry Bridges: The Rise and Fall of Radical Labor in the United States*, New York, 1972, chapter 8 passim, and Sanford Zalburg, *A Spark is Struck! Jack Hall and the ILWU in Hawaii*, Honolulu, 1979, chapters 10 and 11 passim.

18. A similar approach, contrary to AFL policy, was taken by the International Ladies' Garment Workers' Union: see the letter by vice-president Rose Pesotta in *The New Republic*, November 1, 1943.

      The extent to which such statements varied from the enduring anti-Asian position shaped by AFL leaders at the turn of the century cannot be overstated. Energized by Gompers' extreme racism, AFL policy had featured vehement opposition to Asian immigration, the branding of the progeny of Asians and non-Asians as "invariably degenerate," the attribution of "filth," "disease," "vice, and "immorality" to Asians in America, and support for the notion that "the American people would in their just and righteous anger sweep them from the face of the earth." Alexander Saxton, "Race and the House of Labor," in Gary B. Nash and Richard Weiss, eds., *The Great Fear: Race in the Mind of America*, New York, 1970, pp. 114-115. Gompers supported the AFL's notorious pamphlet *Some Reasons for Chinese Exclusion: Meat vs. Rice, American Manhood Against Coolieism, Which Shall Survive?* (1901), which charged that "ninety-nine out of 100 Chinese are gamblers," that "the Yellow Man found it natural to lie, cheat, and murder," and that Chinese men were wont "to prey upon American girls." Philip S. Foner, *History of the Labor Movement in the United States*, Vol. III, New York, 1964, pp. 268-269. Small wonder that Gompers refused to organize Asian workers and acted to undermine the unions they sought to establish or join. His refusal to charter the Sugar Beet and Farm Laborers' Union in Oxnard, California (1903) - organized by the Japanese-Mexican Labor Association - typified the practices which persisted for decades. See Almaguer, "Racial Domination and Class Conflict in Capitalist Agriculture: The Oxnard Sugar Beet Workers' Strike of 1903." Relevant is Ronald Takaki's observation that "tragically for the American labor movement, Gompers had drawn a color line for Asians." Takaki, *Strangers from a Different Shore*, Boston, 1989, p. 200. See also the important article by Herbert Hill, "Anti-Oriental Agitation and the Rise of Working-class Racism," *Transaction: Social Sciences and Modern Society*, Vol. 10 (1973), pp. 43-54.

Part V: African-Americans

The documents which follow survey statements by African-Americans on the situation of Asians in the United States. While several contributions have been placed in other sections of the current volume, it has been thought useful to highlight the remarks of African-American observers below, as indication of the sentiments of one oppressed group about another. The first several documents are taken from letters appearing in *Frederick Douglass' Paper* during the 1850's [Documents 1-3]. Another of the famed orator's journals, *Douglass' Monthly*, offered comment on Chinese-related issues before the Civil War (commonly linked to abolitionist themes) [Document 4]. Frederick Douglass' "Composite Nation" speech [Document 5], given in 1869, is a significant assessment of American nationality. Articles which follow express diverse concerns over the treatment of the Chinese and the impact of Chinese immigration on Black workers. A meeting held before the founding of the Colored National Labor Union in 1869 adopted a statement on that score [Document 6]. William H. Hall, CNLU organizer and frequent contributor to *The Elevator* of San Francisco, opposed harassment of the Chinese, while cautioning that employers would use them to lower Southern wage scales [Document 7]. The *Missionary Record* [Document 8], on the other hand, welcomed the Chinese precisely because their presence would facilitate the promotion of Black labor above a menial status, which the Chinese would then occupy; the editorial from *The Elevator* makes the same argument [Document 9].

On more than one occasion, articles and letters sympathetic to the Chinese appeared in *The New Era* [Document 10], a paper eventually edited by Frederick Douglass.[1] These reflected the broadmindedness of Douglass himself, who continued to offer his vision of a "composite nation" [Document 11]. As the 1870's unfolded, the Bay Area's *The Elevator* kept up with the debate on Chinese immigration, without approximating Douglass' view. Despite its editors' hostility, the paper continued to publish opinions against exclusion [Document 12]. Its editorials, however, became stridently anti-Chinese as the atmosphere of intolerance mounted in San Francisco [Documents 13a-c].

1

Letters from "Nubia," a San Francisco correspondent, appeared in Frederick Douglass' Paper, *founded by the outstanding abolitionist and statesman in 1851 as the successor to* The North Star.[2] *Below, the writer expresses both sympathy for and suspicion of the Chinese in San Francisco.*

....San Francisco presents many features that no city in the Union presents. Its population is composed of almost every nation under heaven. Here is to be seen at a single glance every nation in miniature. - The Chinese form about one-eighth of the population. They exhibit a most grotesque appearance. Their "unmentionables" are either exceedingly roomy or very close fitting. The heads of the males are shaved, with the exception of the top, the hair from which is formed into a plaited tail, resembling "pig tail tobacco." Their habits are filthy, and their features usually devoid of expression. The whites are greatly alarmed at their rapid increase. They are very badly treated here. Every boy considers them lawful prey for his boyish pranks. They have no friends, unless it is the colored people, who treat every body well, even their enemies....

Letter from Nubia, *Frederick Douglass' Paper*, September 22, 1854

2

An emphasis on the dire consequences for African-Americans of official mistreatment of the Chinese accompanied Nubia's coverage of the exclusion issue.

The Legislature is in session. Mr. Flint (one of the members) asked leave to introduce a bill to prevent Chinese and all others not eligible to citizenship, from holding mining claims.[3] If the bill should pass, it will strike a terrible blow at the colored miners, some of whom are in possession of the best claims in the State....

The Chinese have taken the places of the colored people, as victims of oppression. - The poor Chinese are, indeed, a wretched looking set; that they are filthy, immoral and licentious - according to our notions of such things - is unquestionable. But these vices do not justify the whites in oppressing them. The Chinese consider themselves the first people in the world in respect to civilization, and regard the Americans as mere heathen, compared with themselves. - The Chinaman, under the most favorable aspects, is calculated to excite a smile. His vacant Know Nothing face is expressive of nothing but stupidity. His hair is shaved, with the exception of a little at the top of the head; this is formed into a tail, which trails on the ground. His unmentionables resemble a couple of potato sacks sewed together.

Letter from Nubia, *Frederick Douglass' Paper*, April 6, 1855

3

The denial to Chinese (and others unable to obtain citizenship) of the right to establish gold mine claims inspired the concern of Black Californians over the potential deployment of slaves in that state's gold industry during the 1850's.[4] The integrity of the new state's "free soil" status was apparently not assured. Evident in the letter, as in the others excerpted above, is an acceptance of certain anti-Chinese assumptions.

....The Legislature is still is session. Mr. Flint's Bill, to "prevent the Chinese and all others not eligible to citizenship from holding mining claims," has been published. The Chinese cannot be effected half so much by the passage of this bill, as the colored people. The most of the Chinese are worked as "coolies," and are satisfied to make from one to two dollars per day, as it costs them little or nothing to live. The same objections cannot be urged against the colored people, as are urged against the Chinese, viz.: that their habits and customs entirely prevent their amalgamation with Americans; that they degrade labor, because their wants are so few, that they can afford to work for a third of what is necessary to support an American. I am apprehensive that the real object of this bill is to enable owners of slaves to work them in the mines - for, it must be recollected that California is not altogether a free State. (See the so called, Fugitive Slave Bill of California, enacted in 1852, which provides that all slaves brought into the State prior to its admission into the Union, shall be considered subject to their masters for one year.) This privilege the Legislature has extended from year to year, so that at this moment, it is not more free than it was in 1852. My apprehensions are grounded upon the fact, that slaveholders are prevented from taking up claims for their own benefit, on account of their slaves. This is obviously, just for the reason that a slaveholder with a hundred slaves could occupy a 101 mining claim, to the great injury of northern men. This bill allows others (white men) to hold claims for them, (Chinese and negroes.) Thus, it will be seen, by the passage of this bill, that capitalists can hold claims for their coolies, and slaveholders for their slaves....

Letter from Nubia, *Frederick Douglass' Paper*, April 13, 1855

4

> *Douglass' Monthly, a paper edited at Rochester, N.Y. from 1859 to 1863, made occasional reference to the Chinese in a number of contexts - religious, political, social - tied in with the contemporary sharpening battle lines between freedom and slavery. Here, Douglass speaks of the hypocrisy of clergymen who engaged in missionary work in China while shutting their eyes to the sins of slaveholders.*[5]

The venerable and pious John Angel James, who, during more than a half a century, has discharged the duties of a pastor in Birmingham, England, to the same congregation, and has connected his name with most of the benevolent movements of Great Britain during the last thirty years, now calls upon the American churches to avail themselves of the opening made by British cannon for the entrance of the gospel into China. His letter, published in the *Independent* of last week, is a document quite remarkable as coming from a man so well stricken in years. It is alive with zeal, earnestness, hope and enthusiasm, such as a man of thirty might feel under the first awakening of his spiritual nature. Time has done little to quench the ardor of his religious feeling, or his spirit of religious enterprize. He speaks for a cause which reaches eternity, and speaks with his whole heart.

Nevertheless, we think he has spoken to but little effect in the direction of the main purpose of his epistle. His letter contains a few words which cannot be otherwise distasteful to the Evangelical Christians of America. He tears open the great moral and religious "wounds, bruises, and putrifying sores" of America. He removes the polished marble and exposes the rottenness and dead men's bones of American slavery. This offense of his, this irreverence, this meddling with what does not concern him, will very effectually bar the minds of our mind-your-own-business-Christians against his pious missionary suggestions. Mr. James approaches his American brethren with much meekness and humility; but these will hardly excuse the offence already mentioned. - It is all well enough for Evangelical Christians to meddle with the religion and social arrangements of China; but for a venerable English clergyman to call attention to abuses in this Evangelical Christian country, is an impertinence no amount of devotion to the cause of evangelical religion can excuse....

Upon the whole, we do not regret anything which hinders the spread of our American slaveholding religion, or weakens its strength and respectability at home or abroad. It will be no great loss to China if she remains destitute of a religion which steals the babe from the mother, and makes merchandize of the image of God. A church which fellowships the Imp of Hell, who lashes the slave to toil, and pockets the earnings of his blood and sweat, should be confined to a very small corner of our globe. We have no manner of respect either for such a church or for its religion. -And just such a church as this, is the Evangelical Church of America. Her ministers, North and South, are "dumb dogs," and her communion a communion of men-stealers. Once in a while we hear a prayer for universal freedom, but evidently more in apology for the slaveholder than in sympathy for the slave - more as a defence against the charge of pro slavery, than as an earnest outburst of heartfelt compassion for those in chains.

The Rev. John Angel James makes altogether too much of our recent revival of religion, in his appeal. In this, however, he has only fallen into an error, which even those who are better provided than he with the means of forming an intelligent opinion of its character, have fallen into. He looks upon it as an unusual work of grace, a peculiar mark of Divine favor, a genuine regeneration, a vast step towards the destruction of the ways and works of the Devil, when in fact it has left our religious people more at peace with themselves, and with oppression, than they were before, and less disposed to cast out slavery from Christian communion than ever. Both the American Board of Commissioners, and the American Tract Society, are more confirmed in this slaveholding policy than ever, since the revival. In view of the pro-slavery attitude of the American churches, we cannot but feel that every such appeal to them for assistance in the work of evangelizing the world, as that now made, is hurtful to the cause of true religion, in that it assumes that a church can be dead to the claims of humanity at home, and alive to those claims abroad; that a church can be steeped to the lips in guilt of slaveholding, and yet profoundly concerned for the salvation of souls; that men can serve God and Mammon at the same time; that God will be pleased to see their uplifted hands, though they be stained with blood.

The effect of such recognition is bad. Mr. James is a burning and shining light among Congregational Christians in England. That such a man, with all his known piety and benevolence, calls upon American churches, as if they were really Christian churches, to help in making China a Christian country, they will take as another evidence of their goodness. Upon no point are the Christian people of Great Britain more united, than on that which affirms the utter sinfulness of slavery. They hate, loathe and detest it, and pray for its abolition. Thousands of them would be willing to give a portion of their means of living, if, by that, they could purchase the freedom of the American bondman; and yet in one way or another British religious influence is constantly given against the slave and in favor of slavery. It is in the power of the British religious Press and Pulpit to abolish slavery in America. -Those two powers could make slavery an outlaw the world over. Let the British Press and Pulpit but make slaveholding stand with kindred crimes, and refuse in any way to recognize the Christianity of those who deal in the bodies and the souls of men, and slavery would receive a blow which would send it staggering to its grave. It would cheer and encourage the hearts of those who are struggling to free the church here from the guilt of slavery. But to this hour, those who have separated themselves from pro-slavery churches, such as the Wesleyans and Free Mission Baptists, have failed of British recognition, while correspondence, and other tokens of fellowship, are kept up with those churches which still fellowship and defend slavery.

"America Called Upon to Send Evangelical Missionaries to China," *Douglass' Monthly*, February 1859

5

The views of Frederick Douglass on the Chinese question were best articulated in the "Composite Nation" speech, delivered in Boston in 1869. Douglass rejected exclusion as undemocratic and un-American, a break with tradition and a contradiction of the assimilated "composite nationality" that the people of the United States had become. Confident that the Chinese would not long accept the servile status envisioned for them by Southern planters, Douglass proposed investing them with all rights, including the right to vote.[6]

...It is thought by many, and said by some, that this Republic has already seen its best days; that the historian may now write the story of its decline and fall.

Two classes of men are just now especially afflicted with such forebodings. The first are those who are croakers by nature - the men who have a taste for funerals, and especially National funerals. They never see the bright side of anything and probably never will. Like the raven in the lines of Edgar A. Poe they have learned two words, and these are "never more." They usually begin by telling us what we never shall see. Their little speeches are about as follows: You will *never* see such Statesmen in the councils of the nation as Clay, Calhoun and Webster. You will *never* see the South morally reconstructed and our once happy people again united. You will *never* see the Government harmonious and successful while in the hands of different races. You will *never* make the negro work without a master, or make him an intelligent voter, or a good and useful citizen. This last *never* is generally the parent of all the other little nevers that follow.

During the late contest for the Union, the air was full of nevers, every one of which was contradicted and put to shame by the result, and I doubt not that most of those we now hear in our troubled air, will meet the same fate.

It is probably well for us that some of our gloomy prophets are limited in their powers, to prediction. Could they command the destructive bolt, as readily as they command the destructive word, it is hard to say what might happen to the country. They might fulfill their own gloomy prophesies. Of course it is easy to see why certain other classes of men speak hopelessly concerning us.

A Government founded upon justice, and recognizing the equal rights of all men; claiming higher authority for existence, or sanction for its laws, than *nature*, reason, and the regularly ascertained will of the people; steadily refusing to put its sword and purse in the service of any religious creed or family is a standing offense to most of the Governments of the people, and to some narrow and bigoted people among ourselves.

To those who doubt and deny the preponderance of good over evil in human nature; who think the few are made to rule, and the many to *serve*; who put rank above brotherhood, and race above humanity; who attach more importance to ancient forms than to the living realities of the present; who worship power in whatever hands it may be lodged and by whatever means it may have been obtained; our Government is a mountain of sin, and, what is worse, it seems confirmed in its transgressions.

One of the latest and most potent European prophets, one who has felt himself called upon for a special deliverance concerning us and our destiny as a nation, was the late Thomas Carlyle. He described us rushing to ruin, not only with determined purpose, but with desperate velocity.

How long we have been on this high road to ruin, and when we may expect to reach the terrible end our prophet, enveloped in the fogs of London, has not been pleased to tell us.

Warning and advice are not to be despised, from any quarter, and especially not from one so eminent as Mr. Carlyle; and yet Americans will find it hard to heed even men like him, if there be any in the world like him, while the animus is so apparent, better and perverse.

A man to whom despotism is Savior and Liberty the destroyer of society, - who, during the last twenty years of his life, in every contest between liberty and oppression, uniformly and promptly took sides with the oppressor; who regarded every extension of the right of suffrage, even to white men in his own country, as shooting Niagara; who gloats over deeds of cruelty, and talked of applying to the backs of men the beneficent whip, to the great delight of many, the slave drivers of America in particular, could have little sympathy with our Emancipated and progressive Republic, or with the triumphs of liberty anywhere.

But the American people can easily stand the utterances of such a man. They however have a right to be impatient and indignant at those among ourselves who turn the most hopeful portents into omens of disaster, and make themselves the ministers of despair when they should be those of hope, and help cheer on the country in the new and grand career of justice upon which it has now so nobly and bravely entered.

Of errors and defects we certainly have not less than our full share, enough to keep the reformer awake, the statesman busy, and the country in a pretty lively state of agitation for some time to come. Perfection is an object to be aimed at by all, but it is not an attribute of any form of Government. Neutrality is the law for all. Something different, something better, or something worse may come, but so far as respects our present system and form of Government, and the altitude we occupy, we need not shrink from comparison with any nation of our times. We are to-day the best fed, the best clothed, the best sheltered and the best instructed people in the world.

There was a time when even brave men might look fearfully at the destiny of the Republic. When our country was involved in a tangled network of contradictions; when vast and irreconcilable social forces fiercely disputed for ascendancy and control; when a heavy curse rested upon our very soil, defying alike the wisdom and the virtue of the people to remove it; when our professions were loudly mocked by our practice and our name was a reproach and a by word to a mocking earth; when our good ship of state, freighted with the best hopes of the oppressed of all nations, was furiously hurled against the hard and flinty rocks of derision, and every cord, bolt, beam and bend in her body quivered beneath the shock, there was some apology for doubt and despair. But that day has happily passed away. The storm has been weathered, and the portents are nearly all in our favor.

There are clouds, wind, smoke and dust and noise, over head and around, and there will always be; but no genuine thunder, with destructive bolt, menaces from any quarter of the sky.

The real trouble with us was never our system or form of Government, or the principles under lying it; but the peculiar composition of our people; the relations existing between them and the compromising spirit which controlled the ruling power of the country.

We have for a long time hesitated to adopt and may yet refuse to adopt, and carry out, the only principle which can solve that difficulty and give peace, strength and security to the Republic, *and that is* the principle of absolute *equality*.

We are a country of all extremes, ends and opposites; the most conspicuous example of composite nationality in the world. Our people defy all the ethnological and logical classifications. In races we range all the way from black to white, with intermediate shades which, as in the apocalyptic vision, no man can name a number.

In regard to creeds and faiths, the condition is no better, and no worse. Differences both as to race and to religion are evidently more likely to increase than to diminish.

We stand between the populous shores of two great oceans. Our land is capable of supporting one fifth of all the globe. Here, labor is abundant and here labor is better remunerated than any where else. All moral, social and geographical causes, conspire to bring to us the peoples of all other over populated countries.

Europe and Africa are already here, and the Indian was here before either. He stands to-day between the two extremes of black and white, too proud to claim fraternity with either, and yet too weak to with stand the power of either. Heretofore the policy of our government has been governed by race pride, rather than by wisdom. Until recently, neither the Indian nor the negro has been treated as a part of the body politic. No attempt has been made to inspire either with a sentiment of patriotism, but the hearts of both races have been diligently sown with the dangerous seeds of discontent and hatred.

The policy of keeping the Indians to themselves, has kept the tomahawk and scalping knife busy upon our borders, and has cost us largely in blood and treasure. Our treatment of the negro has slacked humanity, and filled the country with agitation and ill-feeling and brought the nation to the verge of ruin.

Before the relations of these two races are satisfactorily settled, and in spite of all opposition, a new race is making its appearance within our borders, and claiming attention. It is estimated that not less than one-hundred thousand Chinamen are now within the limits of the United States. Several years ago every vessel, large or small, of steam or sail, bound to our Pacific coast and hailing from the Flowery kingdom, added to the number and strength of this element of our population.

Men differ widely as to the magnitude of this potential Chinese immigration. The fact that by the late treaty with China, we bind ourselves to receive immigrants from that country only as the subjects of the Emperor, and by the construction, at least, are bound not to naturalize them, and the further fact that Chinamen themselves have a superstitious devotion to their country and an aversion to permanent location in any other, contracting even to have their bones carried back should they die abroad, and from the fact that many have returned to China, and the still more stubborn that resistance to their coming has increased rather than diminished, it is inferred that we shall never have a large Chinese population in America. This however is not my opinion.

It may be admitted that these reasons, and others, may check and moderate the tide of immigration; but it is absurd to think that they will do more than this. Counting their number now, by the thousands, the time is not remote when they will count them by the millions. The Emperor's hold upon the Chinaman may be strong, but the Chinaman's hold upon himself is stronger.

Treaties against naturalization, like all other treaties, are limited by circumstances. As to the superstitious attachment of the Chinese to China, that, like all other superstitions, will dissolve in the light and heat of truth and experience. The Chinaman may be a bigot, but it does not follow that he will continue to be one, tomorrow. He is a man, and will be very likely to act like a man. He will not be long in finding out that a country which is good enough to live in, is good enough to die in; and that a soil that was good enough to hold his body while alive, will be good enough to hold his bones when he is dead.

Those who doubt a large immigration, should remember that the past furnishes no criterion as a basis of calculation. We live under new and improved conditions of migration, and these conditions are constantly improving. America is no longer an obscure and inaccessible country. Our ships are in every sea, our commerce in every port, our language is heard all around the globe, steam and lightning have revolutionized the whole domain of human thought, changed all geographical relations, make a day of the present seem equal to a thousand years of the past, and the continent that Columbus only conjectured four centuries ago is now the center of the world.

I believe that Chinese immigration on a large scale will yet be our irrepressible fact. The spirit of race pride will not always prevail. The reasons for this opinion are obvious; China is a vastly overcrowded country. Her people press against each other like cattle in a rail car. Many live upon the water, and have laid out streets upon the waves. Men, like bees, want elbow room. When the hive is overcrowded, the bees will swarm, and will be likely to take up their abode where they find the best prospect for honey. In matters of this sort, men are very much like bees. Hunger will not be quietly endured, even in the celestial empire, when it is once generally known that there is bread enough and to spare in America. What Satan said of Job is true of the

Chinaman, as well as of other men, "All that a man hath will he give for his life." They will come here to live where they know the means of living are in abundance.

The same mighty forces which have swept to our shores the overflowing populations of Europe; which have reduced the people of Ireland three millions below its normal standard; will operate in a similar manner upon the hungry population of China and other parts of Asia. Home has its charms, and native land has its charms, but hunger, oppression, and destitution, will dissolve these charms and send men in search of new countries and new homes.

Not only is there a Chinese motive behind this probable immigration, but there is also an American motive which will play its part, one which will be all the more active and energetic because there is in it an element of pride, of bitterness, and revenge.

Southern gentlemen who led in the late rebellion, have not parted with their convictions at this point, any more than at others. They want to be independent of the negro. They believed in slavery and they believe in it still. They believed in an aristocratic class and they believe in it still, and though they have lost slavery, one element essential to such a class, they still have two important conditions to the reconstruction of that class. They have intelligence and they have land. Of these, the land is the more important. They cling to it with all the tenacity of a cherished superstition. They will neither sell to the negro, nor let the carpet bagger have it in peace, but are determined to hold it for themselves and their children forever. They have not yet learned that when a principle is gone, the incident must go also; that what was wise and proper under slavery, is foolish and mischievous in a state of general liberty; that the old bottles are worthless when the new wine has come; but they have found that land is a doubtful benefit where there are no hands to till it.

Hence these gentlemen have turned their attention to the Celestial Empire. They would rather have laborers who will work for nothing; but as they cannot get the negroes on these terms, they want Chinamen who, they hope, will work for next to nothing.

Companies and associations may yet be formed to promote this Mongolian invasion. The loss of the negro is to gain them, the Chinese; and if the thing works will, abolition, in their opinion, will have proved itself to be another blessing in disguise. To the statesman it will mean Southern independence. To the pulpit it will be the hand of Providence, and bring about the time of the universal dominion of the Christian religion. To all but the Chinaman and the negro, it will mean wealth, ease and luxury.

But alas, for all the selfish inventions and dreams of men! The Chinaman will not long be willing to wear the cast off shoes of the negro, and if he refuses, there will be trouble again. The negro worked and took his pay in religion and the lash. The Chinaman is a different article and will want the cash. He may, like the negro, accept Christianity, but unlike the negro he will not care to pay for it in labor under the lash. He had the golden rule in substance, five hundred years before the coming of Christ, and has notions of justice that are not to be confused or bewildered by any of our *"Cursed by Canaan"* religion.

Nevertheless, the experiment will be tried. So far as getting the Chinese into our country is concerned, it will yet be a success. This elephant will be drawn by our Southern brethren, though they will hardly know in the end what to do with him.

Appreciation of the value of Chinamen as laborers will, I apprehend, become general in this country. The North was never indifferent to Southern influence and example, and it will not be so in this instance.

The Chinese in themselves have first rate recommendations. They are industrious, docile, cleanly, frugal; they are dexterous of hand, patient of toil, marvelously gifted in the power of imitation, and have but few wants. Those who have carefully observed their habits in California, say they can subsist upon what would be almost starvation to others.

The conclusion of the whole will be that they will want to come to us, and as we become more liberal, we shall want them to come, and what we want will normally be done.

They will no longer halt upon the shores of California. They will burrow no longer in her exhausted and deserted gold mines where they have gathered wealth from bareness, taking what others left. They will turn their backs not only upon the Celestial Empire, but upon the golden shores of the Pacific, and the wide waste of waters whose majestic waves spoke to them of home and country. They will withdraw their eyes from the glowing west and fix them upon the rising sun. They will cross the mountains, cross the plains, descend our rivers, penetrate to the heart of the country and fix their homes with us forever.

Assuming then that this immigration already has a foothold and will continue for many years to come, we have a new element in our national composition which is likely to exercise a large influence upon the thought and the action of the whole nation.

The old question as to what shall be done with the negro will have to give place to the greater question, "what shall be done with the Mongolian" and perhaps we shall see raised one even still greater question, namely, what will the Mongolian do with both the negro and the whites?

Already has the matter taken this shape in California and on the Pacific Coast generally. Already has California assumed a bitterly unfriendly attitude toward the Chinamen. Already has she stamped them as outcasts and handed them over to popular contempt and vulgar jest. Already are they the constant victims of cruel harshness and brutal violence. Already have our Celtic brothers, never slow to execute the behests of popular prejudice against the weak and defenseless, recognized in the heads of these people, fit targets for their shillalahs. Already, too, are their associations formed in avowed hostility to the Chinese.

In all this there is, of course, nothing strange. Repugnance to the presence and influence of foreigners is an ancient feeling among men. It is peculiar to no particular race or nation. It is met with not only in the conduct of one nation toward another, but in the conduct of the inhabitants of different parts of the same country, some times of the same city, and even of the same village. "Lands intersected by a narrow frith, abhor each other. Mountains interposed, make enemies of nations." To the Hindoo, every man not twice born, is Mieeka.[7] To the Greek, every man not speaking Greek, is a barbarian. To the Jew, every one not circumcised, is a gentile. To the Mahometan, every man not believing in the prophet, is a kaffe. I need not repeat here the multitude of reproachful epithets expressive of the same sentiment among ourselves. All who are not to the manor born, have been made to feel the lash and sting of these reproachful names.

For this feeling there are many apologies, for these was never yet an error, however flagrant, and hurtful, for which some plausible defense could not be framed. Chattel slavery, king craft, priest craft, pious frauds, intolerance, persecution, suicide, assassination, repudiation, and a thousand other errors and crimes, have all had their defense and apologies.

Prejudice of race and color has been equally upheld. The two best arguments in its defense are, first, the worthlessness of the class against which it is directed; and, second; that the feeling itself is entirely natural.

The way to overcome the first argument is, to work for the elevation of those deemed worthless, and thus make them worthy of regard and they will soon become worthy and not worthless. As to the natural argument it may be said, that nature has many sides. Many things are in a certain sense natural, which are neither wise nor best. It is natural to walk, but shall men therefore refuse to ride? It is natural to ride on horseback, shall men therefore refuse steam and rail? Civilization is itself a constant war upon some forces in nature; shall we therefore abandon civilization and go back to savage life?

Nature has two voices, the one high, the other low; one is in sweet accord with reason and justice, and the other apparently at war with both. The more men really know of the essential nature of things, and of the true relation of mankind, the freer they are from prejudices of every kind. The child is afraid of the giant form of his own shadow. This is natural, but he will part with his fears when he is older and wiser. So ignorance is full of prejudice, but it will disappear with enlightenment. But I pass on.

I have said that the Chinese will come, and have given some reasons why we may expect them in very large numbers in no very distant future. Do you ask, if I favor such immigration, I answer *I would*. Would you have them naturalized, and have them invested with all the rights of American citizenship? *I would*. Would you allow them to vote? *I would*. Would you allow them to hold office? *I would*.

But are there not reasons against all this? Is there not such a law or principle as that of self preservation? Does not every race owe something to itself? Should it not attend to the dictates of common sense? Should not a superior race protect itself from contact with inferior ones? Are not the white people the owners of this continent? Have they not the right to say what kind of people shall be allowed to come here and settle? Is there not such a thing as being more generous than wise? In the effort to promote civilization may we not corrupt and destroy what we have? Is it best to take on board more passengers than the ship will carry?

To all this and more I have one among many answers, altogether satisfactory to me, though I cannot promise that it will be so to you.

I submit that this question of Chinese immigration should be settled upon higher principles than those of a cold and selfish expediency. There are such things in the world as human rights. They rest upon no conventional foundation, but are external, universal, and indestructible. Among these, is the right of locomotion; the right of migration; the right which belongs to no particular race, but belongs alike to all and to all alike. It is the right you assert by staying here, and your fathers asserted by coming here. It is this great right that I assert for the Chinese and the Japanese, and for all other varieties of men equally with yourselves, now and forever. I know of no rights of race superior to the rights of humanity, and when there is a supposed conflict between human and national rights, it is safe to go to the side of humanity. I have great respect for the blue eyes and light haired races of America. They are a mighty people. In any struggle for the good things of this world they need have no fear. They have no need to doubt that they will get their full share.

But I reject the arrogant and scornful theory by which they would limit migratory rights, or any other essential human rights to themselves, and which would make them the owners of this great continent to the exclusion of all other races of men.

I want a home here not only for the negro, the mulatto and the Latin races; but I want the Asiatic to find a home here in the United States, and feel at home here, both for his sake and for ours. Right wrongs no man. If respect is had to majorities, the fact that only one fifth of the population of the globe is white, the other four fifths are colored, ought to have some weight and influence in disposing of this and similar questions. It would be a sad reflection upon the laws of nature and upon the idea of justice, to say nothing of a common Creator, if four-fifths of mankind were deprived of the rights of migration to make room for the one fifth. If the white race may exclude all other races from this continent, it may rightfully do the same in respect to all other lands, islands, capes and continents, and thus have all the world to itself. Thus what would seem to belong to the whole, would become the property only of a part. So much for what is right, now let us see what is wise.

And here I hold that a liberal and brotherly welcome to all who are likely to come to the United States is the only wise policy which this nation can adopt.

It has been thoughtfully observed, that every nation, owing to its peculiar character, and composition, has a definite mission in the world. What that mission is, and what policy is best adapted to assist in its fulfillment, is the business of its people and its statesmen to know, and knowing, to make a noble use of said knowledge.

I need not stop here to name or describe the missions of other and more ancient nationalities. Ours seems plain and unmistakable. Our geographical position, our relation to the outside world, our fundamental principles of government, world-embracing in their scope and character, our vast resources, requiring all manner of labor to develop them, and our already existing composite population, all conspire to one grand end, and that is to make us the most perfect national illustration of the unity and dignity of the human family that the world has ever seen.

In whatever else other nations may have been great and grand, our greatness and grandeur will be found in the faithful application of the principle of perfect civil equality to the people of all races and of all creeds, and to men of no creeds. We are not only bound to this position by our organic structure and by our revolutionary antecedents, but by the genius of our people. Gathered here from all quarters of the globe by a common aspiration for national liberty as against caste, divine right government and privileged classes, it would be unwise to be found fighting against ourselves and among ourselves; it would be madness to set up any one race above another, or one religion above another, or proscribe any on account of race, color or creed.

The apprehension that we shall be swamped or swallowed up by Mongolian civilization; that the Caucasian race may not be able to hold their own against that vast incoming population, does not seem entitled to much respect. Though they come as the waves come, we shall be all the stronger if we receive them as friends and give them a reason for loving our country and our institutions. They will find here a deeply rooted, indigenous, growing civilization, augmented by an ever-increasing stream of immigration from Europe; and possession is nine points of the law, in this case, as well as in others. They will come as strangers. We are at home. They will come to us, not we to them. They will come in their weakness, we shall meet them in our strength. They will come as individuals, we will meet them in multitudes, and with all the advantages of organization. Chinese children are in American schools in San Francisco. None of our children are in Chinese schools, and probably never will be, though in some things they might well teach us valuable lessons. Contact with these yellow children of the Celestial Empire would convince us that the points of human difference, great as they, upon first sight, seem, are as nothing compared with the points of human agreement. Such contact would remove mountains of prejudice.

It is said that it is not good for man to be alone. This is true not only in the sense in which our women's rights friends so zealously and wisely teach, but it is true as to nations.

The voice of civilization speaks an unmistakable language against the isolation of families, nations and races, and pleads for composite nationality as essential to her triumphs.

Those races of men which have maintained the most separate and distinct existence for the longest periods of time; which have had the least intercourse with other races of men, are a standing confirmation of the folly of isolation. The very soil of the national mind becomes in such cases barren, and can only be resuscitated by assistance from without.

Look at England, whose mighty power is now felt, and for centuries has been felt, all around the world. It is worthy of special remark, that precisely those parts of that proud Island which have received the largest and most diverse populations, are today the parts most distinguished for industry, enterprise, invention and general enlightenment. In Wales, and in the Highlands of Scotland the boast is made of their pure blood and that they were never conquered, but no man can contemplate them without wishing they had been conquered. They are far in the rear of every other part of the English realm in all the comforts and conveniences of life, as well as in mental and physical development. Neither law nor learning descends to us from the mountains of Wales or from the Highlands of Scotland. The ancient Briton whom Julius Caesar would not have as a slave, is not to be compared with the round, burly, aplitudinous Englishman in many of the qualities of desirable manhood.

The theory that each race of men has some special faculty, some peculiar gift or quality of mind or heart, needed to the perfection and happiness of the whole is a broad and beneficent theory, and, besides its beneficence, has, in its support, the voice of experience. Nobody doubts this theory when applied to animals and plants, and no one can show that it is not equally true when applied to races.

All great qualities are never found in any one man or in any one race. The whole of humanity, like the whole of everything else, is ever greater than a part. Men only know themselves by knowing others, and contact is essential to this knowledge. In one race we perceive the predominance of imagination; in another, like the Chinese, we remark its total absence. In one people, we have the reasoning faculty, in another, for music; in another exists courage; in another, great physical vigor, and so on through the whole list of human qualities. All are needed to temper, modify, round and complete.

Not the least among the arguments whose consideration should dispose to welcome among us the peoples of all countries, nationalities and colors, is the fact that all races and varieties of men are improvable. This is the grand distinguishing attribute of humanity and separates man from all other animals. If it could be shown that any particular race of men are literally incapable of improvement, we might hesitate to welcome them here. But no such men are anywhere to be found, and if there were, it is not likely that they would ever trouble us with their presence. The fact that the Chinese and other nations desire to come and do come, is a proof of their capacity for improvement and of their fitness to come.

We should take council of both nature and art in the consideration of this question. When the architect intends a grand structure, he makes the foundation broad and strong. We should imitate this prudence in laying the foundation of the future Republic. There is a law of harmony in all departments of nature. The oak is in the acorn. The career and destiny of individual men are enfolded in the elements of which they are composed. The same is true of a nation. It will be something or it will be nothing. It will be great, or it will be small, according to its own essential qualities. As these are rich and varied, or poor and simple, slender and feeble, broad and strong, so will be the life and destiny of the nation itself. The stream cannot rise higher than its source. The ship cannot sail faster than the wind. The flight of the arrow depends upon the strength and elasticity of the bow, and as with these, so with a nation.

If we would reach a degree of civilization higher and grander than any yet attained, we should welcome to our ample continent all nations, kindreds, tongues and peoples; and as fast as they learn our language and comprehend the duties of citizenship, we should incorporate them into the American body politic. The outspread wing of the American eagle are broad enough to shelter all who are likely to come.

As a matter of selfish policy, leaving right and humanity out of the question, we cannot wisely pursue any other course. Other Governments mainly depend for security upon the sword; ours depends mainly upon the friendship of its people. In all matters, - in time of peace, in time of war, and at all times, it makes its appeal to all the people, and to all classes of the people. Its strength lies in their friendship and cheerful support in every time of need, and that policy is a mad one which would reduce the number of its friends by excluding those who would come, or by alienating those who are already here.

Our Republic is itself a strong argument in favor of composite nationality. It is no disparagement to Americans of English descent, to affirm that much of the wealth, leisure, culture, refinement and civilization of the country are due to the arm of the negro and the muscle of the Irishman. Without these and the wealth created by their sturdy toil, English civilization had still lingered this side of the Alleghanies, and the wolf still be howling on their summits.

To no class of our population are we more indebted to valuable qualities of head, heart and hand than to the German. Say what we will of their lager, their smoke and their metaphysics, they have brought to us a fresh, vigorous and childlike nature; a boundless facility in the acquisition of knowledge; a subtle and far-reaching intellect, and a fearless love of truth. Though remarkable for patient and laborious thought the true German is a joyous child of freedom, fond of manly sports, a lover of music, and a happy man generally. Though he never forgets that he is a German, he never fails to remember that he is an American.

A Frenchman comes here to make money, and that is about all that need be said of him. He is only a Frenchman. He neither learns our language nor loves our country. His hand is on our pocket and his eye on Paris. He gets what he wants, and like a sensible Frenchman, returns to France to spend it.

Now let me answer briefly some objections to the general scope of my arguments. I am told that science is against me; that races are not all of one origin, and that the unity theory of human origin has been exploded. I admit that this is a question that has two sides. It is impossible to trace the threads of human history sufficiently near their starting point to know much about the origin of races.

In disposing of this question whether we shall welcome or repel immigration from China, Japan, or elsewhere, we may leave the differences among the theological doctors to be settled by themselves.

Whether man originated at one time and one or another place; whether there was one Adam or five, or five hundred, does not affect the question.

The great right of migration and the great wisdom of incorporating foreign elements into our body politic, are founded not upon any genealogical or ethnological theory, however learned, but upon the broad fact of a common human nature.

Man is man the world over. This fact is affirmed and admitted in any effort to deny it. The sentiments we exhibit, whether love or hate, confidence or fear, respect or contempt, will always imply a like humanity. A smile or a tear has no nationality; joy and sorrow speak alike in all nations, and they, above all the confusion of tongues, proclaim the brotherhood of man.

It is objected to the Chinaman that he is secretive and treacherous, and will not tell the truth when he thinks it for his interest to tell a lie. There may be truth in all this; it sounds very much like the account of man's heart given in the creeds. If he will not tell the truth, except when it is for his interest to do so, let us make it for his interest to tell the truth. We can do it by applying to him the same principle of justice that we apply to ourselves.

But I doubt if the Chinese are more untruthful than other people. At this point I have one certain test. Mankind are not held together by lies. Trust is the foundation of society. Where there is no trust there can be no society. Where there is society, there is trust, and where there is trust, there is something upon which it is supported. Now a people who have confided in each other for five thousand years; who have extended their empire in all directions till it embraces one-fifth of the population of the globe; who hold important commercial relations with all nations; who are now entering into treaty stipulations with ourselves, and with all the great European powers, cannot be a nation of cheats and liars, but must have some respect for veracity. The very existence of China for so long a period, and her progress in civilization, are proofs of her truthfulness. But it is said that the Chinese is a heathen, and that he will introduce his heathen rights and superstitions here. This is the last objection which should come from those who profess the all-conquering power of the Christian religion. If that religion cannot stand contact with the Chinese, religion or no religion, so much the worse for those who have adopted it. It is the Chinaman, not the Christian, who should be alarmed for his faith. He exposes that faith to great dangers by exposing it to the freer air of America. But shall we send missionaries to the heathen and yet deny the heathen the right to come to us? I think a few honest believers in the teachings of Confucius would be well employed in expounding his doctrines among us.

The next objection to the Chinese is that he cannot be induced to swear by the Bible. This is to me one of his best recommendations. The American people will swear by anything in the heavens above or in the earth beneath. We are a nation of swearers. We swear by a book whose most authoritative command is to swear not at all.

It is not of so much importance what a man swears by, as what he swears to, and if the Chinaman is so true to his convictions that he cannot be tempted or even coerced into so popular a custom as swearing by the Bible, he gives good evidence of his integrity and his veracity.

Let the Chinaman come; he will help to augment the national wealth. He will help to develop our boundless resources; he will help to pay off our national debt; he will help to lighten the burden of national taxation; he will give us the benefit of his skill as a manufacturer and tiller of the soil, in which he is unsurpassed.

Even the matter of religious liberty, which has cost the world more tears, more blood and more agony, than any other interest, will be helped by his presence. I know of no church, however tolerant; of no priesthood, however enlightened, which could be safely trusted with the tremendous power which universal conformity would confer. We should welcome all men of every shade of religious opinion, as among the best means of checking the arrogance and intolerance which are the almost inevitable concomitants of general conformity. Religious liberty always flourishes best amid the clash and competition of rival religious creeds.

To the mind of superficial men, the fusion of different races has already brought disaster and ruin upon the country. The poor negro has been charged with all our woes. In the haste of these men they forget that our trouble was not ethnographical, but moral, that it was not a difference of complexion, but a difference of conviction. It was not the Ethiopian as a man, but the Ethiopian as a slave and a coveted article of merchandise, that gave us trouble.

I close these remarks as I began. If our action shall be in accordance with the principles of justice, liberty, and perfect human equality, no eloquence can adequately portray the greatness and grandeur of the future of the Republic.

We shall spread the network of our science and civilization over all who seek their shelter whether from Asia, Africa, or the Isles of the sea. We shall mold them all, each after his kind, into Americans; Indian and Celt, negro and Saxon, Latin and Teuton, Mongolian and Caucasian, Jew and Gentile, all shall here bow to the same law, speak the same language, support the same government, enjoy the same liberty, vibrate with the same national enthusiasm, and seek the same national ends.

Frederick Douglass, *Composite Nation*, 1869. Typescript in possession of the editors; original in the Douglass Papers, Library of Congress, microfilm, Reel 14. See also John W. Blassingame and John R. McKivigan, ed., *The Frederick Douglass Papers*, Series One, Volume 4: 1864-1880, New Haven, 1991, pp. 240-259]

6

The call to the founding convention of the Colored National Labor Union [see Part IV] made reference to the implications of Chinese immigration for Black labor. Of interest is the wording of the relevant clause, which appears directed against employers intent on manipulating and debasing Chinese workers.[8]

At a State Labor Convention of the Colored men of Maryland, held July 20th, 1869, it was unanimously resolved that a National Labor Convention be called to meet in the Union League Hall, City of Washington, D.C., on the first Monday in December, 1869, to consider:

1st - The present status of Colored Labor in the United States, and its relationship to American Industry.

2nd - To adopt such rules and devise such means as will systematically and effectually organize all the departments of said labor, and make it the more productive in its new relationship to capital, and consolidate the colored working men of the several States to act in co-operation with our white fellow workingmen, in every State and Territory in the Union, who are opposed to distinction in the apprenticeship laws, on account of color, and to so act co-operatively until the necessity for separate organizations shall be deemed unnecessary.

3rd - To consider the question of the importation of contract Coolie labor and its effect upon American labor, and to petition Congress for the adoption of such laws as will prevent its being a system of slavery.

4th - And to adopt such other means as will best advance the interest of the colored mechanics and workingmen of the whole country.

Fellow-Citizens: You cannot place too great an estimate upon the important objects this Convention is called to consider, viz.: your industrial interests. In the greater portion of the United States, colored men are excluded from the United States on account of their color.

The laboring man, in a large portion of the Southern States, by a systematic understanding prevailing there, is unjustly deprived of the price of his labor, and in localities far removed from the Courts of Justice is forced to endure wrongs and oppression worse than slavery.

By falsely representing the laborers of the South, certain interested writers and journals are striving to bring contract Chinese or Coolie labor, into popular favor there, thus forcing American laborers to work at Coolie wages or starve....

"National Labor Convention of the Colored Men of the United States," *The Elevator*, October 15, 1869

7

William H. Hall's views are noteworthy. A prominent Black San Franciscan, he played leading roles in many organizations from the virtual inception of California statehood (1850) through the late nineteenth century. He was associated with the Black press, with local business endeavors, and with the Colored National Labor Union. Hall served as president of the 1857 state convention of Colored Citizens. In the pages of The Elevator,[9] *an African-American paper of long standing (launched originally as the organ of the "Executive Committee of California"), he expressed himself often on the Chinese issue. In the letter below, written from Hamilton, Nevada, his opposition to Chinese persecution and his support for the right of immigration are tempered with the fear that the newcomers would be used to undercut the bargaining position of African-Americans in the South.*[10]

Mr. Editor, - In presenting my views in a series of articles on the expediency of encouraging a large immigration of Chinese in the Southern States, it was not my object to join in the prevailing hue and cry raised throughout the Pacific slope, by the ignorant Democracy, against affording lawful protection to these people in their various pursuits. Like all other loyal Americans, I have ever regarded the amenities of treaty stipulations made between my own government and that of the Celestial Empire of the most sacred and binding force, whereby those claiming to be the superior race of people, should treat their inferiors civilly and fairly, guarding their rights and protecting their persons and property in the same proportion as our citizens demand under the Chinese government. I am still further convinced that the employment of cheap Chinese labor in the States of California, Oregon, Nevada, and all the adjacent territories, where a boundless mineral and agricultural resource is open to industry, and where the population is meagre and heterogeneous which has been attracted to the mountain wilds of new countries, by the desire to obtain sudden wealth, and failing in that object has refused to work insignificant mines, or attempt to reclaim the innumerable acres of swamp land which the patient toil of these people could turn into gold, cotton, silk, rice and tea, thus outstripping the European and American in returning revenue and products from a soil considered useless. But what is seen of advantage to be derived from these people employed on the Pacific side, does not create the same necessity on the Atlantic side, especially in the Southern States, because they have millions of laborers, whose subsistence through life - whose present and future political and social conditions depends upon the chances now offered, to escape the misery and poverty years of slavery entailed upon them. No other race of people upon the score of economy, expediency or revenge should be allowed to compete with the freedmen in the field of labor, until their industry is fairly tested, and if proven successful to go towards their elevation and independence - because the intelligent world must remember that the poor negroes just blessed with freedom, are yet...under the influence of their late masters in devising plans of livelihood; they can deprive them of work - close every avenue of that ease and comfort which the idea of liberty inflames the ignorant mind, and make them believe that their new condition has rendered the change in the labor element essential to the prosperity of the land owners. It is to remove this tremendous control of the dominant and haughty race over the powerless and subject race, and make each others interest identical, that I have opposed Chinese immigration among my defenceless race....

W.H. Hall, "Freedmen versus Chinamen," Letter to *The Elevator*, October 29, 1869

8

Accepting the use of Chinese workers as necessary, and as beneficial to the elevation of African-Americans from the bottom rungs, the Missionary Record *(a Black paper published in Charleston, South Carolina) took issue with anti-immigration arguments, in the context of Reconstruction era struggles for the right to own land and enjoy improved working conditions.*[11]

Just now the Southern people are regaling themselves with the chimera that they will bring coolies here and dispense with colored laborers, and will give no encouragement to colored people. We suggest to them that the negro does not care a fig how many they bring. South Carolina has (19,000,000) nineteen millions of acres of land and only about four and a half millions of this in cultivation. There is room for a hundred thousand of them, and no detriment to the people who are here. We believe it one of the best events that can take place in the South for the colored people, because when coolie labor comes into competition, it will force them to buy lands of their own, and work for themselves, it will by that means compel good wages to be paid for labor performed for the cost of each coolie to the planter, by contract will be about fifteen dollars per month, and they will be compelled to keep them for a term of years; then they cannot discharge them at will as they do colored help. This rise of wages will help the colored people to fix a standard for their labor, which they greatly need just now. The highest average of wages paid by planters is not more than eight dollars per month, and in most cases it is not that, when provisions are taken out, and the real value of purchases considered; there are thousands of hands working now who do not really get 12 cents a day for the work they perform for the planters, while the amount of labor performed is worth to them two dollars, and three dollars per day - computing the price of cotton and returns made to the owner. Think of a planter realizing fifteen and twenty thousand dollars a year off his cotton crop, for which he has possibly paid his hands five hundred dollars, and the actual cost to him all told about seven hundred dollars - twelve hundred dollars producing $15,000 dollars.

There is now no standard of wages fixed for laborers in this State, every one makes such a bargain as he can. The colored people, without education, or comprehension as to what is actually necessary for their support and their families are always behind, by virtue of the poor calculations which they make, and hence, they are always dependent on the land owner for a place to live and a place to work - and being compelled to live somewhere, and work some place, they are compelled to take whatever is offered to them, rather then starve; but when the coolies come, and their wages is fixed by contract, the colored people will have a lawful standard, by which they can compete with coolies, both in work and price of labor performed. Thousands will be driven from the plantations now cultivated, to the new and virgin soil, where they will produce double the produce they do now. Let the coolies come, it will be advantageous to the working classes to have them come!

"Bring on Your Coolies: Who Cares," *Missionary Record*, reprinted in *The Elevator*, November 26, 1869

9

The following editorial sustained the latter position and challenged the views of W.H. Hall.

In reply to our correspondent from Hamilton in reference to the laboring population of the Southern States, we will refer him to an article in the *Elevator* of 26th ultimo, copied from the *Missionary Record* of Charleston, S.C.....The editor of that paper, R.H. Cain is conversant with the South, and the condition of the people, and is deeply concerned in whatever affects the interests of his race. He also says, "there is room for a hundred thousand more laborers, and no detriment to the people who are here." What is true of South Carolina is true of all the Southern States.

Our correspondent asks - "whence did the laborers come from during the dark days of slavery, when the South produced sufficient to make our own country bloom with prosperity, and sent enough cotton, corn and tobacco to different parts of Europe to repay the luxuries our people were extravagantly enjoying?" We have shown that notwithstanding the prosperity of which our correspondent boasts, but a small portion of the land was under cultivation, and the laboring population is not half what it was, "during the dark days of slavery." The census of 1860 made the number of slaves to be about four millions. In those "dark days" as our correspondent well knows, every human being was put to work. Children, as soon as they could walk were put in the field. Women of all ages and in all conditions of life were forced to labor. Under the new regime of freedom these things are different. Young children are now sent to school instead of the cotton-field, and but a small portion of the females will be required to perform agricultural labor. Again the war has reduced the male laboring population to perhaps half its original number, either by the casualties of battle or seeking other avocations. This decrease of population will not decrease the wants of the South. A new condition of life creates new necessities, and freedom consumes more than slavery.

Mr. Hall misquotes us, whether wilfully or unintentionally, we know not - we hope the latter. We did not say, "the Germans seek more independent occupations than the South affords." The latter portion is Mr. Hall's addition. The South affords employment for all who seek it, and in all avocations, and we were speaking of the labor performed by the freedmen and the Chinese. In reference to the Irish we repeat, "we would sooner see the freedmen contending against the Mongolian than the Celt." We have failed to see those "traits of generosity" in the character of the ignorant Irish when their prejudices are excited. They are vindictive, revengeful, fiendish and malicious. Witness the scenes in New York, and the outrages by the Irish in 1863, and then talk of the "generosity of the ignorant Irish."

Another misquotation. We said, "an increase of 500,000 Chinese to the laboring population of the South could not be effected in ten years." A weekly line of steamers could not add over 50,000 a year to the population of the United States, when we make allowances for deaths and returns; for the Chinese do not come to America for a permanent residence. Our correspondent says, "the demand comes from Chicago, New York, and the woollen mills of Massachusetts." If other places offer better inducements than the South, which they undoubtedly will do, where is the probability of that region becoming overrun with hordes of Pagan Mongolians which Mr. Hall and others so much dread? The emigration from Europe to the Atlantic States shows the fallacy of such apprehensions. the number who arrived last year, the largest ever known [,] was about 375,000. The facilities for transportation are far greater than can ever be on the Pacific Ocean. A steamship leaves some port in the Atlantic States almost daily; sailing vessels comprising packet-ships, merchantmen, transient, etc., fully as often, each one bringing from two to ten hundred immigrant passengers, and the number brought does not exceed 375,000.

We are not in favor of Chinese emigration, either here or elsewhere. The country needs labor - where is it to come from? Ireland is nearly depopulated of her laboring classes, a new field is open for them in Algeria, and Lord knows, we have enough of our correspondent and Governor Seymour's friends. The German people will not become hirelings, the negro race has become decimated by the war, and there is no other source from whence labors can be obtained but Asia. There is no danger of Coolieism or peonage ever being introduced in America - Congress will guard against that, and if they come voluntarily as free laborers, we do not fear the result.

"Freedmen and Chinamen," editorial, *The Elevator*, December 17, 1869

10

In the spirit of Frederick Douglass' "Composite Nation" address, strong support for the rights of the Chinese was registered in The New Era.[12] *As it notes the irony of the presence of oppressed Irish immigrants in the anti-Chinese movement, the piece below puts the correspondent generally in the humanist tradition represented by the statements of Phillips, Douglass, and Garrison, among others.*

Based more upon the emptiness of theory than the substance of fact is yet America's boasted freedom. And as the scales of justice slowly balance for the negro, as America begins to fully comprehend that the negro is a man, prejudice must find another victim, and who more suitable than "Wo Lee and his kinsfolk?" The "vast horde of Asiatic scum" sweeping upon our western shores and penetrating to the interior must be stopped. By the ballot? No. By the unanimous protest of America's millions? No. The spirit of Ireland seems not content to rule the main seaport of the Atlantic coast, but it must stretch its riotous hands from the Battery to the Pacific's golden gate. All Ireland would howl were Castle Garden to close its doors against Irishmen; yet Ireland stands to-day with her voice raised in imprecation against this "torrent of Paganism," and with the hand of violence ready to sweep it back.

This question promises to test still further the principles of the Republic. The Chinaman, like the negro, is a patient sufferer; and America has doubtless learned ere this that such races are difficult to exterminate. Their lives possess a sort of tenacity that enables them to greatly ignore class persecution in the hopeful view the future holds out to them. It is plain that large fields of action necessarily require corresponding powers of development; and the main proof of America's completeness will lie in her willingness to receive, and her ability to mould and assimilate, her mosaic population.

In view of the vast tracts of undeveloped land now lying idle, it is evident that the great need of America is more labor. The question of overpopulation is one that will solve itself; for when our resources are balanced by equally developing powers, immigration, in accordance with the national laws that govern all political economy will cease. The principles of nature are self-adjusting. The balance hangs now between China and America. The western end is weighted down with the millions of a country overburdened with humanity, while the eastern, from its very lightness, kicks the beam. The balance must hang even. The laws of supply and demand will, as a matter of course, regulate emigration.

This is a question that will solve itself. But what promises to test American institutions is, not the quantity or quality of emigration, but rather our ability to mould, educate, and adapt these mixed masses to the free principles of our American Government. When we look forward to an entire settlement of the habitable portions of this continent, to the vast population its resources will require, and remember that they have all to become, either directly or otherwise, important elements in the structure of the republic, then, in the light of this consideration, it seems that our peculiar form of government is nothing more nor less than a well-advanced theory. The principles of equality to all men on which the declaration of Independence was based, have yet to be proven a fact. To close the doors against the immigration, or civil and political equality of any particular race, is to remove the foundations upon which the republic stands. The representative American has yet to be born; and it is unreasonable to believe, that he will be either Yankee, Negro, Chinaman, or any one particular race inhabiting this continent. The nation must, in justice to its principles, give all the varied classes of the population equal privileges before the law, and in the Government.

With this point attained, we reach at once the true principles of our Government; but there still remains a great barrier to the completeness of our Republic. The lines of social distinction must be removed. This is no question for politicians, and perhaps not for the present. But it is a problem that the future must inevitably solve. The "squeamishness" of the "superior race" may stave it off for some time. But as the country approaches nearer and nearer to the maturity of perfect development, as the races become more and more harmonized, the result must naturally be the complete removal of all social distinctions as well as political disabilities.

George Rice, "The Completeness of the Republic," Letter to the Editor of the New Era, *The New Era*, March 17, 1870

11

Douglass himself continued to contribute to the Chinese exclusion debate on the side of free immigration and anti-racism.[13]

We are a great nation - not we colored people particularly, but all of us. We are all together now. We are fellow-citizens of a common country. What a country - fortunate in its institutions, in its fifteenth amendment, in its future. We are made up of a variety of nations - Chinese, Jews, Africans, Europeans, and all sorts. These different races give the Government a powerful arm to defend it. They will vie with each other in hardship and peril, and will be united in defending it from all its enemies, whether from within or without....

The New Era, May 5, 1870

12

The following piece by an African-American woman welcomed the Chinese; editors of The Elevator *rebuked her in the same issue for failing to recognize Chinese labor competition as "the thorn festering" in "the vitals" of the American people.*

The tide of Chinese immigration setting towards America is already wonderful, is sure to...increase. Thousands if not millions of them are to be our fellow country men - our fellow citizens. What will be the effect of the mingling of these people with the Americans is no easy matter to describe. Their customs are not moulded after ours; their religion and manners belong to another age....

Many are opposed to the admission of these people upon this continent. The cry is again heard of inferiority and unfitness; mental and physical incapacity; we have become too accustomed to such clamour to be moved by it. The Chinaman is ready, willing and able to work; he seems to delight in the very hardest labor. Are these people to crush and enslave?

Already the Chinese have been subjected to outrages in the Pacific States, in Legislature and society paralleled only by those endured by the Indians and negroes in other parts of the country.

Will the land that has promised protection to all not right this wrong? Alas! for the ideal dream of liberty and equality. Alas! for the proud land that boastingly invites the criticism of the world; the plague spot is within the heart; the leperous defilement is upon its face, it if learn not justice and humanity, if it remove not this barbarism of its civilization. The influence of the Chinese upon our industry, for good cannot be doubted. There is a vast amount of work to be done. Our country is large and new. Cities are to be built; valleys are to be cultivated; mountains are to be leveled, and marshes to be drained - in doing all of which these people are to assist. They are to assist in planting the cotton and in picking it; in sowing the rice and gathering it; in short they are to become laborers to the country in general....

But, if they are to make railroads what will become of the Irishman? If they are to raise cotton what is to become of the negroes? The Irishman as he becomes fully Americanized is to occupy a higher plane in the industry of the country; while the negro, a true American, possessing all his genius and tact, is to be treated no longer as a foreigner in the land of his birth. Liberty, with more generous instinct, will make him welcome to his own; he will be exalted in his rightful station. In common with others he will figure as mechanic capitalist and professional man. But the Chinaman is to have his day of power in our country. If justice be not done him, he will no longer submit to oppression, and he may rise in arms against us, and the result will be another war.

It is the one true wisdom as well as duty to give them cordial welcome. Let us open to them our public schools and our colleges, our sabbath schools and our churches, even our homes. Let them see that our object is not to degrade but rather to elevate them, that they may form one more link in the strong chain which binds our nation together; that they may be gentle and refined in their taste; beautiful and cultivated in their pursuits; heroic in their lives; possessing all the elements that make the perfect man and citizen.

Clarendale, "The Chinese," *The Elevator*, March 8, 1873

13

In editorials, from which samples appear below, The Elevator
*increasingly reflected the influence of the bitter exclusion campaign
which unfolded in California during the 1870's.*[14]

(a)

For many years past, the general theme of conversation in this city
and even throughout our State has been that of "hard times," and many have
inquiringly asked what is the cause of all this, from whence does it arise? Are
capitalists absconding? is there an insufficient amount of money in
circulation? are we destitute of that specific amount of ingenuity which
enables us to contribute towards the necessities of a populace? is it that our
city is too immensely populated?

All these several questions have been penetrated into. Not devoid of
metaphysical reasoning, when finally it was ascertained that the welfare of our
city or State was not annihilated by any source above mentioned, but appeared
from a greater - a more obvious one to the vision and apprehension of an
enlightened race - one which we now have, and, perhaps, ever will have
occasion to repent of, even in the wary hours of senility; namely: the
immigration of a Chinese people; if not, we are destined to a sad mistake.

To our State these people come in vast numbers - not for an
incidental good to us but to do us a grievous wrong. What can our State or
metropolis benefit by encouraging the immigration of a class of people who
use no common dictates of reason while among us, who are pagans in religion,
inhuman in their traits, most scurrilous when their feelings are irritated,
illiterate in intellectual education and of the doctrines of morality, and lastly
wholly incompetent to become true citizens.

We cannot expect to derive any good by associating or negotiating
with them; then why they ever were permitted to flock here in such great and
apparently innumerable hordes when their immigration is in direct conflict to
the prosperity of a country, and when it is in opposition to the obedience of
the wishes of the people in general, is more than human intelligence can
disclose?

Their traits, their mode of living, necessitates the disgust which is
universally bestowed upon them; and although we have but little knowledge
of the best portion of their society, we must naturally be prejudiced against
the whole race. They are a people who are peculiarly adapted to sordid,
insolubrious localities and places of abode which nature, in her estimation

seems to have set apart for them; an unprincipled people, showing not the remotest shadow of hospitality for any industrious and law-abiding citizen, and ultimately are a disgrace to whatsoever position or estate they occupy in that country wherein universal civilization exists....

"The Gentile Chinese: His Immigration, its Detrimental Consequences to a Metropolis, and His Mode of Living," editorial, *The Elevator*, March 29, 1873

(b)

....We felt in those terrible days which called forth the Vigilance Committees and their summary dealing with those who were preying upon the best interests of society, that the imperious law *of self-defense* imperatively demanded it. That a certain element must be gotten rid of. That same imperious law will probably call upon us in the case of the hordes of Chinese who are flocking to our shores and sapping to the foundation our mechanical and labor interests. The manner in which the law of self-defense should be applied to this latter evil must differ materially from that of its application to the thieves and desperadoes which had taken possession of this city and county, and sought to pervert justice and commit with impunity, outrages of every conceivable form and character, but it, nevertheless, becomes necessary to apply it. Under the sanction of statutes and the guiding hand of kindness and humanity - with the aid of National, State and Municipal governments, together with individual assistance in the withdrawal of patronage, so contract their revenue that the moneyed inducements which now bring them here, would cease, and with it their continued influx, at least to the extent that we are now suffering from.

"Chinese Immigration," editorial, *The Elevator*, April 26, 1873

(c)

....We don't think our Congressional Solons can be made to see the extent of our suffering in this matter; and if they did see, they would probably conclude that the benefit to our national commerce was greater and more important than the evil to the prosperity of any individual State. Statesmen of enlarged views will argue that way sometimes; and probably they are right, viewed from a national standpoint, with a statesman's eye. But *self-preservation* is the law under which we are called on to deal with the subject....

"The Vexed Question - Chinese Immigration," editorial, *The Elevator*, May 8, 1873

Notes

1. Major biographies of Douglass include Benjamin Quarles, *Frederick Douglass*, New York, 1948; Philip S. Foner, *Frederick Douglass: A Biography*, New York, 1964; William McFeely, *Frederick Douglass*, 1991.

2. See Foner, *The Life and Writings of Frederick Douglass*, vol. II, New York, 1950, pp. 151-155. The weekly newspaper had a volunteer staff of local reporters writing under pseudonyms. Quarles, pp. 84-86. Two pieces tracing African-American views of Asian immigrants dating back to the 1850's are Arnold Shankman, "Black on Yellow: Afro-Americans View Chinese-Americans, 1850-1935," *Phylon*, Vol. XXXIX, No. 1 (Spring 1978), pp. 1-17, and David J. Hellwig, "Black Reactions to Chinese Immigration and the Anti-Chinese Movement: 1850-1910," *Amerasia Journal*, Vol. 6 (1979), pp. 25-44. See also Leon Litwack, *North of Slavery: The Negro in the Free States, 1790-1860*, Chicago, 1961, pp. 167-168.

3. A number of organized white miners demanded exclusion of the Chinese from the gold fields. A convention in Shasta County, California passed a resolution to that effect in 1855. *Minority Report of the Select Committee on Resolutions of the Miner's Convention of Shasta County*, submitted March 17, 1855, California Senate, Document No. 16.

4. *Pioneer Urbanites: A Social and Cultural History of Black San Francisco*, by Douglass Henry Daniels (Phila., 1980), is useful in understanding the social conditions and attitudes of nineteenth century Bay Area African-Americans.

5. A constant theme in Douglass' antebellum writings and speeches, it also appears in the "Composite Nation" address.

6. See John W. Blassingame and John R. McKivigan, eds., *The Frederick Douglass Papers, Series One, Volume 4: 1864-1880*, New Haven, 1991, pp. 240-259. Blassingame and McKivigan note that Douglass gave much the same address on several later occasions. (pp. 548-549) Waldo E. Martin, Jr.'s *The Mind of Frederick Douglass*, Chapel Hill, 1984, assesses Douglass' "racial vision" in exemplary fashion. (pp. 95-97, 213-219) For the "Composite Nation" speech, Martin gives the date appearing on the typescript copy (1867); Blassingame and McKivigan have corrected the year to 1869.

7. untouchable.

8. This manipulation was seriously contemplated by Southern planters as a solution to the difficult task of compelling former slaves to labor under conditions of subservience and dependence during the Reconstruction period. See Eric Foner, *Reconstruction: The Unfinished Revolution, 1863-1877*, New York, 1988, chapters 3 and 4 passim; Gerald David Jaynes, *Branches without Roots: Genesis of the Black Working Class in the American South, 1862-1882*, New York, 1986, part II passim. Interestingly, the former head of the Freedmen's Bureau, General O.O. Howard, later spoke out against exclusion and persecution of the Chinese. See "Gen. Howard and Chinese," *New York Times*, January 13, 1902.

9. Daniels supplies details on William Hall and *The Elevator*. (pp. 50, 62, 110-111, 114-115, 130).

10. Hall's suspicion was not unfounded. Southern planters directly articulated the anti-Black potential of Chinese labor. See E. Foner, p. 419; Vernon Lane Wharton, *The Negro in Mississippi, 1865-1890*, Chapel Hill, 1947, pp. 97-99; William Ivey Hair, *Bourbonism and Agrarian Protest: Louisiana Politics, 1877-1900*, Baton Rouge, 1969, pp. 94-95; Charles H. Wesley, *Negro Labor in the United States, 1850-1925*, New York, 1927, pp. 196-198. These works note that planters also considered the use of allegedly more pliant European immigrants as an easier alternative to the freedwomen and freedmen. These developments generated tensions in areas far from the South. In San Francisco, where the livelihoods of African-Americans were insecure, "blacks and Chinese were serious job competitors" after the Civil War. (Shankman, p. 5) See also Shankman, *Ambivalent Friends: Afro-Americans View the Immigrant*, Westport, 1982, p. 22. Says another historian: "Ironically, San Francisco's leading Negroes came to be reflectors of certain contemporary white animosities." Leigh Dana Johnsen, "Equal Rights and the 'Heathen Chinee': Black Activism in San Francisco, 1865-1875," *Western Historical Quarterly, January 1980, p. 68*.

11. Other African-American religious papers took this position. See "The Chinese in California," *The Christian Recorder*, July 24, 1869.

12. The weekly *New Era* began in early 1870; under Douglass' editorship, it became the *New National Era* later that year. P. Foner, *Life and Writings of Frederick Douglass*, vol. IV, New York, 1955, pp. 220-22, 566.

13. He denounced the "coolie trade" in the *New National Era*, August 10, August 17, 1871.

14. During the 1870's and 1880's, San Francisco employers often expressed preference for Chinese laborers over African-American workers. Daniels, pp. 67-68.

Part VI: Relocation and Protest

Examples follow of the legal rationale for the evacuation of the Japanese during World War II, accounts of the internment, and statements by or about people - generally not of Japanese descent - who opposed the government's concentration camp policy. The materials also trace the struggle by camp survivors for vindication and reparations.

Executive Order 9066 introduces the argument justifying relocation [Document 1].[1] General DeWitt, commander of the West Coast Command, gives the military rationale for evacuation [Document 2]. Excerpts from a wartime Congressional investigation charge relocation officials with failing to elicit proper displays of loyalty from internees [Document 3]. Confirmation of the bad taste left by the use and potential re-employment of concentration camps (the latter made possible under the Internal Security Act of 1950) is suggested in the Kleindienst letter of 1969 [Document 4].

Organized resistance to evacuation, including legal action, began in the Japanese American community, accompanied by efforts to improve conditions and treatment under internment. Landmark dissents in the Supreme Court challenged the hysteria of the period [Document 5]. An account of the internment experience constitutes Document 6. The internment of Karl Yoneda and the position of the Communist Party are the concerns of Documents 7 and 8. Socialist and civil libertarian Norman Thomas was an outspoken opponent of the relocation [Document 9]. So too was the editor and writer Carey McWilliams, a foremost commentator on racism, labor and the rights of Asian Americans [Documents 10 and 11].

Quaker George Knox Roth worked doggedly in Los Angeles against the evacuation; he paid a heavy price [Document 12]. The endeavors of the Methodist pastor Herbert V. Nicholson, an early proponent of federal reparations for the survivors, are sketched in Document 13. The *Pittsburgh Courier*, a leading African-American paper, reported favorably on a Japanese American's vision of cooperation against racism [Document 14]. The Black scholar and leader W.E.B. DuBois spoke out insistently against the internment; among his avenues of protest was his regular column in the *Amsterdam News* [Documents 15a-c]. The International Longshoremen's and Warehousemen's Union, a West Coast stronghold of the Congress of Industrial Organizations and an outgrowth of the 1934 San Francisco General Strike, included many Japanese Americans (and other Asian Americans as well). That the union stood by them during the war is borne out by Documents 16a-c.

Testimony of one of the camp survivors before a federal commission considering redress demonstrates the mounting pressure on the government during the 1980's [Document 17]. In the same spirit, the Japanese American Citizens League put the issue cogently [Document 18]. Finally, the evolution of the case for redress is traced through a number of reports and commentaries [Documents 19a-d].

1

President Franklin D. Roosevelt's Executive Order 9066 helped set a legal precedent in discrimination against Asian Americans.

Whereas, The successful prosecution of the war requires every possible protection against espionage and against sabotage to national-defense material, national-defense premises and national-defense utilities as defined in Section 4, Act of April 20, 1918, 40 Stat. 533, as amended by the Act of November 30, 1940, 54 Stat. 1220, and the Act of August 21, 1941, 55 Stat. 655 (U.S.C., Title 50, Sect. 104):

Now, therefore, By virtue of the authority vested in me as President of the United States, and Commander in Chief of the Army and navy, I hereby authorize and direct the Secretary of War, and the Military Commanders whom he may from time to time designate, whenever he or any designated Commander deems such action necessary or desirable, to prescribe military areas in such places and of such extent as he or the appropriate Military Commander may determine, from which any or all persons may be excluded, and with respect to which, the right of any person to enter, remain in, or leave shall be subject to whatever restriction the Secretary of War or the appropriate Military Commander may impose in his discretion. The Secretary of War is hereby authorized to provide for residents of any such areas who are excluded therefrom, such transportation, food, shelter, and other accommodations as may be necessary, in the judgment of the Secretary of War or the said Military Commander, and until other arrangements are made, to accomplish the purpose of this order. The designation of military areas in any region or locality shall supersede designations of prohibited and restricted areas by the Attorney General under the Proclamations of December 7 and 8, 1941, and shall supersede the responsibility and authority of the Attorney General under the said Proclamations in respect of such prohibited and restricted areas.

I hereby further authorize and direct the Secretary of War and the said Military Commanders to take such steps as he or the appropriate Military Commander may deem advisable to enforce compliance with the restrictions applicable to each Military area hereinabove authorized to be designated, including the use of Federal troops and other Federal Agencies, with authority to accept assistance of state and local agencies.

I hereby further authorize and direct all Executive Departments, independent establishments and other Federal Agencies, to assist the Secretary of War or the said Military Commanders in carrying out this Executive Order, including the furnishing of medical aid, hospitalizations, food, clothing, transportation, use of land, shelter, and other supplies, equipment, utilities, facilities, and services.

This order shall not be construed as modifying or limiting in any way the authority heretofore granted under Executive order No. 8972, dated December 12, 1941, nor shall it be construed as limiting or modifying the duty and responsibility of the Federal Bureau of Investigation, with respect to the investigations of alleged acts of sabotage or the duty and responsibility of the Attorney General and the Department of Justice under the Proclamations of December 7 and 8, 1941, prescribing regulations for the conduct and control of alien enemies, except as such duty and responsibility is superseded by the designation of military areas hereunder.

Executive Order No. 9066, Authorizing the Secretary of War to Prescribe Military Areas, February 19, 1942, in Lieutenant General J.L. DeWitt, U.S. Army Western Defense Command, *Final Report: Japanese Evacuation From the West Coast*, 1942, Washington D.C., 1943, pp. 26-27

2

> *General J.L. DeWitt was the officer chiefly responsible for*
> *carrying out the Executive Order. His introduction to the official report*
> *on the handling of the evacuation, excerpted below, revealed the racial*
> *dimension of what was purportedly a military need. The implications*
> *for potential singling out of a nationality or ethnic group endowed with*
> *the characteristics he proposes are clear. Studies of the evacuation*
> *indicate his importance and his influence in the operation of the*
> *internment camps.*

The evacuation was impelled by military necessity. The security of the Pacific Coast continues to require the exclusion of Japanese from the area now prohibited to them and will so continue as long as that military necessity exists. The surprise attack at Pearl Harbor by the enemy crippled a major portion of the Pacific Fleet and exposed the West Coast to an attack which could not have been substantially impeded by defensive fleet operations. More than 115,000 persons of Japanese ancestry reside along the coast and were significantly concentrated near many highly sensitive installations essential to the war effort. Intelligence services records reflected the existence of hundreds of Japanese organizations in California, Washington, Oregon and Arizona which, prior to December 7, 1941, were actively engaged in advancing Japanese war aims. These records also disclosed that thousands of American-born Japanese had gone to Japan to receive their education and indoctrination there and had become rabidly pro-Japanese and then had returned to the United States. Emperor worshipping ceremonies were commonly held and millions of dollars had flowed into the Japanese imperial war chest from the contributions freely made by Japanese here. The continued presence of a large, unassimilated, tightly knit racial group, bound to an enemy nation by strong ties of race, culture, custom and religion along a frontier vulnerable to attack constituted a menace which had to be dealt with. Their loyalties were unknown and time was of the essence. The evident aspirations of the enemy emboldened by his recent successes made it worse than folly to have left any stone unturned in the building up of our defenses. It is better to have had this protection and not to have needed it than to have needed it and not to have had it - as we have learned to our sorrow.

Lieutenant General J.L. DeWitt to Chief of Staff, United States Army, War Department, Washington D.C., June 5, 1943, in DeWitt, *Final Report: Japanese Evacuation From the West Coast*, 1942, Washington D.C., 1943, p. vii

3

The House Un-American Activities Committee, established in 1938 and almost immediately identified as a subverter of the Bill of Rights, evidently felt that the government failed to vigorously carry out and enforce the spirit and letter of the evacuation. Key to its 1943 critique of the War Relocation Authority was the charge that the latter had permitted Japanese American organizations and cultural activities to operate in the camps. The character of the accusation - baseless, in any case, since the greater part of Japanese cultural activity was proscribed - is indicated in the following passage from the Committee's report.

PRESERVATION AND PROMOTION OF JAPANESE CULTURAL TIES

Indicative of the same type of negligence which caused the War Relocation Authority to fail to adopt prompt and drastic measures of segregation in the centers was the authority's callous promotion of cultural ties with Japan.

Mr. Myer[2] admitted in his testimony before the subcommittee that at one time the War Relocation Authority was paying at least 90 instructors in Judo at a single center. Judo is a distinctively Japanese cultural phenomenon. It is more than an athletic exercise. By the employment of 90 instructors at one center, the Authority was obviously promoting Judo among Japanese-Americans who did not already know it.[3] Various other forms of so-called recreation which could only have the effect of a tie-back to Japan were likewise promoted in the centers and their promotion was paid for out of the

War Relocation Authority's funds which come ultimately from the taxpayers of this country. The same is true of instruction in the Japanese language. It is one thing for the Government to give instruction in the Japanese language to those who, the Government has reason to believe, will shortly utilize that instruction in some intelligence agency. It is a totally different thing to post notices on the bulletin boards of the centers that one and all may enroll in course in the Japanese language. American citizens are citizens regardless of their ancestry, and there is no possible justification whatever for a program which goes out of its way to stimulate the interest of an American citizen in the culture of a foreign country from which that citizen has presumably been completely separated by the very fact of his American citizenship.

Every fact adduced in evidence before the subcommittee indicated that the War Relocation Authority had before it an almost unparalleled opportunity to inaugurate a vigorous educational program for positive Americanism. At the same time, the committee is unable to arrive at any other conclusion than that the Authority treated this opportunity with the most reprehensible indifference. And not only that, but the Authority proceeded to make outlays of funds for the express purpose of forcibly reminding the residents of the centers that they stemmed from Japan, whereas the loyal at least should have been encouraged by every possible means to regard themselves as Americans and Americans only.

Report and Minority Views of the Special Committee on Un-American Activities on Japanese War Relocation Centers, September 30, 1943, 78th Congress, 1st Session, House of Representatives Report No. 717, p. 8

4

Title II of the Internal Security Act of 1950 provided a procedure for internment of people for political reasons in the event of a threat to national security; Congress overrode President Harry Truman's veto of the Act. Of relevance here was the revival for use under the new law of camps in which Japanese Americans had been interned. As Title II eroded in the wake of successive legal appeals during the 1960's, Attorney General Richard Kleindienst admitted the

*persistence of a constitutionally-based opposition to the original
removal of the Japanese as a factor in his proposal to repeal the Act.*

Dear Senator:

This is in response to your request for the views of the Department
of Justice on S. 1872, legislation to repeal the Emergency Detention Act of
1950.

The Emergency Detention Act was enacted as Title II of the Internal
Security Act of 1950. In brief, the Act established procedures for the
apprehension and detention, during internal security emergencies, of
individuals likely to engage in acts of espionage or sabotage.

Unfortunately, the legislation has aroused among many of the citizens
of the United States the belief that it may one day be used to accomplish the
apprehension and detention of citizens who hold unpopular beliefs and views.
In addition, various groups, of which our Japanese-American citizens are most
prominent, look upon the legislation as permitting a reoccurrence of the
roundups which resulted in the detention of Japanese ancestry during World
War II. It is therefore quite clear that the continuation of the Emergency
Detention Act is extremely offensive to many Americans.

In the judgment of this Department, the repeal of this legislation will
allay the fears and suspicions - unfounded as they may be - of many of our
citizens. This benefit outweighs any potential advantage which the Act may
provide in time of internal security emergency....

Richard Kleindienst to Senator James O. Eastland,[4] Chairman, Committee on
the Judiciary, December 2, 1969, in Roger Daniels, ed., *The Decision to
Relocate the Japanese Americans*, Philadelphia, 1975, p. 131

5

The dissent of Supreme Court justice Frank Murphy in the
Korematsu *case (1944) constituted a significant constitutional
argument against the evacuation; excerpts from his opinion appear
below. (Justice Robert Jackson, later American prosecutor at the
Nuremburg Trials, also dissented.) Fred Toyosaburo Korematsu, a*

*second generation Japanese American in Oakland, had refused to
report for evacuation for plain personal reasons. Ultimately interned,
he pursued the legal road to vindication all the way to the Supreme
Court; the Court upheld the Army's removal of the Japanese,
Korematsu included. Justice Murphy had been governor of Michigan
at the time of the rise of the Congress of Industrial Organizations and
the United Automobile Workers.[5] His sympathy for civil liberties and
labor causes was not unknown, and in fact, his appointment to the
bench by Roosevelt had been part of the latter's re-shaping of what
had been a most conservative Court.*

Mr. Justice MURPHY, dissenting

This exclusion of "all persons of Japanese ancestry, both alien and non-alien,"
from the Pacific Coast area on a plea of military necessity in the absence of
martial law ought not to be approved. Such exclusion goes over "the very
brink of constitutional power" and falls into the ugly abyss of racism.

In dealing with matters relating to the prosecution and progress of a
war, we must accord great respect and consideration to the judgments of the
military authorities who are on the scene and who have full knowledge of the
military facts. The scope of their discretion must, as a matter of necessity and
common sense, be wide. And their judgments ought not to be overruled lightly
by those whose training and duties ill-equip them to deal intelligently with
matters so vital to the physical security of the nation.

At the same time, however, it is essential that there be definite limits
to military discretion, especially where martial law has not been declared.
Individuals must not be left impoverished of their constitutional rights on a
plea of military necessity that has neither substance nor support. Thus, like
other claims conflicting with the asserted constitutional rights of the
individual, the military claim must subject itself to the judicial process of
having its reasonableness determined and its conflicts with other interests
reconciled....

The judicial test of whether the Government, on a plea of military
necessity, can validly deprive an individual of any of his constitutional rights
is whether the deprivation is reasonably related to a public danger that is so
"immediate, imminent, and impending" as not to admit of delay and not to

permit the intervention of ordinary constitutional processes to alleviate the danger....Civilian Exclusion Order No. 34, banishing from a prescribed area of the Pacific Coast "all persons of Japanese ancestry, both alien and non-alien," clearly does not meet that test. Being an obvious racial discrimination, the order deprives all those within its scope of the equal protection of the laws as guaranteed by the Fifth Amendment. It further deprives these individuals of their constitutional rights to live and work where they will, to establish a home where they choose and to move about freely. In excommunicating them without benefit of hearings, this order also deprives them of all their constitutional rights to procedural due process. Yet no reasonable relation to an "immediate, imminent, and impending" public danger is evident to support this racial restriction which is one of the most sweeping and complete deprivations of constitutional rights in the history of this nation in the absence of martial law.

It must be conceded that the military and naval situation in the spring of 1942 was such as to generate a very real fear of invasion of the Pacific Coast, accompanied by fears of sabotage and espionage in that area. The military command was therefore justified in adopting all reasonable means necessary to combat these dangers. In adjudging the military action taken in light of the then apparent dangers, we must not erect too high or too meticulous standards; it is necessary only that the action have some reasonable relation to the removal of the dangers of invasion, sabotage and espionage. But the exclusion, either temporarily or permanently, of all persons with Japanese blood in the veins has no such reasonable relation. And that relation is lacking because the exclusion order necessarily must rely for its reasonableness upon the assumption that *all* persons of Japanese ancestry may have a dangerous tendency to commit sabotage and espionage and to aid our Japanese enemy in other ways. It is difficult to believe that reason, logic or experience could be marshalled in support of such an assumption.

....The main reasons relied upon by those responsible for the forced evacuation, therefore, do not prove a reasonable relation between the group characteristics of Japanese Americans and the dangers of invasion, sabotage and espionage. The reasons appear, instead, to be largely an accumulation of much of the misinformation, half-truths and insinuations that for years have been directed against Japanese Americans by people with racial and economic prejudices - the same people who have been among the foremost advocates of the evacuation. A military judgment based upon such racial and sociological considerations is not entitled to the great weight ordinarily given the judgments based upon strictly military considerations. Especially is this so when every charge relative to race, religion, culture, geographical location, and legal and economic status has been substantially discredited by independent studies made by experts in these matters.

The military necessity which is essential to the validity of the evacuation order thus resolves itself into a few intimations that certain individuals actively aided the enemy, from which it is inferred that the entire group of Japanese Americans could not be trusted to be or remain loyal to the United States. No one denies, of course, that there were some disloyal persons of Japanese descent on the Pacific Coast who did all in their power to aid their ancestral land. Similar disloyal activities have been engaged in by many persons of German, Italian[6] and even more pioneer stock in our country. But to infer that examples of individual disloyalty prove group disloyalty and justify discriminatory action against the entire group is to deny that under our system of law individual guilt is the sole basis for deprivation of rights. Moreover, this inference, which is at the very heart of the evacuation orders, has been used in support of the abhorrent and despicable treatment of minority groups by the dictatorial tyrannies which this nation is now pledged to destroy. To give constitutional sanction to that inference in this case, however well-intentioned may have been the military command on the Pacific Coast,is to adopt one of the cruelest of the rationales used by our enemies to destroy the dignity of the individual and to encourage and open the door to discriminatory actions against other minority groups in the passions of tomorrow.

No adequate reason is given for the failure to treat these Japanese Americans on an individual basis by holding investigations and hearings to separate the loyal from the disloyal, as was done in the case of persons of German and Italian ancestry....It is asserted merely that the loyalties of this group "were unknown and time was of the essence." Yet nearly four months elapsed after Pearl Harbor before the first exclusion order was issued; nearly eight months went by until the last order was issued; and the last of these "subversive" persons was not actually removed until almost eleven months had elapsed. Leisure and deliberation seem to have been more of the essence than speed. And the fact that conditions were not such as to warrant a declaration of martial law adds strength to the belief that the factors of time and military necessity were not as urgent as they have been represented to be.

Moreover, there was no adequate proof that the Federal Bureau of Investigation and the military and naval intelligence services did not have the espionage and sabotage situation well in hand during this long period. Nor is there any denial of the fact that not one person of Japanese ancestry was accused or convicted of espionage or sabotage after Pearl Harbor while they were still free, a fact which is some evidence of the loyalty of the vast majority of these individuals and of the effectiveness of the established methods of combatting these evils. It seems incredible that under these circumstances it would have been impossible to hold loyalty hearings for the mere 112,000 persons involved - or at least for the 70,000 American citizens - especially when a large part of this number represented children and elderly men and women. Any inconvenience that may have accompanied an attempt to conform to procedural due process cannot be said to justify violations of constitutional rights of individuals.

I dissent, therefore, from this legalization of racism. Racial discrimination in any form and in any degree has no justifiable part whatever in our democratic way of life. It is unattractive in any setting but it is utterly revolting among a free people who have embraced the principles set forth in the Constitution of the United States. All residents of this nation are kin in some way by blood or culture to a foreign land. Yet they are primarily and necessarily a part of the new and distinct civilization of the United States. They must accordingly be treated at all times as the heirs of the American experiment and as entitled to all the rights and freedoms guaranteed by the Constitution.

323 U.S. 233-235, 239-242

6

There have been a large number of reminiscences by former internees. Among them is that of Yuri Kochiyama, published by the

American Committee for the Protection of the Foreign Born during the late 1960's. Congress was then debating the future of the internment clause of the Internal Security Act of 1950. A resident of California, Kochiyama had been evacuated to a camp in Arkansas during the war.

"WITHIN 48 HOURS"

On January 29th, the Attorney General ordered evacuation of Japanese from certain strategic areas. Terminal Island was one. On February 2, 1942, a swarm of FBI agents descended on Terminal Island and arrested 336 Issei on presidential warrants as potential enemy agents. They were all fishermen. This meant that practically all men, heads of families, were incarcerated. Then came a confusion of government orders: to move out - to stay put. Finally and suddenly, everyone was told to evacuate within 48 hours. Panic ensued as the Island community was flooded with profiteers, vultures looking for an easy buy of refrigerators, radios, cars, furniture, fishing equipment.

Throughout February and March 1942, public officials from Congressman Rankin[7] of Mississippi to Mayor Bowron of Los Angeles, Governor Warren[8] and General DeWitt of California vociferated on "getting the Japs out." On February 19, 1942, President Roosevelt issued Executive Order 9066 which authorized commanding generals to designate military areas forbidden to civilians.

Organizations wishing to "get rid of" the Japanese were growing by leaps and bounds - political groups, labor unions, veterans' organizations, immigration committees, Oriental exclusion leagues, chambers of commerce, social clubs, lodges, merchants, farmers, realtors, press and tradition-setters such as the Sons and Daughters of the Golden West.

That much of the clamor was decidedly more racial than political or economic cannot be denied. Also, false charges of sabotage, wild rumors and fanciful tales were expanded and the flames of suspicion fanned. To be a friend of the Japanese was not only unpopular but "un-American" and jeopardizing. Also, other Orientals, not of Japanese ancestry, were often mistaken for "Japs" and attacked. Finally, buttons sprouted on lapels reading, "I'm not a Jap!"

On March 18, 1942, President Roosevelt established the War

Relocation Authority and promulgated Executive Order 9102, the directive to formulate and effectuate a program for relocation, maintenance and supervision.

About March 27, residents of the Los Angeles Harbor Area were issued directives to be ready to move in a week. That was our area. On April 3, my mother, my oldest brother and I, along with residents of Long Beach, Wilmington, San Pedro, Torrance, etc., left in a car-caravan for the assembly center which was the Santa Anita Race Tracks. We were allowed to take whatever we could carry in our hands, so we limited ourselves to absolute essentials, bedding, some cooking utensils, silverware and rough camp-type clothes.

Every assembly center was a race track or fair grounds, serving as temporary headquarters until "relocation" or concentration camps could hastily be built in desert areas, swamplands or mountain regions.

HOME IN A HORSE STALL

A horse stall became our home. Army cots and straw-filled mattresses were the only furnishings given to each family. Boxes had to be converted into tables, chairs, and dressers. Later, internees brought in more household goods or had neighbors from back home send necessary equipment.

My twin brother by then was in language intelligence training in Minnesota, ready to ship out to the South Pacific.

Since the move to the assembly center was in the Spring, there was no climatic hardship. The second evacuation to concentration camps in the interior posed many problems. Utah, Idaho, Arizona, Wyoming, Arkansas were the states selected, as well as Manzanar and Tulelake in California. If it was not the dust storms, heat and flies in Arizona, it was the freezing cold of Wyoming, or the sticky mud of Arkansas. It was very hard on the aged, the chronically ill and mothers with small children.

Camp life functioned communally. There was a community mess hall, the community latrine, bath-house, laundry facility. For everything, it was lining up. Post offices and P.X.'s were set up. Schools, churches and hospitals were readied. In Santa Anita, the grandstand bleachers became school and church. The garage under the grandstand became the first hospital. As a nurse's aid, I remember measle cases, TB, broken legs, mental patients, mothers in labor and infants thrown in one large room with doctors sleeping in between. Later partitioned wards were built.

In camp, practically every person not attending school worked. The pay-scale was: $8.00 a month for unskilled laborers, $12.00 for semi-skilled, $16.00 to $19.00 for professionals. There were many things that all who were able participated in without pay. Every able-bodied male in Arkansas camps went to the forests and chopped down trees for firewood. In some blocks, women dragged these trees in like teams of horses. Anyone who could lift a shovel helped dig the drainage system around their block. Play areas were cleared by block people.

There were marriages, births and deaths. There were family squabbles, differences with administration, rumors of cop-infiltration, confrontations, fights, riots, political beatings and a couple of killings.

Material losses, physical upheaval and being stigmatized were part of the war-time experience. We also suffered, as did other Americans, the loss of a large per cent of our young men who were killed in combat. The 442nd,[9] the Japanese-American Combat Team, distinguished themselves in Europe by becoming the most highly decorated unit in U.S. history....

Yuri (Mary) Kochiyama, *Concentration Camps USA: It Has Happened Here*, American Committee for the Protection of the Foreign Born, New York, no date, pp. 4-6

7

Veteran labor organizer and Communist Karl Yoneda [see Part IV] was also a victim of the evacuation. He was interned in the Manzanar Relocation Center in Eastern California; both his wife (who was not Japanese) and their young son eventually joined him there. Yoneda was active in efforts to improve camp conditions and to combat those few who were indeed supporters of Japanese imperialism. He was later among those who testified at the pivotal Federal Commission Hearings on the internment in 1981.

The day of departure for Manzanar dawned. That Monday my thoughts were occupied by many questions. What is in store for us? When will we be a family again? Will I be able to enlist? About eight hundred thirty "volunteers" gathered at the Santa Fe Station. We were assigned ID and train coach numbers. I was #596 on coach no. 13. There were armed soldiers everywhere to "protect" us. Maryknoll priests and nuns, plus hundreds of relatives and friends, milled around. Newspaper reporters were busy trying to get interviews. One reporter told us that three hundred Issei and Nisei in a hundred forty cars had rolled out from the Pasadena Rose Bowl headed for the same destination that morning.

As the train pulled out, I watched Elaine, Tommy, Joyce, and my in-laws until they disappeared from view. The train stopped more than a dozen times. At every crossroad and bridge the MP's got out to check to make sure that it was safe to move forward.

Everybody wondered what kind of a place Manzanar would be. A few pro-Japanites boasted that they were "one step ahead of the FBI." They started rumors that the U.S. will have to pay each of us three thousand dollars after Japan wins the war, that the U.S. would detain us like Indians in camps, and that we would be fed leftover army supplies.

John Umemoto, a young Hawaii Kibei sitting in our coach, began to slander President Roosevelt loudly. My cousin Saito told him, "Keep still, if you keep this up you'll go to Montana," referring to an enemy alien detention camp.

At 10:00 P.M. we finally arrived at the small town of Lone Pine. It took thirteen hours for the two-hundred mile journey! U.S. Army trucks took us to the camp eight miles away. Those who had arrived earlier by car caravan led us to the barracks. There were no lights, stoves, or window panes. My two cousins and I, together with seven others, were crowded into a 25 x 20 foot room. We slept on army cots with our clothes on.

The next morning we discovered that there were no toilets or washrooms. The one outside faucet was frozen. We walked around and saw that the construction of army-type barracks was progressing in two shifts. Building materials were strewn over the premises. The administration building, post office, and clinic had been completed and were ready for business.

We saw GIs manning machine guns in the watchtowers. The barbed wire fence which surrounded the camp was visible against the background of the snow-covered Sierra mountain range.

"So this is the American-style concentration camp," someone remarked....

After Elaine, Tommy, and I shared a few days in the room with the six strangers, we moved to Block 4, Barrack 2, "Apartment" 2. Our lives were not any easier because we had to share the new area with a seventy-five year-old blind man and his fifteen-year-old nephew. These two were the overflow from the Nishimura family of nine crammed into "Apartment" 1. Elaine's parents sent us sheets, some of which we used to curtain off our three cots. I garnered all the scrap lumber I could to build shelves, a table, and chest, and used empty nail kegs for chairs, as others did. Months later, after many complaints, the partition between "Apartments" 1 and 2 was moved to make our space 20 x 20. The Nishimuras' now measured 20 x 30 and "able to accommodate" all nine members of the family. Thus we had 4-2-2 all to ourselves.

We often complained to the front office on matters relating to the gross mishandling of human needs. For example, the latrines were built without doors or partitions between the two back-to-back rows of five toilet bowls each. The shower area lacked curtains.

Elaine pointed out to me that something had to be done about the conditions of the latrines because many young girls hesitated to use the facilities. On April 10 she went to the office and complained to Service Director J.M. Kidwell about the situation. He shrugged his shoulders and told Elaine, "It is army specifications." "To hell with specifications," Elaine said, pounding his desk. "If you don't do something soon, there may be mass hysteria and even some suicides." Shortly thereafter, doors, partitions, and curtains were installed.

In order to introduce "self-government" in Manzanar, the administration appointed Nisei and Issei to various positions and committees. These committees dealt with a constitution and by-laws, block leadership, night checkers, family relations, cooperatives, education and press, grievance and complaints, and camp police and firemen.

I was appointed to act as Block 4 leader of three hundred fifty occupants until a regular election was held. I was also appointed to a five-member Constitution and By-Laws Committee.

As block leaders, or "blockheads" as we were commonly called, we transmitted project policies to the block residents and in turn carried their beefs and suggestions back to the Block Leaders Council. Despite ideological and language difficulties, we held many meetings and did much paper work which brought many results. Meetings were conducted in English and Japanese without translations.

Karl Yoneda, *Ganbatte: Sixty-Year Struggle of a Kibei Worker*, Los Angeles, 1983, pp. 126-127, 131-132

8

Caught up in the anti-Japanese hysteria following the Pearl Harbor attack and eager to demonstrate "loyalty," General Secretary Earl Browder and other leaders of the Communist Party supported the evacuation and suspended all members of Japanese descent (and, where relevant, their non-Japanese spouses[10]). Interestingly, the suspension pre-dated FDR's internment order by two months. The document below, demanding an apology, suggests an attempt to fully come to grips with the implications of that wartime move.

Whereas: When the Japanese imperialists attacked Pearl Harbor on December 7, 1941, the Communist Party, USA "pledged its loyalty, its devoted labor and the last drop of its blood in support of our country in this greatest of all crises that ever threatened its existence." The Party called for "Everything for National Unity!" "Everything for victory over world-wide fascist slavery!" Eventually 15,000 members of the C.P. and YCL [Young Communist League] served with the U.S. armed forces, including many Japanese Americans, and

Whereas: On December 8, 1941, the Japanese American members of the Party dispatched the following telegram to President Roosevelt: "ON BEHALF OF ONE HUNDRED FIFTY READERS AND SUBSCRIBERS IN SAN FRANCISCO BAY AREA OF *DOHO*, JAPANESE AMERICAN NEWSPAPER, WE PLEDGE FULL COOPERATION IN ALL ENDEAVORS TO SECURE VICTORY FOR DEMOCRACIES. WE STAND READY TO JOIN THE RANKS OF FIGHTING FORCES

UNDER YOUR COMMAND TO DEFEAT THE VICIOUS MILITARY FASCISTS OF JAPAN. Signed by Karl Yoneda, editor, Karl Akiya, circulation agent," and

Whereas: On the same day, an instruction from then C.P. General Secretary Earl Browder read "In the name of national unity, all members of Japanese ancestry and their non-Japanese spouses shall be suspended from the C.P. for the duration of the war." The rationale for this racist suspension, according to Browder, was that "The best place for any Japanese fifth columnist was in C.P. ranks, consequently no Japanese American should be kept while the war against Japan is going on." On the same morning, Nori Ikeda, Japanese American woman C.P.er, was discharged from the San Francisco P.W. [*People's World*] office for the above reason, and

Whereas, on February 19, 1942, President Roosevelt issued Executive Order 9066 which resulted in the incarceration of more than 110,000 Japanese Americans and Japanese aliens without trial or hearing, into 10 concentration camps, which was a blatant violation of the U.S. Constitution and democratic human rights, and

Whereas: The Communist Party did not speak out against the evacuation order, and

Whereas: In spite of injustice inflicted on the Japanese Americans many hundreds of them volunteered for the U.S. Military Intelligence and served in the Pacific and Asiatic war zones, many others enlisted from behind barbed wire for the 442nd Combat Team and heroically fought in European fronts, and

Whereas: Many years after WWII [a] redress/reparation movement emerged within the Japanese community, later supported by the C.P., ILWU and other groups, small numbers of former Nisei employees of the city [and] county of Los Angeles, San Francisco and Sacramento who had been fired right after Pearl Harbor received a check of $5,000 redress money; Aleuts are being given $12,000 redress money from the USA; Japanese Canadian evacuees are getting $20,000 redress money since 1988, and

Whereas: After many days of hearings from more than 750 witnesses in 1981 and 1982, the Commission on Wartime Relocation and Internment of Civilians came to the following conclusion regarding the evacuation: "The promulgation of Executive Order 9066 was not justified by military necessity...the broad historical causes which shaped these decisions were race prejudice, war hysteria and a failure of political leadership, widespread ignorance of Japanese Americans contributed to a policy conceived in haste and executed in an atmosphere of fear and anger at Japan." The Commission recommended to the Congress: 1) The U.S. Government issue an official apology to the former evacuees of Japanese ancestry; 2) To pay a check of $20,000 each to 60,000 surviving evacuees. The Congress adopted the Commission's recommendation and President Reagan signed the redress/reparation bill on August 10, 1988, and payment began on October 1, 1990. Therefore be it

Resolved: That this is an opportune time for our Party to issue a comprehensive apology to all former evacuees and past and present members of the Party, although the Party in its 20th Convention in 1972 passed a resolution: "One of the most serious of those errors being our failure to mount a struggle against the racist incarceration in 1942 of more than 110,000 people of Japanese ancestry in US concentration camps." Be it Further

Resolved: That the Party pledges to eliminate racism with a new depth and seriousness that is worthy of our Party, bringing to bear upon this subject full resources of information and program of Asian Pacific and other minority peoples.

Asian Pacific American Commission, "Call for a Public Apology by CPUSA to WWII Evacuees of Japanese Ancestry," *Dialog*, January 1991, pp. 42-43

9

A prodigious labor organizer and the major Socialist Party figure after the death of Eugene Victor Debs, Norman Thomas was one of the earliest opponents of the evacuation. His position contrasted with that of his own party and most left-wing organizations. A longtime civil libertarian and a leader of the American Civil Liberties Union, Thomas was among the first non-Japanese Americans to pronounce the evacuation process a challenge to the Constitution: in this regard, he differed with most other ACLU leaders, who did not protest.[11] His humanitarian concern with the post-war status of the evacuees is indicated in the selection below. Thomas was initially an isolationist in World War II; only reluctantly did he extend "critical support" for the war effort.[12]

THE ISSUES

Greater than the quantitative sufferings of 130,000 Japanese in a world of suffering are the issues for all of us implicit in this story.

Humanitarian

The first and most obvious of these issues is humanitarian, and to that the American people, on the whole, have not been blind. Within the Army itself, and still more within the War Relocation Authority there has been much evidence of a conscientious effort to do a distasteful job as well as it could be done. No one accuses the American concentration camps of paralleling in sheer and deliberate brutality the camps which, even before the war, were so black a disgrace to the Nazis.

Many American churches have been aware of the humanitarian aspects of the problem and in particular have tried to keep fellowship with the very considerable number of Japanese Christians who are at the camps. But since at least half the Japanese are Buddhists, or at any rate not connected with any Christian church, they are more or less untouched by the activities of the churches and their representatives. If the Japanese American Citizens' League can continue its work, and become more and more truly the democratic spokesman of the evacuated, much will be gained.

Relocation Camps

While the immediate humanitarian problem concerns the treatment of the Japanese in the assembly centers, that phase of the situation will be pretty well over by next fall, or at worst by the end of the year. The more important questions then will concern conditions in relocation camps, wage scales and work opportunities, and ultimately the re-absorption of the Japanese into the American community.

Common sense confirms the views expressed by many students of the situation that as a result of this policy of evacuation we are threatened with the permanent establishment of a group of second class American citizens. We are creating an American pale like the old Russian pale for Jews. The best government camps cannot be permanent for a racial group unless that racial group is to be stamped with inferiority.

When the war is over, there certainly will be no automatic solution of the problem. The same forces which were so active in bringing about evacuation will be active against the return of Japanese to their old homes and businesses. These will have passed into others' hands who will have a vested interest in them. Racial prejudice and greed will have been sharpened by the war experience. Even in time of peace other cities and states will scarcely want to take colonies of those whom the west coast has turned out.

The problem here is one of relocating Japanese not in large colonies, but by families, or relatively small groups of families, in communities where they can be absorbed into the general American life. They have shown their capacity to make their way economically and their excellence as citizens.

Placement of Students

One beginning of this process which has found in theory governmental approval is the placement of Japanese American students in colleges and universities outside the prohibited areas. This process is going far more slowly than it ought. A number of important colleges and universities have refused to take these Japanese American citizens, to say nothing of aliens. It is reported that some army authorities have tried to impose such preposterous conditions as: (1) that no Japanese be taken by colleges and universities doing defense research for the Government - that means all the good ones; and (2) that no Japanese be allowed to go to an educational institution within twenty-five miles of a railroad station. And that rule would leave the theoretical right an empty and hypocritical thing. There are also financial difficulties. But all these obstacles are likely to be removed or lessened by the higher authorities and the beginning of better things will not be wholly on paper.

At best it will be a very small beginning. What will happen to these young men and women after they are through college? Must they return to camps or may they be absorbed in the general American community? If they can, what about the others less fortunate who will be left behind in camps?

Work Furloughs

The War Relocation Authority, it is understood, contemplates an effort eventually to place Japanese at regular work in widely scattered American communities. They have arranged for work furloughs from camps as a beginning, with requirements that men furloughed for paying jobs send back money for the maintenance of their families.

The *Pacific Citizen*, organ of the Japanese-American Citizens' League, reports that 500 Japanese workers sent to Idaho "have helped save virtually all of the state's $16,000,000 sugar beet crop." The usefulness of these workers in Idaho sheds an interesting light on the Governor's previous declaration that "Japs are rats." The Japanese in Idaho were not put under armed guard but deputy sheriffs were assigned to the camps and the movements of the inmates were restricted, particularly at night. Visitors were allowed only under special circumstances. It would be easy for this sort of regulation to stiffen into real military or police surveillance of work camps after the order of Stalin's camps for political prisoners. Against this all decent Americans must be on guard.

The best relocation plans of the government cannot go far unless there is a more cooperative attitude among the people and less race feeling than is now the case....

Civil Liberty

In these obviously humanitarian tasks it is already evident that a great many people will interest themselves who will not face the basic issue of civil liberty implicit in our story.

The theory of justice frankly acknowledged in every totalitarian state is that the interest of the state as interpreted by the dictator is supreme. The individual has no right against it. As far as there is any theory behind brutal anti-Semitism in Nazi Germany, it is that whatever may be occasional excellencies of certain Jews, the presence of the Jewish people in Germany of itself menaces the well being of the German state and the highest good of the German people.

This is precisely the theory, and the only theory, on which the government's treatment of American citizens of Japanese ancestry can be explained. It is recognized in our domestic law and in whatever may be left of International law that during a war men and women of alien nationality, resident in a country, may be restricted in their movements or interned altogether. In camps they are supposed to be treated decently, and there is always fear that any nation which treats enemy aliens with cruelty will invite reprisals on those of its own nationality in the land of the enemy.

On the whole, enemy aliens have been fairly well treated in this country during this war. To a considerable degree they have received hearings before civilian boards. Those enemy aliens on the west coast, Japanese as well as German and Italian, who were interned by the order of the Department of Justice, pending inquiry, in Missoula, Montana, are in some respect better treated than Japanese aliens and American citizens, against whom the F.B.I. presented no charges.

Bill of Rights

The legal issue, therefore, which we are now discussing concerns the rights of citizens, which rights we were led to believe we were guaranteed in the Bill of Rights of our Federal Constitution. Certainly there is nothing in that famous document, or in the American tradition, or in the logic of American institutions which gives the President or his agents the right to remove any or all of us out of the districts in which we have lived and worked for reasons the validity of which he and his agents are the sole judges. This is the power asserted in the Presidential Proclamation of February 19th. It is strictly in line with totalitarian, not American, theory. The truth of that statement is not refuted by alleging that it is only a temporary measure, and by asserting, what is fortunately the truth, that the intentions of the Government with regard to these Japanese-Americans are better than the intentions of the German Government towards the Jews. More than once in history men have acceded to dictatorial power in the hands of a man with good intentions only to find that they have laid the basis for dictatorship unredeemed by pious aspirations.

Democracy and Japanese Americans, New York, The Post War World Council, 1942, pamphlet, pp. 24-29

10

On the night of July 15, 1943, the radio show "Town Meeting of the Air" was broadcast from Santa Barbara, California, before a live audience. The main question of the program, which featured debates on controversial subjects (the next topic, aired two weeks later, was "Should the Government Be Responsible for Our Natural Resources?"), was "Should All Japanese Continue to Be Excluded from

*the West Coast for the Duration?" (of the war). Assembled to discuss
the matter were four experts, including Congressman John M. Costello
(D-CA) and journalist Carey McWilliams, who then headed the state
Division of Immigration and Housing. Costello was a member of the
House Un-American Activities Committee: it was he who presented the
special HUAC report excerpted in Document 3 above. Extracts from
the debate, in which McWilliams followed Costello to the microphone,
are illustrative of the contention evoked by the topic in California. The
work of McWilliams against anti-Asian, anti-Black, and anti-Semitic
prejudice mark him as a foremost protagonist of democratic racial and
ethnic relations. Recent literature, however, indicates that McWilliams
overstated the benign treatment of Hawaiians of Japanese descent
following Pearl Harbor. [See Gary Okihiro,* Cane Fires: The Anti-
Japanese Movement in Hawaii, 1865-1945, *Temple University Press,
1991.]*

Congressman Costello:

In my opinion, all the Japanese should continue to be excluded from
the west coast for the duration of the present war. The same considerations
which justified the evacuation of all persons of Japanese ancestry from the
pacific coast will continue in effect throughout the period of the war.

The original evacuation of the Japanese was not a hastily conceived
program brought on by any sudden hysteria resulting from the shock of the
treacherous attack on this country at Pearl Harbor. On the contrary, the
evacuation order was not put into effect until the February following Pearl
Harbor. At that time the possible threat of attacks by the Japanese on the
west coast, or attempted invasion, was quite real. The possible landing of
saboteurs from submarines was equally real. And the danger of sabotage and
the treachery of espionage were all factors considered by the military
authorities....

Because of the danger to internal security, the military authorities,
under a partial application of martial law, directed the evacuation of those
persons of Japanese ancestry, alien and citizen alike, only because their
presence on the Pacific coast was the prime source of danger. For that reason,

the loyal Japanese-Americans had to be excluded along with the known disloyal. Because of the military necessity, the constitutional rights of these persons were not violated any more than the rights of any citizens are violated in denying them access to any restricted military area such as an airfield, war industry, military fortification, or a naval shipyard....

One must not lose sight of the fact that the United States is at war with Japan. And the first effort of every person in this country should be to effectively win that war. Nothing should be permitted that will in any way jeopardize the internal security of the country or our total war effort.

Return of these Japanese to the Pacific Coast would unquestionably be a very definite threat to our conduct of the war. I can only say that the Japanese can best contribute to the war effort by not seeking to return to the Pacific coast at this time....

Mr. McWilliams:

My answer to this question is "No," with, however, some important qualifications. For example, there are about 2,000 Japanese who were taken into custody immediately after Pearl Harbor and who are now being held in detention camps. Each of these individuals is being held for good cause after full investigation and an impartial hearing. There are also several thousand evacuees in relocation centers who have expressed a desire for repatriation or have indicated a disinclination to renounce all allegiance to Japan.

Obviously neither of these groups should be released. It is equally obvious that no person should be released from a relocation center without a searching and vigorous investigation. Once such an investigation has been made, then those suspected as potentially dangerous should be held in separate relocation centers for the duration.

But those whose records are approved should be released as rapidly as they can be relocated. The longer their release is delayed, the more complicated the entire problem becomes. This is particularly true of the third generation, made up of children born in this country of parents born in this country. These children have already been made far too conscious of the fact that they have Japanese faces.

Whether any of those released should be permitted to return to the west coast is primarily a military question, since the area has been declared a theater of war. There are special hazards in a theater of war which it would be folly to minimize. Only the military can appraise these hazards, since they alone possess the requisite information. Since it is their responsibility, they should make the decision. If and when the authorities relax the ban, as they have already done in the case of furloughed soldiers, then evacuees should be permitted to the coast if they so desire.

As a citizen, I express the hope that the ban may be relaxed before the war is over and for the following reasons: Hawaii is certainly no less important strategically than the west coast. Our policy of not removing persons from the islands has been entirely successful. While there were only 126,000 persons of Japanese descent on the west coast on December 7, 1941, approximately one per cent of the population, there were 157,000, constituting 37 per cent of the population, in Hawaii. No acts of sabotage have been reported in Hawaii either before or after Pearl Harbor. (*Cries of "No" and applause.*) The conduct of the Japanese has, in fact, won official commendation by General Emmons. That there was less race prejudice and therefore less political agitation of the question merely indicates that political and strictly military considerations may have played too large a part in shaping policy on the mainland.

The present agitation against the return of any evacuees is, in fact, being conducted with primary regard to nonmilitary considerations. No attempt is made to disguise the fact that this agitation has for its real purpose the permanent exclusion of all Japanese from the west coast. (*Applause and cries of "Sure" and "Why not?"*) Its avowed purposes include such objectives as stripping the American-born Japanese of their American citizenship, establishing rigid economic barriers against them, and laying the foundation for their eventual deportation. If this emerging pattern is permitted to take form now, it is likely to result in the indefinite postponement of the restoration of full citizenship even to those who have never been suspected of disloyalty.

Since this was not our intention in ordering mass evacuation, we should either promptly restore full citizenship rights or give an immediate guarantee of such restoration the moment the military emergency terminates. We cannot ignore the fact that this current agitation is being largely predicated, now as in the past, upon dangerously irrelevant so-called racial considerations, unsupported by a shred of scientific evidence.

To make a race issue of this problem is to do precisely what Tojo is trying to do: namely, to convince the colored peoples of the Far East that this is a race war. How we handle the evacuee problem is, therefore, one measure to our intention to apply the four freedoms to all peoples regardless of color. The peoples of India and China, as well as our own colored minorities, are watching the development of race feeling in the United States with the deepest concern. There can be no doubt but that the manner in which the evacuee problem is being discussed on the west coast today has tended to heighten race tension in a dangerously irresponsible fashion. Since race agitation seems to be cumulative in its intensity, scope, and consequences, any attempt to appease race bigotry can only result in stimulating further aggressions, not merely against the particular minority, but against all minorities.

As a Nation, we stand firmly committed to the great ideal that distinctions based upon race, color, or creed have no place in American life in peace or in war. (*Applause.*) If we permit the concept of citizenship to be broken down at one point for one group, we're undermining the very structure of American citizenship. We have never tolerated the notion that there could be different levels of citizenship with rights withheld from some citizens which were freely granted others. Political subdivisions of the Nation, therefore, should not be encouraged in the arrogant assumption that they can set up their own canons of citizenship. As I recall, there are forty-eight States in the Union. Not forty-five, and certainly not forty-seven.

Once investigated and released, no cloud of suspicion should follow the evacuees. Unity is imperative in the war effort, but unity cannot be achieved if we listen to those who believe that loyalty is only skin deep. In the relocation centers today there are men who are veterans of the first World War. Today, also, several thousand citizens of Japanese descent are serving with the armed forces of this Nation. When on furlough, these soldiers are now permitted to visit the west coast on military passes. They are to me, as I am sure they are to most Americans, living symbols of the greatness and strength of American democracy. To suggest that race can be a test of loyalty is as insulting to these soldiers and to their families as it is to some sixteen million other American citizens whose skins happen to be red or black, yellow or brown. Such a suggestion is utterly at variance with American ideals and is well calculated to jeopardize America's magnificent opportunity for world leadership in an unprecedented crisis in human affairs. As President Roosevelt has reminded us, Americanism is a matter of the mind and heart. Americanism is not, and never has been a matter of race or ancestry.

Town Meeting: Bulletin of America's Town Meeting of the Air, Vol. 9, No. 11, July 15, 1943, pp. 4-6, 9-11

11

McWilliams' pamphlet on the subject, which came out the following year, dealt more fully with the relevant issues. In addition to his manifold other activities (including editing The Nation), *McWilliams was a contributor to the work of the Institute of Pacific Relations. The IPR, founded by YMCA representatives in the 1920's as a liberal body of scholarly inquiry, went on to make an important impact in Asian and Pacific studies in the United States. A non-partisan body with a wide range of contributors and publications, the IPR fell victim to McCarthyism in the wake of the Chinese revolution of 1949.[13]*

Unlike Other Immigrant Groups
Not only were the Japanese a late immigrant group, but they were racially different from the others and were also set apart by sharp cultural differences. Noting that the rate of assimilation for the Japanese was somewhat slower than for other immigrant groups, west-coast residents hastily concluded that the cultural difference was accounted for in terms of race. It must be remembered, however, that the American-born or Nisei generation had not, by December 7, 1941, assumed the leadership of the Japanese communities, although they would clearly have done so in another decade. In 1930, slightly more than half of the Japanese in America were foreign-born; but in 1940 the ratio had declined to slightly more than one-third. In other words, the war struck the west-coast communities just at the moment when the American-born and American-educated generation was beginning to

displace the alien generation in positions of social and economic leadership.

Thus there existed on the west coast, on December 7, 1941, a deep fissure in the social structure of the region. This fissure separated the relatively small Japanese minority from the rest of the population. Like the earthquake fissures that run along the Pacific Coast, this particular fissure was deeper in some areas than in others; it had been dormant for some years, but it was still potentially active. As fifty years of prior social history had shown, almost any jar or shock was capable of disturbing it. The attack on Pearl Harbor was more than a jar; it was a thunderous blow, an earthquake, that sent tremors throughout the area in which the fissure existed. The resident Japanese were victims of this social earthquake. This is the root-fact, which precipitated the mass evacuation of the west-coast Japanese - which has been accurately described as "the largest single forced migration in American history...."

Racial Considerations

General DeWitt's report makes it clear that his interpretation of "military necessity" involved a judgment on sociological grounds. "The continued presence," writes General DeWitt, "of a large, unassimilated, tightly-knit racial group, bound to the enemy by strong ties of race, culture, custom, and religion, constituted a menace which had to be dealt with." There is at least some question as to whether the task of weighing these "ethnic affiliations" was a proper assignment for a military commander. Sociologists, who had been studying the problem for years, have drawn an entirely different conclusion from the same facts. The prompt arrest of all "dangerous enemy aliens" and the fact of the war itself had served to cut whatever ties had bound the west-coast Japanese to their homeland. If these "ethnic affiliations" were deemed so dangerous on the west coast, why were the same affiliations in Hawaii regarded as unimportant? There has been no mass evacuation of the Japanese in Hawaii, where they constitute 37 per cent of the entire population, and all the authorities agree that, there, the local Japanese have conclusively demonstrated their loyalty.

Racial considerations were evidently regarded as part of the "military necessity" requiring mass evacuation. "The Japanese race," states General DeWitt in his report, "is an enemy race, and while many second- and third-generation Japanese born on United States soil, possessed United States citizenship, have become 'Americanized,' the racial strains are undiluted...."

Testifying on April 13, 1943, before the House Naval Affairs Subcommittee, he also volunteered this remark:

...[The Japanese-Americans] are a dangerous element, loyal or not. There is no way to determine their loyalty...it makes no difference whether he is an American; theoretically, he is still a Japanese and you can't change him.... You can't change him by giving him a piece of paper.

This reference to citizenship as "a piece of paper" and the frank admission that "loyalty" was not even a factor certainly indicate that the racial consideration was uppermost in General DeWitt's mind. This same consideration was uppermost in the minds of the influential public officials who were mobilizing a public opinion in favor of mass evacuation and who were bringing pressure to bear directly upon General DeWitt. Governor Earl Warren of California (then Attorney-General) told the Tolan Committee early in 1942 "that when we are dealing with *the Caucasian race* we have methods that will test the loyalty of them," but that no such determination could be made in the case of the Japanese. The many demonstrations of the loyalty of the west-coast Japanese were apparently regarded as an immaterial consideration. Racial distrust was the chief factor prompting mass evacuation....

What About Our Japanese-Americans?, New York, Public Affairs Committee, Inc., 1944, pp. 4-5, 9-11

12

George Knox Roth was an ardent anti-evacuation protester in Southern California during the peak of the internment. A Quaker, he made a series of radio broadcasts challenging the constitutionality of the procedure and defending the integrity of Japanese Americans.[14] For this, his career as educator suffered dramatically. The Pacific Citizen *was and is the newspaper of the Japanese American Citizens League.*

"Friends of George Knox Roth" and the Pacific Southwest JACL District Council are about to honor a truly unsung hero of the Japanese American because when practically every public official and organization was screaming to send them all to concentration camps, Roth stood up and publicly attempted to prevent the tragic event.

The honors will be accorded the Roth family at a fund-raising dinner to be held on Saturday, Aug. 13, 7:30 p.m. at the Little Tokyo Towers, 455 E. 3rd St.

Roth was 35 years old then, father of three children, a teacher and starting a political career in 1942.

Based on his belief in human rights, his friendship and admiration of the Japanese people, Roth worked with several Nisei to prevent the Evacuation despite they hysteria of the times.

The Friends of the George Knox Roth Committee, co-chaired by Mrs. Mitsu Sonada and Sam Minami, this past week revealed Kay Sugahara, Sam Minami and the late Joe Shinoda were the three Nisei who helped provide the money which Roth used to purchase radio time to counteract the pro-Evacuation broadcasts for a period of six weeks, during which he emphasized the positive and valuable contributions which were being made by the Japanese American community. Roth appealed for their basic rights as Americans.

State Sen. Jack B. Tenney of Los Angeles (the county then had only one state senator), chairing the Senate Fact-Finding Committee on Un-American Activities in California, subpoenaed Roth and demanded the names of those Nisei who were "behind" his broadcasts. Upon his refusal to cooperate, he was tried and found guilty of contempt of the committee. Appeals were unsuccessful. It was recalled even his lawyer friends or ACLU would not handle his case.

His file with the State Superintendent of Public Instruction was red-tagged "Nisei sympathizer" and he was convicted "on contempt of Un-American Activities Committee." The record followed him throughout his teaching career for 20 years after the war. Because of this, Roth was never able to gain tenure in any school district and was forced to cash in any accumulated retirement benefits in order to make ends meet during periods between jobs.

"As a result of the penalty that the Roths had to pay for taking a courageous stand in 1942, today they are living on social security and whatever else his ingenuity is able to earn," according to Henry Sakai, PSWDC ethnic concerns chairman who now wonders if there are any other unsung heroes who sought to prevent the Evacuation.

Sakai declared the Japanese American community "owes the Roths a tremendous debt and thanks for the stand he took 35 years ago." He hopes Nisei around the country will participate in this fund-raising tribute....

Harry Honda, "George Knox Roth: He publicly tried to prevent Evacuation," *Pacific Citizen*, June 24, 1977

13

Another particularly active Quaker was Herbert V. Nicholson, who had been a missionary in Japan and a pastor to Japanese Methodists in Los Angeles. His contacts in the Japanese American community, and among the clergy, as indicated by the extracts which follow, were substantial.

The ugly history of locking up tens of thousands of loyal Japanese-Americans in domestic concentration camps during World War II has recently been documented in a long and often eloquent report, *Personal Justice Denied*, issued earlier this year by the federal Commission on Wartime Relocation and Internment of Civilians.

....In its focus on the process of policymaking during the course of the internment, however, the report leaves out an important part of the story: the fact that some white Americans did protest the evacuation.

This all-but-forgotten crusade was led by one tireless man - Herbert V. Nicholson, a lanky, bespectacled Californian.

Nicholson, then in his 50's, had been a Quaker missionary in Japan for 25 years, from 1915 until the approach of war interrupted his evangelistic work. He settled in Pasadena in 1940 and worked as interim pastor at a Japanese Methodist Church in west Los Angeles. The day after Pearl Harbor, his flock began to scatter under the spur of government round-ups.

Stunned by the forced evacuation, he immediately began working against it. For the next 18 months, he became a combination traveling social worker and circuit riding preacher to the internees, visiting the isolated camps in California, Arizona and Texas. He carried parcels of their belongings and took messages to and from their separated family members.

He also tried to organize protests against the internment. He started the day after Pearl Harbor, visiting the Los Angeles FBI office and the regional director of naval intelligence, indignantly insisting that they hysterical newspaper stories about alleged Japanese-American sabotage in Hawaii were false and should be corrected. The naval intelligence director agreed that the reports were erroneous, but said that there was nothing he could do. Later that day, Nicholson took his plea to a meeting of a local church federation, only to be denounced and tossed out of the session.

Friends of the American Way

Finally he and a handful of others, mostly Quakers, formed Friends of the American Way, which did relief work and wrote letters objecting to the treatment of the Japanese-Americans.

They didn't make much headway, however, until February of 1944 when Dillon Myer, the head of the War Relocation Authority, met with Nicholson and a delegation from the American Friends Service Committee at the Quaker meetinghouse in Pasadena. By that time, many young Japanese-Americans had been proving their loyalty in battle as volunteers and the Selective Service System had begun drafting them out of camps for military service. Nicholson confronted Myer with the cruel hypocrisy of calling these men out to defend a system that held their relatives captive.

As Nicholson remembers the conversation, Myer agreed with his criticism but said he couldn't do anything about it. The decision to release the Japanese-Americans would have to come through proper channels - namely from Assistant War Secretary John McCloy, who was in charge of interned citizens....

It took him several weeks to get across the country....Once he got to the Pentagon, he was surprised to find several old acquaintances from Japanese religious missions working there, in intelligence operations. It was these old colleagues who smoothed his way into McCloy's office.

McCloy also agreed with his contention that the Japanese-Americans should be released. The roadblock to releasing the internees, McCloy said, was public opinion. He showed Nicholson a stack of letters, mostly from the West Coast, insisting that no Japanese-Americans should be allowed to return to their homes. "We get very few letters on the other side of the issue," he said. McCloy pointed to his desk, and added, "If you can fill this other basket on my desk with letters saying 'We want our Japanese friends back again,' we'll open the camps as soon as we're sure that public opinion is not 100 percent against it."

Nicholson left McCloy's office and headed straight to the Western Union office to send telegrams to the Friends of the American Way and contacts at several camps, telling them to start writing letters. Then he caught the train to Philadelphia, where he passed the word on to the American Friends Service Committee headquarters and the National Council of Churches....

Nicholson says that within four months more than 150,000 letters were sent to Washington, mainly from the West Coast. Even so, the officials hesitated. There was an election coming on and anti-Japanese hostility was still prevalent. Some Japanese were eventually allowed to leave the camps if they could find work away from their homes on the West Coast, but circumstances forced most to remain.

In the summer of '44, McCloy wrote to the Friends of the American Way indicating that he was willing to test public reaction by releasing a single youth to leave the camps and stay on the West Coast by enrolling at Pasadena Junior College. A young woman named Esther Takei was chosen - she was said to be bright and personable and her brother had been killed fighting with the 442nd Battalion of Nisei volunteers. A Quaker family took her in and she started college in September 1944.

For the first month or so, there was a lot of harassment: threatening phone calls and cars parading past the house. But there were also many messages of encouragement, and within weeks the harassment faded away. Takei proved very popular with other students and there were no incidents. By December 1944, plans were underway to open the camps, and by early 1945 many Japanese were able to return to their home areas. Nicholson still believes that it was the deluge of letters and Esther Takei's success that pushed the government into recognizing the loyalty of the Japanese-Americans and letting them out of the camps....

In August 1981...he testified in Los Angeles before the Commission on Wartime Relocation and Internments of Civilians. He called on the government to establish a memorial fund for those who died in the concentration camps. As he left the room, the capacity crowd burst into loud applause.

That was not the first time he had spoken out for redress. In April 1973, when a historic marker was dedicated at the site of the Manzanar camp, 200 miles out in the desert east of Los Angeles, Nicholson was invited by the Nisei master of ceremonies to make the opening remarks. His main plea, he recalls, was to ask the Nisei on behalf of his countrymen, "Will you please forgive us as we pledge wholeheartedly to join you in the determination that such a thing shall never happen again in our beloved country?"

Chuck Fager, "Days of Infamy," *In These Times*, May 18-24, 1983

14

Of interest in the following document is the sympathy with which the Pittsburgh Courier, *a major Black newspaper, reports the appeal of* Pacific Citizen *editor Larry Tajiri for cooperation against racist discrimination. The anti-Japanese campaign, beginning to ebb by 1944, had nevertheless not run its course.*

"The problem of Japanese Americans being predominantly one of color and race, its ultimate solution will depend on correlation with other problems of color and race in America." That is the conviction expressed by the vigorous Japanese American writer, Larry Tajiri, editor of the *Pacific Citizen*, national organ of the Japanese American Citizens' League, in the latest issue of *Common Ground* magazine, under the caption, "Farewell to Tokyo."

Mr. Tajiri admitted that much of the problem of assimilation is individual, and obviously so, but insisted that the problem is much wider and deeper. He expressed inability to see how Japanese Americans can resolve their present situation wholly on an individual plane, for, while this predicament has certain economic and political aspects, it is a racial problem - a racial problem imbedded deeply in the racial attitudes of the dominant white majority, especially on the West Coast.

More and more, Mr. Tajiri, confessed, Japanese Americans are learning that their fate is tied up inextricably in the fate of other minorities - granting that, in the past, regional prejudices against Filipinos, Mexicans, Negroes and Jews have been accepted by many Japanese Americans, just as these particular victims of discrimination sometimes echo the propaganda of the professional anti-Japanese "yellow peril" mongers.

EVACUATION, BIG REVELATION

Evacuation had to come before Japanese Americans finally came to a sweeping awareness of the urgent and demanding color problems of the American Negro, the militant editor wrote. He said it drove home to all Japanese Americans the delayed revelation that their problem, too, is inescapably one of color - and is part of the unfinished business of democracy.

Mr. Tajiri cited a number of bizarre racial experiences encountered by Japanese Americans in the South as an illustration of the degree to which the Japanese American problem is essentially one of color - like that of the American Negro and, in some cases, even more pernicious and peculiar.

FATES SIMILAR AND DIFFERENT

In one case, "Jim Crow" found a corollary in "Jap Crow," it was described, with the result that Japanese Americans were treated as Negroes and subjected to the same intense prejudice and discrimination.

In other cases, it was explained, Japanese Americans, to maintain peace and harmony, have assumed that they were regarded as colored and have taken their places in jim crow train cars, only to be hied into white coaches by irate conductors who have ordered them away from the Negro passengers.

Still a rarer instance was mentioned where the Japanese American is acceptable to neither white nor Negro Americans, as in the case of a segregated USO in Hattiesburg, Miss.

"'Japanese-Americans' Fate Tied Up With That of Other Minorities,' Editor Writes," *Pittsburgh Courier*, July 1, 1944

15

In his Amsterdam News *column, "As the Crow Flies," W.E.B. DuBois commented upon and reacted to a wide range of wartime developments, both at home and abroad. On more than one occasion therein, DuBois took issue with the evacuation of Japanese Americans and discrimination against them. Selections are taken from several columns.[15]*

(a)
OUR BALANCE SHEET AFTER ONE AND A HALF YEARS OF WAR
Debit

Our jim-crow army.

Discrimination in southern army camps.

Failure to convict known lynchers and promoters of peonage.

Failure of the FEPC.[16]

Continued discrimination against Negroes in labor unions especially in the railway unions.

The encouragement of hate against the Japanese as a race people without regard to whether they are citizens, friends or enemies.

Continued discrimination against China.

Refusal openly to support the aspirations of India.

Refusal to note the extremes of race discrimination in Kenya and the Union of South Africa....

"As the Crow Flies," *Amsterdam News*, June 26, 1943

(b)
AMERICAN JAPANESE

Ten thousand Americans of Japanese descent, torn from their homes, despoiled of their savings and threatened with mob law have been settled in south central Arizona on 17,000 acres of land. The land was worth $24 an acre when they arrived. They are raising now $250 worth of produce on each acre.

Yet no American community welcomes these folk.

"As the Crow Flies," *Amsterdam News*, March 4, 1944

(c)

RACE HATE ON WEST COAST

Most people do not realize that outbreaks of so-called "racial hate" are practically always organized and not spontaneous. The driving out of people of Japanese descent on the West Coast was not the only attempt to confiscate their savings without return, but to foment and prolong racial antagonism. The persons back of this wanted to keep serf Japanese labor in the Hawaiian Islands and prevent the Japanese from working anywhere in the United States outside the West Coast.

The leaders said in 1942, "We should strike now, while the sentiment over the country is right. The feeling of the East will grow more bitter before the war is over and if we begin now to try to shut out the Japanese, after the war we have a chance of accomplishing something." Among the organizations back of this movement is the American Educational League and the Homefront Commandos, Inc., whose slogan is "Slap the Jap Rat" and "No Jap is Fit to Associate With Human Beings."

The Native Sons are the real force behind the movement in California. They have a membership of 25,000 and are not merely anti-Japanese, but anti-Oriental, anti-Mexican and anti-Negro.[17]

"As the Crow Flies," *Amsterdam News*, June 10, 1944

16

The International Longshoremen's and Warehousemen's Union on the West Coast compiled an unrivalled record in combatting racial discrimination. Under a left-wing leadership headed by Harry Bridges (1900-1990), the union had opened its doors to workers of all nationalities and races. One of the first unions to recognize the dangers of fascism, the ILWU had refused to stow scrap iron aboard ships bound for Japan during the late 1930's, thus winning the admiration of all who sympathized with that nation's chief victim: China. The high esteem in which Chinese and Chinese Americans, for example, held the ILWU, is indicated by the numerous messages of gratitude the union received for its stance against Japanese aggression, years before Pearl Harbor. When the latter was attacked, the union did not succumb to the anti-Japanese racism prevailing on the Pacific Coast, but on the contrary reinforced its opposition to discrimination.[18] Despite anti-Japanese sentiment in one local,[19] the ILWU as a whole stood for solidarity of all workers and defied the racist norms of the period and the region.

(a)

Matt Meehan, veteran Local 8 member and former secretary-treasurer of the ILWU, returned last week from the Hawaiian Islands, where he spearheaded the start of an organizing drive.[20]

"The workers in the huge sugar milling industry in the Islands are ready as never before for unions," he said.

Some 35,000 potential unionists work in this important industry. More than 5,000 workers are already organized in the CIO. ILWU members principally on the waterfront, provided an organizing base when the ILWU approached key workers in the refining mills.

"The response was immediate. Substantial majorities were signed up in three of the mills, with Hawaiian and Filipino members of the ILWU leading the organizing drive," Meehan reported.

A virtual melting pot, with a mixed population of Japanese and Portuguese, as well as Hawaiians and Filipinos, the Islands have racial problems which have deterred organization in the past.

The Hawaiian sugar industry, ruled by the "Big Five," is notorious for its efforts to keep apart the people of different national backgrounds.

"In the CIO tradition," Meehan pointed out, "these groups are coming together into the ranks of the ILWU."

Because of the loyalty of the Japanese and their whole-hearted cooperation in the war effort, attempts to persecute Japanese Americans have sharply failed.

Meehan stressed that Filipinos and Hawaiians, together with those of Japanese and Portuguese descent, keenly feel the need for organization. To them the war of liberation means liberation from slave labor....

"Meehan Back with Report on Hawaii," *The Dispatcher*, June 16, 1944

(b)

Memories of unionists who befriended him gave hope to a Japanese-American during the trying days after Pearl Harbor, Staff Sergeant Alex N. Yorichi wrote in a letter to the union last week.

Recalling this union friendship, Yorichi called again on Local 6 to aid him in discharging his voting responsibilities as a "good American citizen and a good rank and filer."

"I received my official election war ballot for the general election in Alameda County," he states.

"Since I'm not acquainted with the recommendations of the Alameda County CIO nor of the CIO Political Action committee, I would like to learn of their candidates, including write-ins.

"I'm a book member in the A.C.W.U., CIO, San Francisco and was a permit man in your union after Pearl Harbor, so I thought I could ask and enlist your help on this matter.

EVACUATED TO STABLE

"You may still have old records in your permit files which will show that I, a Japanese American, was given a job through your union. Like all the other Americans of Japanese ancestry, I was evacuated to a stable in a race track and then later to a barbed-wire enclosed camp in the middle of a desert. But during my 'captivity' in that demoralizing environment, I remembered my faithful friends back in California, especially the union brothers who befriended me during those trying days.

"As a good American citizen and a good rank and filer, I have been voting regularly. Now I would like to learn of the political situation in Alameda County, so I can vote intelligently.

"It is ironical but through absentee balloting I voted in the November 1942 election during a dust storm at a relocation center, and now in 1944, I'm voting in the monsoon period near the jungles."

Needless to say, the information requested by Yorichi was sent to him with the union's hope that soon he can return to an America in which brighter days will wipe out entirely the memories of his experiences in the post-Pearl Harbor era.

"Japanese-American Sergeant Recalls Union Friendship; Asks Voting Aid," *The Dispatcher*, November 17, 1944

(c)

ILWU President Harry Bridges hailed the War Department order permitting Americans of Japanese ancestry to return to their homes on the West Coast as "clearly in line with the anti-fascist purposes of the war," in a statement released December 18.

"Our union has never believed that the test of loyalty should be the color of a man's skin," said Bridges. "Our brother Americans of Japanese descent have shown their patriotism the hard way, as evidenced by our own members on the battlefront. It has been their unfortunate lot to have to prove themselves by doing an even better job on the home front and on the fighting front than anybody else.

"The order must be welcomed as proof that America will not accept either the Nazi or the Japanese imperialist theories of a superior race."

"Bridges Lauds End of Japanese Ban," *The Dispatcher*, December 29, 1944

17

On the basis of the increasingly widespread conviction that the evacuation and internment had been thoroughly unjust, the notion of compensating survivors for their suffering and losses was widely discussed during the 1970's and 1980's. In hearings held in a number of cities during 1981, a federal commission took testimony from hundreds of surviving internees, including first, second, and third generation Japanese Americans. The remarks of one witness appear below.

My name is Adaso Kadoya, I was born in Lynwood, California; I am a Nisei.

The months following Pearl Harbor were so terrifying that I shall never forget them.

I was living in Los Angeles when Pearl Harbor was bombed. My husband and his two brothers owned produce markets in the Hawthorne-Inglewood area. One day, three men who claimed they were from the FBI ordered all of the men to go to the police station and register for the army. They all left within minutes; then the men made advances at me, pulled my blouse open and tried to rape me. I was so horrified, I froze. Fortunately my husband and his brothers returned. They said that they were made fools of because the police did not know anything about registration.

I never told my husband or anybody else about what happened that day, there was no reason to but now I feel there is.

Being a citizen, I was proud and loyal. When we were ordered to evacuate I could not believe it! The only country I knew was the USA. Japan to me was as remote as China, Turkey or Russia!

The FBI took my father, for what, I do not know. He was a truck farmer and raised his family never defying the law. He was taken to jail that night and the following day to a place (I do not remember the name). It may have been Tujunga or La Tuna.

When I saw my father and all the men behind the high barbed wire fence, I felt sorry for them. The MP told me to stop talking in Japanese to my father. While I was still talking, the MP grabbed me and took me away. I was pregnant at the time and when I arrived home, I started to bleed. The doctor said that he was not sure whether there would be any medical facilities where we were going. He said that my life would be in danger and suggested an abortion which I agreed.

As you know, the Hawthorne-Inglewood area was one of the first to be blacked out because it was close to the airport. That meant that it was off limits to the persons of Japanese ancestry. We did not have time to sell anything. Having no alternative, we decided to go to Manzanar on 1 April, 1942.

We had our truck full with our belongings when we were notified that we could take only what we could carry. Of course we had to leave everything behind. With so many things happening we did not know what to expect next.

With our suitcases we boarded the train. It was a weird feeling with so many military police guarding us. My first thought when we arrived was: "Is this where we are going to live?" So many barracks just half constructed, barbed wires and sentries, so much confusion, what had we done that we were to be sent to this desolate place?

My husband worked as a cook for $19.00 and I, $16.00 for working in the mess hall.

There was a shortage in Montana for sugar beet workers; we volunteered and spent some months there. The farmers were surprised that we weren't dangerous as they had thought. We were treated kindly.

With my father in New Mexico and my brother in the army and we in camp, I was confused and bitter. When we were questioned about our loyalty, I could not truthfully say "yes" at that time. Consequently, we were sent to Tule Lake.

When it was time to relocate, we did not have any money. We had spent the little money we had to supplement our needs. My husband had $45.00 when he left for Chicago. He had to go first to find a place for us to live and some money to buy food, bedding and clothes. We lived in a hotel. I washed clothes and dished in the bathtub. We lived there for several months.

At Tule Lake, my husband was told to contact the WRA in Chicago as they would help him find a job and a place to live. they did not. It took him a while to send for us - our two little daughters and myself.

Even though the children were three and four years old, I had to work as my husband was making seventy-six cents an hour. He took the graveyard shift at a printing company and I worked at a corset company. It was very hard on both of us.

The company nurse where I was employed, asked me why I was so thin and sickly. I told her of my backache. She made an appointment for me with a doctor. When he examined me, he was surprised how I could work in my physical condition. He scheduled me for surgery immediately. The doctor said that the doctors at the concentration camp had been careless and negligent.

After six weeks of recuperating, I returned to work. We returned to Los Angeles, after three years. We both continued to work until our retirement in 1976.

I feel as though the United States government owes me full restitution for what we lost due to this unjust internment. We were uprooted from our lives, forced into concentration camps and again forced to relocate.

Those of us who experienced life behind barbed wire fences know of the suffering, humiliation and unfairness of this horrible act of the United States government.

The Commission on Wartime Relocation and Internment of Civilians: Selected Testimonies from the Los Angeles and San Francisco Hearings, *Amerasia Journal*, 8:2 (1981), pp. 65-68

18

From the Japanese American Citizens League, which played an important role in bringing the reparations issue before the government and the public, came the following argument for redress.[21]

REDRESS

By custom and tradition, any American who has been injured by false accusation, arrest or imprisonment is expected to bring the responsible parties into court and obtain a judgment clearing his or her name and collecting damages as redress. Freedom is considered so precious by Americans that even a few days in false imprisonment have been compensated with large monetary sums.

German Jews experienced the horrors of the Nazi death camps. Japanese Americans experienced the agonies of being incarcerated for an indeterminate period. Both were imprisoned in barbed wire compounds with armed guards. Both were prisoners of their own country. Both were there without criminal charges, and were completely innocent of any wrongdoing. Both were there for only one reason - ancestry. German Jews were systematically murdered en masse - that did not happen to Japanese Americans, but the point is that both Germany and the United States persecuted their own citizens based on ancestry.

West Germany has made a 25 billion dollar restitution payment to

Jews and Jewish institutions, and another 10 to 15 billion dollars will be paid. The fact that the victorious Allied Powers initially imposed on Germany the concept of reparations to the victims of the Third Reich does not diminish the righteousness or the justice of the act. The Federal Republic of Germany has stated that it is giving precedence to the payment of compensatory damages to "those who suffered in mind and body, or had been deprived unjustly of their freedom." In subsequent legislation Germany went far beyond the responsibilities assumed in the earlier agreements.

More recently, the United States government designated an American Jewish organization to negotiate with East Germany on restitutions. The United States has informed the German Democratic Republic that a refusal to acknowledge the necessity for a meaningful restitution would delay the establishment of normal diplomatic relations.

The mass expulsion and incarceration of American citizens without trial did happen here in the United States. As a professed leader in civil and human rights throughout the world, the United States must take meaningful action to correct its own mistakes.

President Gerald R. Ford rescinded the Executive Order 9066 on February 19, 1976 - exactly 34 years after its promulgation - and stated: "An honest reckoning must include a recognition of our national mistakes as well as our national achievements. Learning from our mistakes is not pleasant, but as a great philosopher once admonished, we must do so if we want to avoid repeating them."

Redress for the injustices of 1942-1946 is not just an isolated Japanese American issue; it is an issue of concern for all Americans. Restitution does not put a price tag on freedom or justice. The issue is not to recover what cannot be recovered. The issue is to acknowledge the mistake by providing proper redress for the victims of the injustice, and thereby make such injustices less likely to recur.

The National Committee for Redress, Japanese American Citizens League, *The Japanese American Incarceration: A Case for Redress*, San Francisco, 1976, pp., 23-24

19

Materials taken from press reports outline the difficult road to vindication and redress, culminating in the federal government's 1988 agreement to compensate surviving internees.

(a)

Newly found documents show that the United States government deliberately misled the Supreme Court in three landmark cases during World War II that challenged the evacuation of 120,000 Japanese Americans, attorneys representing the defendants said yesterday.

They said the documents prove that Navy officials, Justice Department attorneys and Charles Fahy, the U.S. solicitor general at the time, knowingly "suppressed key evidence" in the cases of three Japanese Americans who refused to obey the government's evacuation orders in 1942.

"The evidence will show that high government officials suppressed, altered and even destroyed key evidence to influence the outcome of the (Supreme Court) decisions," said Donald Tamaki, director of the Asian Law Caucus in Oakland and member of a national legal committee representing the three men.

The documents also show that Justice Department attorneys writing briefs for the cases knew that an Army report by General John L. Dewitt accusing Japanese Americans of espionage on the West Coast was an "intentional falsehood," the attorneys said.

The legal action is not related to the Japanese American community's drive for redress from the government for World War II internment.

"There's no money involved here," said Tamaki. "We want to set the historical record straight because many people still believe evacuation was justified by military necessity."

He said petitions asking for the cases of Fred Korematsu, Gordon Hirabayashi and Minoru Yasui to be reopened will be filed today in federal courts in San Francisco, Seattle and Portland, Ore.

All three men - now in their 60s - challenged the military orders that led to the four-year internment of 75,000 Japanese American citizens and 41,000 Japanese aliens in "relocation" camps throughout the western United

States. The three were given jail terms after they refused to obey military orders to go the camps.

They lost their appeals in 1943 and 1944 when the Supreme Court ruled that the Army used legal war powers when it ordered the mass evacuation. Yasui served nine months in an Oregon county jail and Hirabayashi served six months in federal prison in Washington.

Korematsu, a San Leandro resident, spent 60 days in county jail and served five years of probation. All three men also stayed at relocation camps for the duration of the war.

The attorneys said they have discovered a 1944 memo from Edward Ennis, head of the Alien Control Unit of the U.S. attorney's office in Washington, to Assistant Attorney General Herbert Wechsler. Ennis wrote: "It is highly unfair to this racial minority that these lies being put out in official publications go uncorrected."

The "official publication" referred to an Army report released by General John L. Dewitt that accused the Japanese in America of being a threat to the nation's security. Despite findings to the contrary, the government used the report to justify evacuation, according to the attorneys.

They also said that the Federal Communications Commission - after investigating suspected shortwave radio transmissions from West Coast Japanese residents to enemy ships - told the FBI that no cases of such espionage could be found.

"This is the first time in the history of the Supreme Court where you have government officials and attorneys lying and suppressing evidence on a major Supreme Court case," Tamaki said.

"You had people making cold, cynical decisions, knowing that contrary information existed and suppressing it."

The attorneys said the declassified documents were received through Freedom of Information Act requests and dug out of government archives by Peter Irons, a law professor in the political science department at the University of California at San Diego.

"U.S. Reportedly Lied to Justify Japanese Camps," *San Francisco Chronicle*, January 19, 1983

(b)

The internment of 120,000 West Coast Japanese Americans during World War II resulted from "race prejudice, war hysteria and a failure of political leadership" - not military necessity - a congressional commission said yesterday.

While citing the causes of "this shameful page in American history," the nine-member Commission on Wartime Relocation and Internment of Civilians put off the politically tough question of whether the victims of "this grave injustice" should be paid reparations.

Later this year, the commission will make recommendations based upon the report to Congress. The recommendations could range from a presidential proclamation of apology to the payment of $3 billion in reparations.

The commission, which conducted an 18-month study of the causes of the internment, was created in 1980. Its members were appointed by congressional leaders.

Chairman Joan Bernstein insisted that the commission was not trying to duck the reparations question, but did not want its 467 pages of findings overshadowed.

"Too few Americans really know about the mass exclusion and detention of American citizens of Japanese ancestry and their resident-alien parents," she said.

"What happened after Pearl Harbor is particularly sobering because men of the greatest stature, with careers of the most distinguished public service - Democrat and Republican, conservative and liberal, judges, legislators and Cabinet members, the president himself - were personally involved in a course of action which today we can only find gravely unjust and deeply injurious," Bernstein said at a press conference.

President Franklin D. Roosevelt, Secretary of War Henry Stimson, Attorney General Francis Biddle and Lieutenant General John Dewitt, the West Coast military commander, all shared major responsibility for rounding up Japanese Americans and moving them to inland relocation camps where they were kept under armed guard, the commission said.

"Secretary Stimson and President Roosevelt did not subject this program to sufficiently close and critical scrutiny," Bernstein said. "The attorney general did not believe the program necessary, but acceded to it when proposed by the War Department.

"The opinions of those with intelligence responsibility, such as the FBI, who believed that there was no sound basis for mass exclusion, were ignored or drowned out in the frightened uproar of the time."

The commission also found that Roosevelt was unwilling to end the internment until after the presidential election of 1944 - even though Stimson had told him that there was no military justification for continuing the policy.

The commission also criticized Roosevelt and others for failing to make it clear to the American public that there was no evidence to support statements by Navy Secretary Frank Knox that the attack on Pearl Harbor had been aided by sabotage by Japanese residents in Hawaii.

"This policy of exclusion, removal and detention was executed against 120,000 people without individual review, and exclusion was continued virtually without regard for their demonstrated loyalty to the United States," the report said.

"All this was done despite the fact that not a single documented act of espionage, sabotage or fifth column activity was committed by an American citizen of Japanese ancestry or by a resident Japanese alien on the West Coast.

"Thus the country was unfairly led to believe that both American citizens of Japanese descent and resident Japanese aliens threatened American security....On the West Coast, where there had been a long history of prejudice and discrimination against the ethnic Japanese, there were sustained and ever louder demands for the exclusion of Japanese Americans...."

"Japanese Internment Called Needless, Racist," *San Francisco Chronicle*, February 25, 1983

(c)

President Reagan, moving to "right a grave wrong," signed legislation today that apologizes for the Government's forced relocation of 120,000 Japanese-Americans in World War II and establishes a $1.25 billion trust fund to pay reparations to those who were placed in camps and to their families.

"Yes, the nation was then at war, struggling for its survival," Mr.

Reagan said at the White House. "And it's not for us today to pass judgment upon those who may have made mistakes while engaged in that great struggle. Yet we must recognize that the internment of Japanese-Americans was just that, a mistake."

Under the law, the Government will issue individual apologies for all violations of civil liberties and constitutional rights. And, through the office of the United States Attorney General, an award of $20,000 in tax-free payments will be given to each eligible intern or the designated beneficiary of the approximately 60,000 surviving Japanese-Americans who were driven from their homes and placed in internment camps in the war. Legislation providing the money must still be enacted.

Veto Had Been Threatened

Mr. Reagan had threatened to veto the measure but went ahead and signed it today. The White House spokesman, Marlin Fitzwater, said that the president had been concerned about the price tag of the bill, not its concept. In signing the legislation, Mr. Reagan endorsed the position that Vice-President Bush staked out in June on the eve of the California primary.

About 40 percent of those affected by the legislation live in California, according to Congressional estimates.

The White House denied, as it has frequently done in recent weeks, that Mr. Reagan's initial opposition to the measure was reversed in part to help Mr. Bush in California.

When asked whether Mr. Bush's electoral prospects were responsible for Mr. Reagan's change of heart, Mr. Fitzwater replied, "No, they were not a factor in any way...."

Annual Appropriation Limited

No more than $500 million will be appropriated annually, Mr. Fitzwater added. And, in accepting the money, internees must agree to drop all legal claims pending against the Government....

Mr. Reagan, in his remarks in the Old Executive Office Building to 200 Japanese-Americans and Congressional supporters of the bill, took special note of the "scores of Japanese-Americans" who volunteered to serve in the United States armed forces in the war.

"The 442nd Regimental Combat Team, made up entirely of Japanese-Americans served with immense distinction to defend this nation, their nation," the President said. "Yet back at home, the soldiers' families were being denied the very freedom for which so many of the soldiers themselves were laying down their lives."

"....No payment can make up for those lost years," Mr. Reagan said. "What is most important in this bill has less to with property than with honor. For here we admit wrong."

"President Signs Law to Redress Wartime Wrong," *New York Times*, August 11, 1988

(d)

President Bush's recent signing of a bill appropriating $1.2 billion for the surviving 60,000 Japanese "was long overdue," says former internee George Kondo. "It is too bad the money [will not be] available until october 1990, seeing that 200 [internees] die every month."

Tsuyako Kitashima, who spent nearly three-and-a-half years in internment camps, told the *PDW*, "It was a terrific victory for us to go into the Halls of Congress and win, not just for us, but for the whole country. It is a lesson to our government not to repeat this against any other people."

Kondo, regional director of the Japanese American Citizens' League, believes the 1983 court decision repealing the wartime conviction of Fred Korematsu for evading internment and the 1989 entitlement law signed by President Bush will also widen the constitutional rights of other groups.

On Dec. 3, several hundred persons celebrated the signing of the redress entitlement bill at the Japanese Cultural Center. Taking part were Korematsu, Kitashima, 95-year old Ryoko Maruoka and other activists in the Japanese reparations campaign.

"Promises after promises were broken but we learned from our struggles what can be accomplished in a united effort," said Kitashima. The reparations money was initially promised in a 1988 bill, which formally apologized for the government's action but cynically provided no funds.

It took over 40 years to begin to repair the damage. When the internees were released after the war, they had lost their security, their dignity and a lifetime's work. Japanese immigrants to the United States had gone "through 100 years of discrimination, were denied jobs in American firms and there was a lot of anti-Japanese legislation back then," recalls Kondo.

"The Constitution was just a piece of paper in those days - it didn't work for us at all. Also, our generation were the 'quiet Nisei.' We didn't go on marches then," says Kitashima, a full-time volunteer at the Kimochi Senior Center....

The internment planted the seeds of a movement carried forward by the third generation of Japanese-Americans, Sansei. "The older generation said, 'Forget it, we'll never get any money,' but the youth raised the issue of reparation," remembers Karl Yoneda, veteran activist and member of the National Coalition for Redress and Reparation.

Sansei organized the NCRR, a grassroots coalition begun on the West Coast with no funds, in late 1979. It brought victims from as far away as Japan to testify at commission hearings called by President Carter. Despite a year one-half of testimony, two redress bills had died in Congress, recalls Kitashima, who works with the NCRR.

Then began a letter-writing campaign to the president, Congress, even local governments. Over 25,000 were sent from the Bay Area, 10,000 in one year alone, Kitashima reports. The NCRR went back to Congress in 1984, 1987 and 1988, winning victory in 1989. The JACL also lobbied in Washington. "Everybody contributed to this victory. It was everybody's effort," says Kondo....

While the signing of the Japanese reparation bill and the exoneration of Fred Korematsu begin to redress the 40-year old injustice against Japanese-Americans, Kitashima believes that "the same racism that put us in the camps is still around, because we are scapegoated for what Japan sells." Today, "we're still fighting racism," he said. "But we all have to have equal rights."

"Progress Won on Road to Reparations," *People's Daily World*, December 13, 1989

Notes

1. Roger Daniels' *Concentration Camps USA: Japanese Americans and World War II*, New York, 1971, superbly synthesizes the sources, issues, and contexts of the evacuation. His study of the relocation experience in both Canada and

the USA has uncovered evidence that both North American governments considered evacuation well before Pearl Harbor: "I think that it now must be agreed that at least a step toward pre-planning had been taken." Daniels, "The Decision to Relocate the North American Japanese: Another Look," *Pacific Historical Quarterly*, Vol. LI (February 1982), pp. 71-77.

2. Dillon Myer, head of the War Relocation Authority.

3. Judo, originating during the sixteenth century, was banned by the Allied military occupation of Japan after World War II as an ostensibly acute expression of martial values. Donn F. Draeger, *Modern Bujutsu & Budo*, New York, 1974, p. 48.

4. Eastland (Democrat-Mississippi) was an arch-segregationist and Cold Warrior, a powerful force in Southern and national decision-making circles.

5. See Henry Kraus, *The Many and the Few: A Chronicle of the Dynamic Auto Workers*, Urbana, 1985 (1947), pp. 266-286.

6. There was a relocation of numbers of German and Italian "enemy aliens," which in no sense approximated the treatment accorded Japanese Americans but nonetheless induced dislocation and suffering among many, while placing constitutional procedure in forfeit. See Stephen Fox, *The Unknown Internment: An Oral History of the Relocation of Italian Americans during World War II*, Boston, 1990. A visitor who toured Italian and German relocation camps throughout the country recalled his impression that the majority of those he met were loyal to the United States. Jerre Mangione, *An Ethnic at Large: A Memoir of America in the Thirties and Forties*, New York, 1978, p. 321.

7. Rankin was another rabid segregationist.

8. Earl Warren, later governor of California and Chief Justice of the U.S. Supreme Court, fully supported the evacuation. He was state Attorney-General, not governor, in early 1942. Daniels, *Concentration Camps USA*, pp. 51-52, 75-77, 149.

9. The 442nd Regimental Combat Team is studied in Masayo Umezawa Duus, *Unlikely Liberators: The Men of the 100th and 442nd*, Honolulu, 1987. Among the deeds for which it was hailed, the 442nd helped liberate Dachau concentration camp. S. Don Shimazu, "Nisei Too Liberated Dachau," *Jewish Currents*, April 1990, pp. 5-6.

10. A solid account is Vivian Raineri's *The Red Angel: The Life and Times of Elaine Black Yoneda, 1906-1988*, New York, 1991, especially pp. 182-190. See also Karl Yoneda, *Ganbatte: Sixty Year Struggle of a Kibei Worker*, Los Angeles, 1983, pp. 115-116. Party conventions in 1959 and 1972 briefly criticized the war-time suspensions. Yoneda, pp. 214-215.

11. The ACLU's stance on the internment is thoroughly conveyed in Peter Irons, *Justice at War*, New York, 1983. Irons demonstrates that Thomas stood with a lonely minority in the ACLU Board which opposed the evacuation. Among the majority were several civil libertarians of previously impeccable humanitarian reputations.

12. Biographies of Thomas include W.A. Swanberg, *Norman Thomas: The Last Idealist*, New York, 1976; Bernard K. Johnson, *Pacifist's Progress: Norman Thomas and the Decline of American Socialism*, Chicago, 1970; Harry Fleischman, *Norman Thomas: A Biography, 1884-1968*, New York, 1969.

13. The Institute of Pacific Relations is discussed in Frederick Vanderbilt Field, *From Right to Left: An Autobiography*, Westport, 1983, Chapters 9, 12, 13, 15, 17.

14. Other Quakers spoke in like tones, but Quaker publications occasionally equivocated. Thus, an unusually sensitive and evocative booklet, aimed at young readers, described hardships in the camps while claiming that Japanese had been relocated "in as democratic method as possible, kindly, but systematically, orderly and with great haste," evacuated for their own good. American Friends Service Committee, *American Refugees: Outline of a Unit of Study About Japanese-Americans*, Phila., 1943, p. 17.

15. Du Bois' developing wartime outlook is perceptively treated in Manning Marable, *W.E.B. Du Bois: Radical Democrat*, Boston, 1986, pp. 159-164, and Gerald Horne, *Black and Red: W.E.B. Du Bois and the Afro-American Response to the Cold War, 1944-1963*, Albany, 1986, chapters 2-4. In 1944, Du Bois expressed direct support for the work of the Japanese American Citizens League. Horne, p. 228.

16. The Fair Employment Practices Committee was set up in 1941 to ensure non-discriminatory employment in war industries. See John Hope Franklin and Alfred A. Moss, Jr., *From Slavery to Freedom: A History of Negro Americans*, New York, 1988, pp. 399-400.

17. The Native Sons of the Golden West was a racist organization with an anti-Asian focus, founded in 1875. The group counted prominent businessmen and politicians among its members from the turn of the century to the time of the evacuation. Carey McWilliams, *Prejudice - Japanese-Americans: Symbols of Racial Intolerance*, Boston, 1944, pp. 22-24.

18. ILWU and California state CIO leader Louis Goldblatt denounced the evacuation before a Congressional committee in the immediate wake of Executive Order 9066: "This entire episode of hysteria and mob chant...will from a dark page of American history." Raineri, pp. 197-198.

19. See Harvey Schwartz, "A Union Combats Racism: The ILWU's Japanese-American 'Stockton Incident' of 1945," *Southern California Quarterly*, Vol. LXII, No. 2 (Summer 1980), pp. 161-176.

20. For the ILWU in Hawaii, see Sanford Zalburg, *A Spark is Struck! Jack Hall and the ILWU in Hawaii*, Honolulu, 1979. See also Michi Kodame-Nishimoto et. al., eds., *Hanahana: An Oral History Anthology of Hawaii's Working People*, Honolulu, 1984, pp. 3-15, 75-92. Gary Y. Okihiro has shown that Hawaiian race relations were not as ideal as reputed. Okihiro, *Cane Fires: The Anti-Japanese Movement in Hawaii, 1865-1945*, Phila., 1991, pp. 195-276. That the ILWU was exceptional is suggested by Bruce Nelson: "The triumph of the ILWU in Hawaiian agriculture brought about a degree of fraternization across racial lines that few had thought possible." *Workers on the Waterfront: Seamen, Longshoremen, and Unions in the 1930's*, Urbana, 1988, p. 260.

21. According to Ronald Takaki, the JACL was established in 1930 "on the conservative and accomodationist strategies of enterprise and self-help." There was an apparent effort by leaders to downplay the organization's challenge to racism. Takaki, *Strangers from a Different Shore: A History of Asian Americans*, Boston, 1989, pp. 222-224. Karl Yoneda recalls his wartime impression that most JACL leaders were "conservative, anti-labor professionals." Yoneda, p. 119. Regarding the group's response to the evacuation, Roger Daniels likewise suggests that "JACLers collaborated actively with the government" to better "influence both government policy and public opinion and thus make easier their return to a normal life and facilitate their fuller acceptance into American society." Daniels, *Concentration Camps USA*, p. 144. The JACL later spearheaded the redress effort, along with a battery of community, legal, and civil rights groups, among them the Coalition for Redress and Reparations, the Asian Law Caucus, and the Asian American Legal Defense and Education Fund. AALDEF, *Outlook*, Spring 1989.

Select Bibliography

Books

Asher, Robert and Stephenson, Charles, eds. *Labor Divided: Race and Ethnicity in United States Labor Struggles, 1835-1960*. Albany: State University of New York Press, 1990.

Barth, Gunther. *Bitter Strength: A History of the Chinese in the United States, 1850-1870*. Cambridge: Harvard University Press, 1964.

Beechert, Edward D. *Working in Hawaii: A Labor History*. Honolulu: University of Hawaii Press, 1985.

Chan, Sucheng. *Asian Americans: An Interpretive History*. Boston: Twayne Publishers, 1991.

Entry Denied: Exclusion and the Chinese Community in America, 1882-1943. Philadelphia: Temple University Press, 1991.

This Bittersweet Soil: The Chinese in California Agriculture, 1860-1910. Berkeley: University of California Press, 1986.

Cheng, Lucie and Bodnacich, Edna, eds. *Labor Immigration Under Capitalism: Asian Workers in the United States Before World War II*. Berkeley: University of California Press, 1984.

Chiu, Ping. *Chinese Labor in California, 1850-1880: An Economic Study*. Madison: State Historical Society of Wisconsin, 1963.

Christgau, John. *"Enemies": World War II Alien Internment*. Ames: Iowa State University Press, 1985.

Collins, Donald E. *Native American Aliens: Disloyalty and the Renunciation of Citizenship by Japanese Americans During World War II*. Westport: Greenwood Press, 1985.

Daniels, Roger. *Coming to America: A History of Immigration and Ethnicity in American Life*. New York: HarperCollins, 1990.

Concentration Camps USA. New York: Holt, Rinehart and Winston, 1971.

The Politics of Prejudice. Berkeley: University of California Press, 1961.

Daniels, Roger, Taylor, Sandra C., and Kitano, Harry H.L., eds. *Japanese Americans: From Relocation to Redress*. Salt Lake City: University of Utah Press, 1986.

Drinnon, Richard. *Keeper of Concentration Camps: Dillon S. Myer and American Racism*. Berkeley: University of California Press, 1987.

Duus, Masayo Umezawa. *Unlikely Liberators: The Men of the 100th and 442nd*. Honolulu: University of Hawaii Press, 1987.

Girdner, Audrie and Loftis, Anne. *The Great Betrayal: The Evacuation of the Japanese-Americans During World War II*. New York: Macmillan, 1969.

Glenn, Evelyn Nakano. *Issei, Nisei, War Bride: Three Generations of Japanese American Women in Domestic Service*. Philadelphia: Temple University Press, 1986.

Ichioka, Yuji. *The Issei: The World of the First Generation Japanese Immigrants, 1885-1924*. New York: Free Press, 1988.

Irons, Peter. *Justice at War: The Story of the Japanese American Internment Cases*. New York: Oxford University Press, 1983.

Kachi, Teruka Okada. *The Treaty of 1911 and the Immigration and Alien Land Law Issue, 1911-1913*. New York: Arno, 1978.

Kawakami, K.K. *The Real Japanese Question*. New York: Macmillan, 1921.

Kitigawa, Daisuke. *Issei and Nisei: The Internment Years*. New York: Seabury Press, 1967.

Kodame-Nishimoto, Nishimoto, Warren S., and Oshiro, Cynthia A., eds. *Hanahana: An Oral History of Hawaii's Working People*. Honolulu: Ethnic Studies Oral History Project, University of Hawaii at Manoa, 1984.

Kwong, Peter. *Chinatown, New York: Labor and Politics, 1930-1950*. New York: Monthly Review Press, 1979.

Leighton, Alexander H. *The Governing of Men*. Princeton: Princeton University Press, 1945.

McWilliams, Carey. *Prejudice - Japanese-Americans: Symbols of Racial Intolerance*. Boston: Little, Brown, 1944.

Miller, Stuart Creighton. *The Unwelcome Immigrant: The American Image of the Chinese, 1785-1882*. Berkeley: University of California Press, 1964.

Minnick, Sylvia Sun. *Sanfow: The San Joaquin Chinese Legacy*. Fresno: Panorama West Publishing Group, 1988.

Myer, Dillon. *Uprooted Americans: The Japanese Americans and the War Relocation Authority during World War II*. Tucson: University of Arizona Press, 1971.

O'Brien, David J., and Fugita, Stephen S. *The Japanese American Experience*. Bloomington: Indiana University Press, 1991.

Okihiro, Gary S. *Cane Fires: The Anti-Japanese Movement in Hawaii, 1865-1945*. Philadelphia: Temple University Press, 1991.

Riggs, Fred W. *Pressures on Congress: A Study of the Repeal of Chinese Exclusion*. Westport: Greenwood Press, (1950) 1972.

Sandmeyer, Elmer Clarence. *The Anti-Chinese Movement in California*. Urbana: University of Illinois Press, (1939), 1991.

Saxton, Alexander. *The Indispensable Enemy: Labor and the Anti-Chinese Movement in California*. Berkeley: University of California Press, 1971.

Shankman, Arnold. *Ambivalent Friends: Afro-Americans View the Immigrant*. Westport: Greenwood Press, 1982.

Siu, Paul C.P. *The Chinese Laundryman: A Study of Social Isolation*. New York: New York University Press, 1987.

Spicer, Edward H., Hansen, Asael T., Luomala, Katherine, and Opler, Marvin K. *Impounded People: Japanese Americans in the Relocation Centers*. Tuscon: University of Arizona Press, 1969.

Takaki, Ronald. *Iron Cages: Race and Culture in Nineteenth Century America*. New York: Alfred A. Knopf, 1979.

        Strangers from a Different Shore: A History of Asian Americans. Boston: Little, Brown, 1989.

Tateishi, John. *And Justice For All: An Oral History of the Japanese American Detention Camps*. New York: Random House, 1984.

Tsai, Shih-Shan Henry. *The Chinese Experience in America*. Bloomington: Indiana University Press, 1986.

Yoneda, Karl. *Ganbatte: Sixty-Year Struggle of a Kibei Worker*. Los Angeles: UCLA Asian American Studies Center, 1983.

Zalburg, Sanford. *A Spark is Struck: Jack Hall & the ILWU in Hawaii*. Honolulu: University of Hawaii Press, 1979.

Articles

Almaguer, Tomas. "Racial Domination and Class Conflict in Capitalist Agriculture: The Oxnard Sugar Beet Workers' Strike of 1903." *Labor History*, Vol. 25 (1984): 325-349.

Corbett, P. Scott, and Corbett, Nancy Parker. "The Chinese in Oregon, c. 1870-1880." *Oregon Historical Quarterly*, Vol. 78 (1977): 73-85.

Daniels, Roger. "The Decision to Relocate the Japanese: Another Look." *Pacific Historical Review*, Vol. LI, (February 1982): 71-77.

Hellwig, David J. "Black Reactions to Chinese Immigration and the Anti-Chinese Movement: 1850-1910." *Amerasia Journal*, Vol. 6, No. 2 (Fall 1979): 25-44.

Johnsen, Leigh Dana. "Equal Rights and the 'Heathen Chinee': Black Activism in San Francisco, 1868-1875." *Western Historical Quarterly*, Vol. 11 (1980): 57-68.

Karlin, Jules Alexander. "Anti-Chinese Outbreaks in Seattle, 1885-1886." *Pacific Northwest Quarterly*, Vol. 39, No. 2 (April 1948): 103-129.

Lai, H.M. "Historical Survey of Organizations of the Left among the Chinese in America." *Asian America*, Vol. 4, No. 3 (Fall 1972): 10-20.

McKee, Delber L. "The Chinese Must Go! Commissioner General Powderly and Chinese Immigration, 1897-1902." *Pennsylvania History*, Vol. 44 (1977): 37-51.

Miller, Sally, "Americans and the Second International." *Proceedings of the American Philosophical Society*, Vol. 120, No. 5 (October 1976): 372-387.

Paul, Rodman. "The Origin of the Chinese Issue in California." *Mississippi Valley Historical Review*, Vol. 25, No. 2 (September 1938): 181-196.

Quinn, Larry D. "Chink Chink Chinaman: The Beginning of Nativism in Montana." *Pacific Northwest Quarterly*, Vol. 58, No. 2 (April 1967): 82-89.

Salyer, Lucy. "Captives of the Law: Judicial Enforcement of the Chinese Exclusion Laws, 1891-1905." *Journal of American History*, Vol. 76, No. 1 (June 1989): 91-117.

Schwartz, Harvey. "A Union Combats Racism: The ILWU's Japanese-American 'Stockton Incident' of 1945." *Southern California Quarterly*, Vol. LXII, No. 2 (Summer 1980): 161-176.

Seager II, Robert. "Some Denominational Reactions to Chinese Immigration to California, 1856-1892." *Pacific Historical Review*, Vol. 28 (February 1959): 49-66.

Shankman, Arnold. "Black on Yellow: Afro-Americans View Chinese Americans, 1850-1935." *Phylon*, Vol. XXXIX, No. 1 (Spring 1978): 1-17.

Shimazu, S. Don. "Nisei Too Liberated Dachau." *Jewish Currents* (April 1990): 5-6.

Spoehr, Luther W. "Sambo and the Heathen Chinee: Californians' Racist Stereotypes in the Late 1870's." *Pacific Historical Review*, Vol. XLII, No. 2 (May 1973): 185-203.

Stahler, Michael L. "William Speer: Champion of California's Chinese." *Journal of Presbyterian History*, Vol. 48 (1970): 113-129.

Tsai, Shih-Shan H. "Reaction to Exclusion: The Boycott of 1905 and Chinese National Awakening." *The Historian*, Vol. XXIX (1976): 95-110.

"The Workingmen's Party of California, 1877-1882." *California Historical Society Quarterly*, Vol. 55 (1976): 58-71.

Yu, Connie Young. "The Chinese in American Courts." *Bulletin of Concerned Asian Scholars*, Vol. 4, No. 3 (Fall 1973): 22-30.

Index

About the Editors

PHILIP S. FONER is Professor Emeritus of History at Lincoln University. He is the author of many books, including *The History of Black Americans* (3 vols., Greenwood, 1975, 1983, 1983) and (with David Roediger) *Our Own Time: A History of American Labor and the Working Day* (Greenwood, 1988).

DANIEL ROSENBERG is University College Preceptor at Adelphi University. He is the author of *The Human Condition in the Modern Age* (1991) and *New Orleans Dockworkers* (1988).